Books are to be returned on or before
the last date below

Bo

- 4 DEC 2012

KT-558-174

New Cultural Studies

Series Editors
Joan DeJean
Carrol Smith-Rosenberg
Peter Stallybrass
Gary A. Tomlinson

A complete list of books in the series
is available from the publisher.

Body, Self, and Society

The View from Fiji

Anne E. Becker

PENN

University of Pennsylvania Press

Philadelphia

Portions of this book have been previously published in a chapter adapted from this book as "Nurturing and Negligence: Working on Others' Bodies in Fiji," in *Embodiment and Experience*, ed. Thomas J. Csordas (Cambridge: Cambridge University Press, 1993).

Permission is acknowledged to reprint material from the following sources:

e.e. cummings, "maggie and milly and molly and may," *Complete Poems: 1904–1962*, ed, George J. Firmage, copyright © 1956, 1984, 1991 by the Trustees for the E. E. Cummings Trust, reprinted by permission of Liveright Publishing Corporation.

Adrian Furnham and Naznin Alibhai, "Cross-Cultural Differences in the Perception of Female Body Shapes," *Psychological Medicine* 13 (1983): 829–837, adaptations of Figure 1 (p. 831), Figure 2 (p. 835), Table 4 (p. 835), copyright © 1983 by Cambridge University Press, reprinted by permission of Cambridge University Press and Adrian Furnham.

Vladimir Nabokov, *Pale Fire*, copyright © 1962, 1980 by Random House, Inc., reprinted by permission of Random House, Inc.

Christina Toren, *Making Sense of Hierarchy: Cognition as Social Process in Fiji*, copyright © 1990 by Christina Toren, reprinted by permission of Athlone Press.

Cover: Adapted from a traditional Fijian barkcloth painting by Feoko Mele. Courtesy of the artist and Fiji Government Handicraft Centre.

10 9 8 7 6 5 4

Published by
University of Pennsylvania Press
Philadelphia, Pennsylvania 19104-4011

Library of Congress Cataloging-in-Publication Data

Becker, Anne E.
    Body, Self, and society: the view from Fiji/Anne E. Becker.
        p.   cm.—(New cultural studies)
    Includes bibliographical references and index.
    ISBN 0-8122-3180-5 (cloth: alk. paper).—ISBN 0-8122-1397-1
(pbk.: alk. paper)
    1. Ethnology—Fiji—Singatoka (Western Divison)
2. Ethnopsychology—Fiji—Singatoka (Western Divison)   3. Identity
(Psychology)—Fiji—Singatoka (Western Division)—4. Body image—
Fiji—Singatoka (Western Division)   5. Body, Human—Social aspects—
Fiji—Singatoka (Western Division) ts.   6. Singatoka (Western
Division, Fiji)—Social life and customs.   I. Title.   II. Series.
GN671.F5B43   1995
155.8' 099611—dc20   95-22730
                                                                 CIP

DEDICATION

This book is dedicated with respect and gratitude to the memory of Ratu Jocame Rokomatu and to the Nahigatoka villagers.

Na ivolajukujuku hewa okwe me sa na lemu, Tai Simoko, qenia na lemutou na lewe ni rara i Nahigatoka; qi varokorokotakinike-mutou valevu dina hara ga, qi vavinavinatakinia hara ga muni na lemuju kawaitakiniau.

Contents

Figures

Preface

may came home with a smooth round stone
as small as a world and as large as alone.

For whatever we lose(like a you or a me)
it's always ourselves we find in the sea

e. e. cummings

The day I re-entered Nahigatoka Village in January 1988, after an absence of several years, members of the chiefly household gathered to welcome me, some holding new babies to show me, others telling me who was now married or who was new to the village. My hostess, Adi, told me I would be living with them in their newly built house, since the bamboo one I had stayed in earlier had been destroyed by Cyclone Oscar in 1983. She explained that her father, Tai Mosese, would be staying there too, although he rightfully belonged in his chiefly *were levu.* Tai's sleep, however, was often disturbed by an assortment of Melanesian *niju*-spirits wandering through his room, and he preferred to sleep in the company of his namesake and adopted grandchildren. Adi correctly supposed that I was exhausted after my long journey, and she showed me where to lie down while they prepared the room next to Tai Mosese's for me.

When I recall my arrival in Nahigatoka for fieldwork, I think often of that overwhelmingly hot January day as I lay in the midst of late morning activity, enveloped in the confusion of unfamiliar sounds and images. As I reformulate my field experience in a written analysis, I have all but forgotten the initial frustration and emotional sea that attended the experience — the cacophony of village noises and once-unfamiliar dialect, the multitude of flies and mosquitoes, and the oppressive humidity are virtually screened from my memory. I realize, rather helplessly, that I have edited the experience at every retrospective pause.

What I do recall is the long period during which I was considered a *vulagi*, or guest, and my friends and hosts dutifully translated and explained what they felt I needed to know. Often they apologized for what they imagined I could not see or feel — the face of a *niju* peering through the window, their exhilaration when the *cigana* fish first appeared for the season in the river, or their sheer delight and amusement in retelling a joke about their *cavu*, or totems — and indeed, I could not. Otherwise they qualified their statements to me by adding, "That's what the old people used to say," or by hedging, "That's what they used to believe." Usually they advised me not to be bothered with their *vabausia*, their beliefs — they did not apply to other races, just to Fijians, they said.

What I had not expected, however, was the advent of seeing — having *niju* visit me in my dreams, finding the jokes about their totems hilarious, and wrapped in the sweet sleepiness produced by evening stories accompanied by drinking kava, not wanting to remove myself into privacy. I was not prepared for the blurring of boundaries between these people and myself.

My hosts, too, were fascinated by our differences, and yet our capacity for common experience, and I frequently found myself the object of gentle interrogation. Once I sat cross-legged next to Adi on some mats at the head of a large circle of women crowded into a room, where she entertained questions from the gathering about my recent visit by an American friend. "You do not mind if I answer some questions about European dating customs?" she inquired. "These people are curious." At another time, after taping a long interview about traditional medicines and spirit illnesses in the chiefly *were levu* in Keiyasi, the village chief asked me to share my "beliefs" for the edification of the elders who were gathered. When we finished, they played back the cassette to recap my words.

When I was unoccupied with my work, I joined my friends on fishing excursions. These women were good-natured about taking me, and my inevitably meager day's catch provided the substance for much joking. My ineptitude as a fisherwoman left me grateful for skills in other areas, such as an acceptable degree of competence in scraping coconuts, for which my hosts never failed to profess amazement.

This confusion of boundaries — between being an ethnographer and simply being myself among friends — inescapably informs my impressions of the community in Nahigatoka. It is only with a retrospective lens that I have accepted that my understanding of differences between the Fijian and American/Western self was born of the irritation, frustration, and miscomprehension of human behavior — when people I knew, respected, and loved conducted themselves in ways I resented or simply could not comprehend — and that it was the encounter with my own reactions to the bewildering, the terrifying, the pleasant, and the ridiculous from which my insight into Fijian experience emerged. These emotional currents are inseparable from the ethnography.

On a final note, I wish to acknowledge perhaps the single most instrumental factor in fostering my integration into and understanding of the Fijian collective in the family, the *mataqwali*, and the village: my Fijian hosts' immense generosity of spirit and limitless patience in overlooking my naive transgressions and inherent awkwardness in that setting, and assisting me in joining them and knowing myself as a self within a community.

Acknowledgments

Although I alone bear responsibility for the ideas set forth in this book, many mentors, colleagues, and friends have assisted and supported me in formulating them. I am deeply indebted to Professors Arthur Kleinman, Byron Good, and Mary-Jo DelVecchio Good for their enthusiastic guidance and helpful criticism of this work. I am also grateful to Dr. Leon Eisenberg for his supportive role in this project. I owe an enormous debt to two anonymous readers whose commentary was indispensable in refining my ideas.

I received generous financial support for my research from both a Fulbright IIE Scholarship and an M.D./Ph.D. joint degree fellowship sponsored by the MacArthur Foundation.

I am grateful to the Fijian Ministries of Home Affairs, Fijian Affairs, and Health, and the Fiji Immigration Department for their permission to conduct research in Fiji from January 1988 through April 1989 and again in the spring of 1994; and to the chiefs, *turaga ni koro*, and people of Bemana, Keiyasi, Lomanikaya, Nadroumai, and Wauosi for allowing me to conduct my survey in their villages. Special thanks go to the many district nurses, village health workers, and persons who helped to orchestrate and administer the survey questionnaire.

For support of my research in Fiji, I am indebted to Robert Laing, Marcia Kline, Ateca Williams, Katalina Rakai, and the entire staff of the United States Information Service in Fiji. In addition, I thank the staff of the Fiji National Food and Nutrition Committee, Dr. Mataitoga, Dr. Savou, Mrs. Susan Parkinson, and in particular Ms. Vigil Aguilar for their assistance and enthusiasm; Dr. Lander, Dr. A. A. J. Jansen, and Dr. Annette Robertson at the Fiji School of Medicine, and Drs. Rudy and Aida Gerona, Dr. M. V. Mataitoga, Dr. Angila Kant, Mere Babau, Sr. Naituyaga, Sr. Mataitoga, and Sr. Matavesi of the Sigatoka District Hospital; and the Fiji Museum staff—and in particular Sela Rayawa for his help in using the museum resources. I am also grateful to Mrs. Bale, Mrs. Toganivalu, and students at the University of the South Pacific for assisting with and participating in my survey. Professor Asesela Ravuvu provided invaluable guidance for the development of my research ideas.

I thank Eileen Dunn, Robert Kennedy, and George Mohammed for providing me with places to work in Fiji. I am also indebted to Master Isaia Gonewai for his patience and persistence in teaching me the Nadroga dialect and to Dr. Paul Geraghty for serving as a mentor in matters of Fijian language and culture. I am grateful to Joan Taresevich for her assistance in drawing figures for my questionnaire, Susan Santangelo for her help in the statistical analysis of the data, John Tobias for his time in turning these data into a graphic presentation, Ann Hawthorne for her editorial work, and the members of the Thesis Writers' Group in the Department of Anthropology at Harvard, the members of the Writing Seminar in the Department of Psychiatry at the Massachusetts General Hospital, and, in particular, Dr. Paul Hamburg for their helpful comments on my work in progress. Thanks go to other friends and family in Fiji and in America, especially my husband, Eric Isselbacher, who have lent their wisdom and support to this endeavor. I would like to thank Patricia Smith at the University of Pennsylvania Press for her encouragement and guidance in developing this text.

I am particularly grateful to Professor Bill Aalbersberg not only for introducing me to Fiji and Nahigatoka in 1982, but also for his substantial contributions to my research and his overwhelming generosity and hospitality during my work in Fiji.

Finally, I am indebted to the many villages and families in which I was so graciously received. In particular I thank the people of Nahigatoka— who shall remain anonymous, and who include my chief, the *turaga ni koro*, the leders and my "Nana," "aunties," "uncles," "sisters," "brothers," my research assistant and friend, and my *tavale*—for their generosity in allowing me to share in their community and in their lives. In addition to the practical help they offered in my ethnographic study, I acknowledge with gratitude the many other lessons they taught me with their patience and grace.

Mequ lama i sinia, qi vinasia mequ vavinavina ivuara yahila na matavuwere qeinia na virara qu lei qwaravi ke. Qi vabibitatakinia na lequ vavinavina i vuara na koi Nahigatoka—na viagwane na taukei ni rara, na turaga ni koro, kura na juqwaqwa, lequ Tai, lequ Nana, lequ jita, lequ koko, lequ "sista," lequ "braca," lequ tavale, qeinia lequ i vukevuke ni vajijike—i na ledra yalo vina qei sa vohosia, i na lequ lama i vimaliwai qera i na ledra rara, kodaki muni na juku yecola yahila i na gauna qu la mai no koto ke.

Qi mata vavinavinatakinia na ledra vivuke i na vitalanoa na ledra ivarau qeinia na ledra vavuliciau. Vina valevu na yalohavu. Vina valevu. A muni na vikawaitaki. Qi kilasia ke, ni qu kawaitaki koto i na lequ cakacaka, qu dania ni toso rewarewa hara. Qi kilasia niqu tasi numideinia rewa na lemuju itovo vina vuau. A qei kodaki koto koni na kea levu.

Introduction

> The person is no longer diffuse. It disengages itself from the socio-mythic domain in which it was caught. The body ceases to be the old social costume smothering the person. The personage, having no further role to play, disappears. The person locates itself within man himself. The psychological self we saw wandering everywhere, far from the body, is finally fixed: I have a body.
>
> —Leenhardt (1979.165)

The following inquiry into the relationship of embodied experience to the social context of selfhood unfolds from an ethnographic paradox and a clinical puzzle. My arrival in Nahigatoka for doctoral research in anthropology was greeted with enthusiasm and then perplexity on the part of my Fijian hosts on hearing about my interest in their interest in body shape. They were not, they politely clarified, especially attuned to body shape. This occasioned my own equal perplexity, in turn, since I had spent the previous months framing a study on what I felt was nothing short of a cultural preoccupation with food, eating, and body size in Fiji. But as it turned out they spoke truthfully. Notwithstanding the local idiom of greeting, insult, and compliments replete with allusions to body shape and fluctuations in weight, Fijians are not self-reflexive about their bodily habitus. What very much piques their interest, however, are other people's bodies—how they are fed, what weight they have gained or lost, how they are shaped, what illnesses afflict them. Body morphology is a primary lexicon of social processes, not a means of self-presentation; it is a matter of social, not personal, concern.

When I returned several years later, newly trained as a psychiatrist specializing in the treatment of eating disorders, I gave my hosts new cause for perplexity when I spoke of the diseases I treat and wondered whether similarly disordered eating ever occurred in Fiji. My usually

deferential hosts were quite bemused by the clinical descriptions of bulimia and anorexia nervosa. How, they wondered, can people do these
things to their bodies? How can they abuse food and their appetites in
these ways? They dismissed this sort of eating pathology as quite out of
the realm of local possibility[1] and (finding the syndrome quite prepos-
terous) suggested with casual irony that I send my patients to Fiji for
treatment.

Indeed, how is it that bodily experience, clearly so influenced by
the social gaze in both Fijian and American culture, can accompany
such profoundly different experiences of connection or isolation from
a person's social milieu? Only recently have social scientists rekindled
inquiry into the mutual shaping of cultural patterning and embodied
experience (see Giddens 1991; B. Turner 1992; Shilling 1993; Csordas
1994), although there is a long, distinguished, and unresolved debate
in the social science literature concerning the variability of selfhood
and its contingency to social context. This book borrows from the latter
material in exploring the relationship of embodied experience to folk
models of the moral and social context of selfhood in Fiji. It is an ethnographic illustration of the variations inherent in the bodily context of
experience; that is, how personal embodied experience and knowledge
are relocated in the socio-cosmic corpus and how social processes are,
in turn, reconstituted in individual bodies. The transcendent possibilities of embodied experience in Fiji fundamentally challenge Western
folk models of bodily experience as personal and circumscribed. The
complicated relationship between self, body, and society in Fiji highlights aspects of self and body boundaries, agency, identity, and their
relationship to mental illness that are not always visible to the Western
clinical gaze.

The Problem of the Self

Since we are going to explore how the embodiment of the self is structured by the self's grounding in its social milieu, we will first need to
identify salient features of the cultural variability constituting selves.
Specifically, we are interested in how (in very broad strokes) the "Fijian
self" differs from the "Western self."[2] Clifford Geertz has observed
that the

Western conception of the person as a bounded, unique, more or less integrated
motivational and cognitive universe, a dynamic center of awareness, emotion,
judgment, and action organized into a distinctive whole and set contrastively
both against other such wholes and against its social and natural background, is,

however incorrigible it may seem to us, a rather peculiar idea within the context of the world's cultures. (1983:290)

Classically, ethnographers have described two contrasting patterns of selfhood referring to the degree of affiliation of a self with its social milieu. The Western concept of an "individuated" self abstracts a person from his or her social role (Shweder and Bourne 1984:168). This individuated self is located in the context of cultural valuation of "independence, autonomy, and differentiation," whereas the "unindividuated" self includes "a wide variety of significant others" (Marsella 1985:290). For example, the traditional Chinese self is conceived of as "a configuration of role relations with significant others," in contrast with a primary orientation to the "individual self" in American culture (Chu 1985:259). Similarly, American selves may be construed as "independent," with primary emphasis on guarding autonomy and "discovering and expressing their unique inner attributes," in contrast with Asian selves, which are often construed as "interdependent," seeking to attend to others in order to safeguard harmonious relationships (Markus and Kitayama 1991:224).

Clearly the Western self is partially misrepresented in this monolithic depiction. The very concept implies a homogeneity that simply cannot account for variations in gender, generation, geographical location, and ethnicity. For example, Carol Gilligan has found that American women's assessment of self is informed by "a standard of relationship, an ethic of nurturance, responsibility, and care" that grounds morality in connection (1982:159–60). Although independent/interdependent or individuated/unindividuated dichotomies are helpful in grasping primary orientations, certainly elements of both these polarities are expressed by selves in a variety of cultural contexts. Furthermore, the experience of selfhood may not be fixed against shifting contexts even within a particular culture (Ewing 1990).

On the other hand, while acknowledging that these representations may be overly polarized and generalized (see Markus and Kitayama 1991; Murray 1993; Spiro 1993; Holland and Kipnis 1994; Boyarin and Boyarin 1995; Battaglia 1995), we must draw on characterizations about fundamental differences in orientation between "Western selves" and other selves to their respective social matrices for several reasons. Regardless of their ultimate validity, Western folk models provide insight into culturally particular representations of selfhood that identify core cultural values. They consistently portray the idealized self as autonomous and unrelated (Spiro 1993:141). In the West, moral philosophies that espouse the "individualism of self-fulfillment," relating this to authenticity (Taylor 1991:14–16), further articulate these core values. Hazel Rose Markus and Shinobu Kitayama have written convincingly of the usefulness of approaching cognition, emotion, and motivation with a sophisticated understanding of local self-construals in contrast to earlier "monocultural" analyses of these attributes (1991:224).[3]

Hence self experience is unequivocally culturally patterned. Even if the "Western self" is an inadequate foil for broaching the complexities of comparative selves across cultures, this portrait, as captured in a brief pose it strikes, vividly illuminates the contrasting features of selfhood that mold Fijian experience. Whether or not folk models fully match experience, and regardless of their propensity to stereotype, they do identify tendencies that are useful for heuristic purposes. My use of reified folk models for comparative purposes reflects a pragmatic concern with simplifying the parameters for comparison, as well as a conviction that profiling cultural tendencies provides a reasonable substrate for inquiry into how self representations—whether alluded to in folk models or moral philosophies—inform embodied experience.

To begin, Western folk models firmly anchor the self to a body (Fisher 1974:x; Illich 1986:1326; Zegans 1987:32, 34). On the other hand, among Pacific Island societies the self is not so much conceived of as a body, but "as a locus of shared social relationships, or shared biographies" (Lieber 1990:74). The Melanesian person is construed as a "composite site of relationships" (Strathern 1988:13) that is not "coterminous or even synonymous with individual bodies" (Foster 1990:432). The traditional Melanesian's self-awareness was as a set of relationships. Experience was diffused among persons, not considered specific to the individual until contact with the Western world, which imported the notion of "the circumscription of the physical being" (Leenhardt 1979:153, 163–64).

Pacific notions of selfhood are "fundamentally interpersonal" and sustained by the "assumption that sociability and relatedness underlie personal existence" (Kirkpatrick and White 1985:25).[4] For instance, Samoans "focus on things in their relationships" rather than in themselves (Shore 1982:136). Similarly, the Ifaluk of Micronesia conceive of themselves as "oriented primarily toward other people" (Lutz 1985:68). In the Eastern Caroline Islands, the Kapinga understand the person as "a locus of social relationships, of shared biographies" (Lieber 1990:74). The Hawaiian self-concept is "based on interpersonal bonds of emotional exchange and reciprocity"; for them, "self is a socially interactive concept tied to correct social behavior," which prescribes generosity, cooperation, and extension of mutual aid to others (Ito 1985:301, 320). And the Melanesian Solomon Islanders make "solidarity" an explicit

ideal and attribute misfortune to bad feelings incurred in strained interpersonal relations (White 1985:349–50).

In Fiji, as in many other Oceanic societies, self-experience is intimately grounded in its relational context, its kin and village community.
Individual action is ideally aimed at engaging and inculcating social relationships and promoting community interests. Character demonstrating self-effacement and generosity in deference to community needs is
highly valued. Social action is guided by notions of persons' embeddedness in their communities.

Embodiment and Selfhood in Fiji

The chapters that follow explore the context of embodied experience
in Fiji as it emanates from the notion of selves deeply embedded in a relational matrix. The Fijian ethos of social relatedness is well-established
in the ethnographic literature (see especially Ravuvu 1987). Chapter 1
reviews select features of the fundamental nature of the Fijian orientation toward engaging in social relationships since they are relevant to
understanding the illustrations of the intercalation of self, body, kin,
and community relationships that follow.

Chapter 2 examines the ways in which the positioning and orientation
of self within a social matrix structures the representational use of the
body. That is, while core cultural symbols may be encoded or inscribed
in body shape, in Fiji the authorization for the manipulation of these
symbols rests with the community, not the individual. The body is not
formulated as a project of the self, as it can be in Western representations of experience. This challenges the notion that the body is an
apparatus of the self.

Chapter 3 demonstrates how social processes, notably caring, are embodied in individuals via feeding and evidence of weight fluctuation.
The Fijian core emphasis on expression of care (best represented in
the local idiom of *vikawaitaki*), is concretized in formal exchange, feast
preparation, and routine food sharing in the community. Cultivation of
bodily space is further established as collective enterprise rather than a
personal pursuit.

Chapter 4 reviews the public visibility and social appropriation of the
personal body in Fiji as reflected in stories relating non-disclosure of
pregnancy to cosmologic mishaps. These narratives reflect the cultural
construal of bodily behavior as entwined in and regulated by cosmologic
forces and allow for the possibility that somatic experience transcends
the individual body. Hence, bodies do not circumscribe individual experience.

Chapter 5 further investigates the social appropriation of bodies in the use of illness as a forum for articulating social conflict and negotiating moral meaning. The possession of bodies by *niju* (parahuman beings), and the displacement of selves from bodies manifest in the wandering *yalo* (disembodied selves) further corrupt self-agency.

Chapter 6 concludes this study by reviewing how the intrinsic moral binding of self to community in Fiji lays the groundwork for both the embodiment of social processes within the personal body and the disembodiment of its agency and identity. Socio-moral transgression, manifest as physical symptom, as well as care, are located and concretized in individual anatomic space, allowing for enhanced integration into one's universe of kin and social relations. These processes raise questions about social isolation or integration and their inception in embodied experience, and they fundamentally challenge the Western notion of bodily experience as personally authored and circumscribed.

Addendum

Subsequent to the completion of this study, preliminary data collection on attitudes toward diet and body shape among secondary school young women in the Sigatoka area has revealed the presence of some behaviors and attitudes consistent with symptoms seen in bulimia nervosa, including increased concern among some women regarding being overweight. More than likely, the appearance of these phenomena is secondary to a shift away from the traditional experiences of self and body in Fiji as young men and women have increasing exposure to Western values and lifestyles through the media and the influx of tourists to their country. The views expressed in this text most likely reflect traditional views that continue to evolve with exposure to these values and lifestyles. It appears that cultural traditions that may protect against the preoccupations, behaviors, and distress that accompany eating disorders may not, unfortunately, be able to buffer against the influx of encroaching cultural traditions that may precipitate or support these symptoms. Continued research may clarify this issue.

Chapter 1
Cultural Bearings:
Identity and Ethos in Fiji

Fiji is an archipelago of approximately 300 islands located south of the Equator on the 180th meridian (Figure 1.1), both geographically and culturally straddling the conventional border between Melanesia and Polynesia. Fijian lifeways draw elements from both Polynesian and Melanesian cultural traditions[1] and reflect an orientation toward identity characteristic of other Pacific Island cultures. This chapter traces the roots of Fijian identity and ethos. It also introduces the microcontext of this monograph, Nahigatoka Village, which provides the ethnographic backdrop to the exploration of the relationship between food exchange, care, body, self, and society in the following chapters.

Nahigatoka: The Field Site

The primary field site, Nahigatoka,[2] is the chiefly village of the Jubuniwai District. This district, comprised of seven villages clustered near the mouth of the Sigatoka River, is located in the Nadroga Province on the western side of Viti Levu (Figure 1.2), the largest island in the Fiji group. Located within walking distance of Sigatoka Town, Nahigatoka is a relatively large village of fifty households and 338 inhabitants. Villagers visit the market and supermarkets to supplement their own daily harvests from the reef, river, and plantation.[3] Like most other villages in this area, Nahigatoka has a small shop selling basic food items and necessities, a community hall, and a Wesleyan Protestant church.[4] Individual families cultivate plots on the village plantation, situated on a river island that runs parallel to the village and extends to the river mouth.

The village's proximity to Sigatoka Town and its central location in Fiji's prime tourist area, the Coral Coast, make it more vulnerable to the intrusions and temptations of Western culture than are rural and valley villages.[5] Considerable intergenerational tension has evolved re-

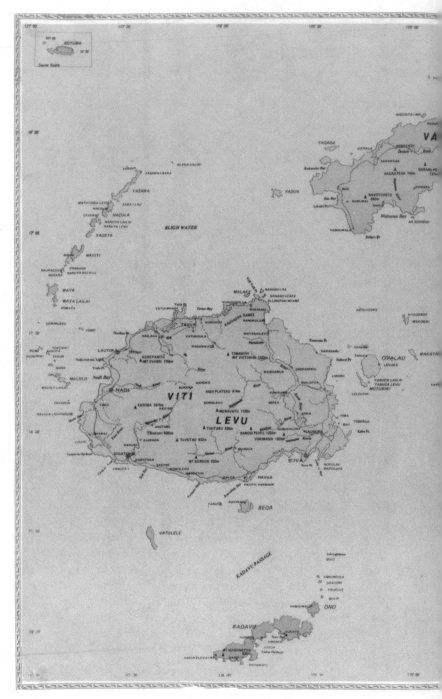

Figure 1.1. Map of the Fiji Islands. Courtesy of Fiji Times Ltd.

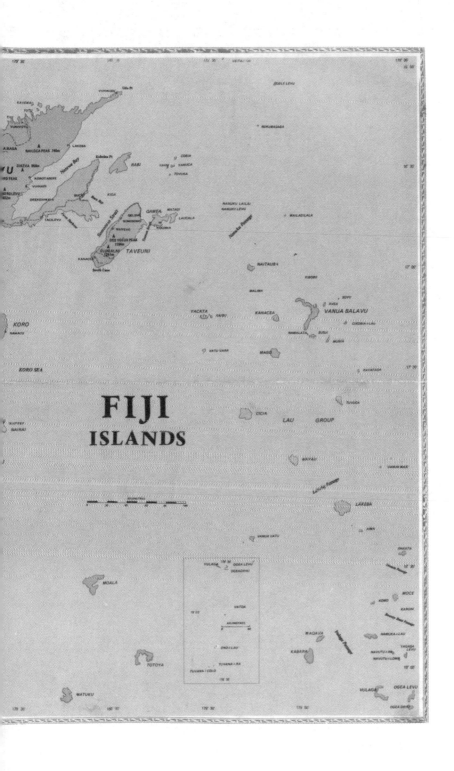

FIJI
ISLANDS

LAU GROUP

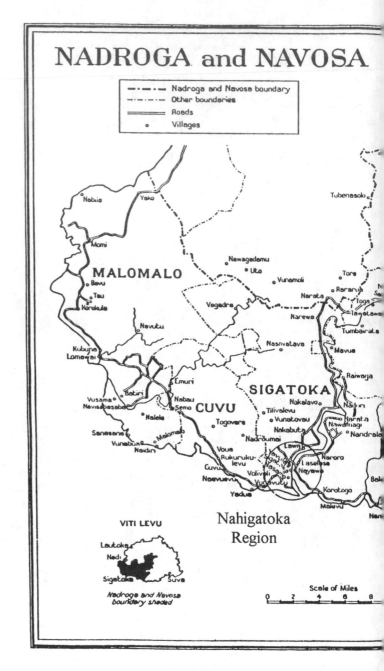

Figure 1.2. Map of Nadroga and Navosa, showing a detailed view of the Nahigatoka region. Reprinted with permission from Cyril Belshaw, *Under the Ivi Tree: Society and Economic Growth in Rural Fiji*, copyright © 1964 by the Regents of the University of California.

garding elements of Western lifestyle perceived as eroding various traditional lifeways.[6] For example, the consumption (and sometimes abuse) of alcohol often upstages traditional *yaqona* drinking.[7] Social strain becomes apparent when adolescents and young adults experiment with Western-style relationships, food, dress, or cosmetics, and is commonly precipitated by instances of persons leaving the village to work or study in the multi-ethnic urban areas. These conflicts are expressed and negotiated through discussion, joking, indirect criticism (insults and gossip), and storytelling (*talanoa*) within various group contexts, typically during *yaqona* drinking or food preparation. In any such gathering, people are as much engaged in the listening to and telling of stories as in their ostensible activities.

Village Routines

Daily village life in Nahigatoka, like that in other Nadroga villages, consists of varied routine tasks related to the cultivation of root crops, the gathering of supplemental greens, the harvesting of sea and river foods, and the preparation of meals. The days are punctuated by meals (three or four each day), afternoon rest periods, frequent church activities, and long evenings of quiet gatherings and conversations over many bowls of *yaqona*. Although men and women do sometimes work together on their plantations, tasks are usually gender segregated; women attend to food gathering, meal preparation, and childcare while men cultivate crops and maintain the village. Many daily tasks are accomplished as group activities. For example, women go to the reef together to fish or prepare food collectively as they discuss political, village, and domestic events. A cookhouse scene described in my journal portrays the microcontext of these village routines.

    I joined Lausana[8] and Via, who were seated cross-legged on the floor plucking the leaves off sea grapes; the edible part was tossed into a basin, and the stems were dropped onto a burlap sack already laden with rubbish from the morning's cooking. Seated at the table were Josefa and Atelaite, finishing their bread, tea, and rice. Next to me Tai Vani was lying on her back as a neighbor carefully plucked her eyelashes. She was suffering from *vuluki*, a condition in which tiny eyelashes grow in — in this case attributed to sitting for long hours in a smoke-filled cookhouse — causing itching and redness.

    Across from us a Bombay pot filled with plantains, breadfruit, and cassava was boiling over a fire. The hearth was cleared of its usual coconut husks, and smoke had not yet filled the cookhouse. The two doors facing the village were wide open. Outside, frangipanis and palm trees stood out against a brilliant blue sky. A large turtle shell was hanging in a tree to dry.

    Against one wall of the corrugated tin building, and resting on banana-leaf stands, were three clay cooking pots that Tai Vani had made in the last few days

for an upcoming bazaar. Fishing nets hung over them in the corner. Next to the
burlap sack with rubbish was a small Bombay pot with the morning's leftover
rice, a heap of papayas, some breadfruit, and a bunch of the leafy *waci*. On the
other side of the door were baskets and suitcases full of clothes. Above them on
a shelf were bottles of fragrant body oil (*waiwai*) and a hurricane lantern. On
the floor were two tins, one full of pounded *yaqona* and the other full of money
from its sale. Mats, foam mattresses, and pillows were piled on the far side of
the door.

As we prepared the sea grapes, Vasiti, who had placed a heap of hibiscus on
the floor, started to break off twigs of a branch and to impale the yellow, orange,
pink, and red blooms on the exposed ends. These were to be taken to the church
for the service later in the morning.

After she finished with Tai Vani's eyelashes, the guest was thanked and ushered
to the side of the cookhouse, where there were coconuts she wished to purchase.
Tai Vani sat up to confront her eighteen-month-old great-grandson who toddled
by her. "*Yato* Tai Fani," she encouraged, and the child cooperated by stooping a
little closer to the ground in imitation of his great-grandmother's walking posture. The exercise was greeted by laughter and approval by those present; then
the child, tired of the game, circulated among the various people present, naming each by her relationship to him. Several times as he passed by me he paused
to gaze at my hair, fastened in a ponytail, and on his last pass he finally tugged
at it. Three generations of women reprimanded him for this *tabu* action.

Jita collected the *waci* leaves and began to roll them in tight bundles to drop
into the boiling coconut cream. She sniffed and asked me for a tablet for her
runny nose; I ran to fetch it for her.

The daily itinerary of subsistence, church, and recreational activities
is punctuated with feasts (*magisi*), fundraisings (*holi*), and other ritual
presentations or exchanges within and among the villages in the area,
including weddings, funerals, formal visits to the family of a new child
(*roqoroqo*), and visits to the construction site of an important building
(*visiko*). Indeed, gatherings to coordinate the labor and accumulate the
resources for a *holi* or a *magisi* are frequent events in the social calen-
dar, especially that of the chiefly *mataqwali* (clan). It is in these ritual
presentations, in the everyday rendering of household and subsistence
tasks, and in the serious or lighthearted telling of stories around the
yaqona bowl that the essence of the Fijian ethos — *vikawaitaki* and *viqwaravi* (caring about and taking care of) — is experienced and shared.

Health Care in Nahigatoka

A variety of options are available for the diagnosis and treatment of illnesses in Nahigatoka. Villagers here, like Fijians elsewhere, employ a
kind of eclectic pragmatism in seeking help for medical complaints. Em-
pirical experience guides them to Westernized medical facilities for a
variety of mundane afflictions such as fevers, skin infections, and lacera-
tions. The Fiji School of Medicine, located in Suva, trains physicians who

are then stationed in district hospitals around Fiji. Nahigatoka is served by the Sigatoka District Hospital as well as the Health Sister station, both within walking distance.

Coexisting with and still flourishing alongside these Western biomedical services, Fijian traditional medicine maintains a vast and sophisticated pharmacopoeia administered in the popular sector. These traditional medications (*dranu*) are prepared from roots, stems, and leaves by pounding, chopping, grating, boiling, and often mixing with other plants or with water to make an elixir. *Dranu* selection and dosage are specific to symptoms and the age of the afflicted. Massage is an important adjunct to pharmacologic therapy. While some healers specialize in massage directed against particular ailments, family and friends routinely massage the back, limbs, and abdomen of individuals suffering an illness. With the typically vigorous massage, a generous amount of Fijian oil (*waiwai*) — scented with sandalwood, flowers, and coconut — is applied. Moreover, certain health problems are understood to have a spirit etiology that is rooted in social conflict or a breach of *tabu*. These illnesses may accordingly be managed within the kin group, by addressing the perceived social precipitant or with the assistance of specialists called *daurairai*, or seers.

Historical Perspectives on Fijian Ethnic Identity

Archaeologic and linguistic evidence suggests that proto-Oceanic peoples settled in Fiji approximately 3,500 years ago and later dispersed to the various other island groups of Polynesia (Geraghty 1983; Routledge 1985:21). Additional migrations from Melanesia some 900 years ago had a profound impact on material culture and on the practice of warfare in Fiji (Routledge 1985:21). During the last several centuries there has been some intermarriage with and cultural borrowing from the nearby island Kingdom of Tonga.

An immense mountain range which crosses the main island, Viti Levu, from north to south, has influenced the evolution of many distinguishing features in the cultural traditions among Fijians in the eastern and western provinces. Despite Fiji's political unification since coming under British sovereignty in 1874, a degree of linguistic and cultural diversity has continued to characterize the ethnic Fijian population.[9]

Beyond its own cultural multiformity, Fiji has become ethnically diverse through the arrival of explorers, missionaries, colonists, immigrant laborers, and developers.[10] In the middle of the nineteenth century, having found the indigenous Fijians averse to working harder than required for subsistence, British colonists brought indentured laborers from India to Fiji to develop the sugar industry. The immigrant Indians progressively carved out a niche in the commercial economy, and with their expanding population today slightly outnumber ethnic Fijians. The two dominant ethnic moieties in Fiji have maintained their respective languages, cultural traditions, and political parties. At present, institutionalized practices such as separate programming of radio news and music, segregated classes, and printed news in several languages (Standard Fijian, Hindustani, Fiji Hindi, and English) reflect the continuing sociocultural rifts. Further ethnic admixture has come with the arrival of settlers from China and Rotuma and an influx of students coming to be educated at the University of the South Pacific and the Fiji School of Medicine in Suva, Fiji's capital city.

The superimposition of colonialism, capitalism, and Western lifeways on traditional practices of land tenure, legitimate authority, and distribution of resources has often made Fijians feel that both their cultural autonomy and their traditional lifeways have been compromised by accommodating groups they still consider to be guests in their country.[11] In 1987 the predominantly Indian party (though with an ethnic Fijian leader) won a majority of seats in Parliament, thus unseating the (primarily Fijian) Alliance Party, which had enjoyed a majority since Fiji's independence from Great Britain in 1970. Two military coups led to the declaration of Fiji as a republic and restored political control to the ethnic Fijians and their traditional paramount chiefs. The ensuing constitution enshrines Fijian political dominance. The interethnic tension, having been further exacerbated by the military coups of 1987 and the revision of the constitution, has set the stage for proactive ethnic solidarity among the Fijian population.

Despite criticism of this perceived institutionalization of racial discrimination by members of the British Commonwealth, the Fijians persist in their intention to safeguard indigenous culture and interests and to invest traditional structures with legitimate authority. In a letter to the editor of the *Fiji Times*, the coup leader, Brigadier General Sitiveni Rabuka, cautioned that Fijians need beware the erosion of the traditional chiefly authority and common values of sharing and caring that bind the Fijian community in harmony,[12] noting that Western democratic and capitalist values had infiltrated Fijian society and were "eating away our mutual trusts, bonds and kinship" (Tiko 1988a:6). The enhanced awareness of Fijian ethnicity and of both Indian and Western infringement on indigenous lifeways occasioned a popular movement, supported by the chiefly leaders, to return to indigenous custom. In addition to sanctions against excessive alcohol consumption and for the revitalized observance of tabus concerning demeanor and dress within the villages, a discourse affirming traditional ways has evolved through informal evening gatherings, most dramatically in *talanoa* (stories) regarding the superiority of traditional lifeways. For example, oral tradition maintains that Fijian ancestors were physically more robust than their modern counterparts, and that this good health resulted from crops that were both larger and of greater nutritional value than the present crops, which many believe have been progressively corrupted by Western agricultural technology. In 1988, when part of an ancient burial site about two to three thousand years old alongside the mouth of the Sigatoka River was unearthed by high winds, reports of "giant" skeletons were advanced as archaeological proof of the modern decline of Fijian physiognomy.[13]

In some ways, the mobilization of ethnic Fijian identity is a post-traditional movement that has emerged from the reflexive awareness of the threatened integrity of Fijian lifeways. Historically, Fijians have been eager to test and even incorporate outside cultural elements as their own. Yet Linnekin and Poyer note a more recent pan-Pacific phenomenon wherein ethnic constructs are created against the intrusive foreign presence:

In espousing *kastom*, the Pacific Way, the Micronesian Way, Maoritanga, and so on, Pacific Islanders are asserting their right, their capability, and their willingness to reject aspects of Western culture and to retain crucial features of indigenous lifeways and world view. From an anthropologist's point of view this commitment to cultural diversity, a phoenix rising from the ashes of the threat of Western uniformity, is a hopeful sign for the future. (Linnekin and Poyer 1990:15)

This emerging grassroots sentiment, through which Fijians consolidate their identity by noting their differences from other groups, presents a marked departure from traditional South Pacific modes of social inclusiveness of outsiders (Howard 1990:271; see also Lévi-Strauss 1985:160). In fact, it is through the projection of contrasting values onto white, colonial society that the definition of the Fijian way (*na itovo vavisi*) emerges, since "for many Oceanic intellectuals, white society, with its emphases on individualism, material consumerism, and racialism, provides an oppositional category that allows clearest self-definition" (Howard 1990:276).

An Ethos of Relatedness

In Fiji, as in other Melanesian and Polynesian cultures, social action is guided by the tight affiliation of individuals with their communities. Fijian identity is grounded in one's connections to the immediate kinship group and social network. Ideally, individual activity is devoted to developing and reinforcing social relationships and promoting collective interests. Characterological traits and practices demonstrating self-sacrifice, generosity, and self-effacement in deference to community goals are highly valued and actively cultivated.

Marshall Sahlins writes that in Fiji, "the main relationships of society are at once projected historically and embodied currently in the persons of authority" (1985:47). Early in this century, the Reverend W. Deane noted the Fijians' proclivity for communalism. He observed:

Individualism has had to fight for its existence in Fiji, as, perhaps, in no other community. Under the ancient system of communism there was no room for personal initiative. (Deane 1921:149)

Asesela Ravuvu maintains that although British rule and Christian influence may have "offered an opportunity for the growth of individuality in the Fijian character," the Fijian still finds it "difficult to separate himself completely from his own people" (Ravuvu 1987:289). He also comments:

Individualism is loathed and discouraged for the sake of group solidarity and harmony. Few alternatives are available. Individual desires and wants are thus constrained, though everyone's basic needs are satisfied within the social and cultural framework of the kin group. (Ravuvu 1988:14)

Innumerable mechanisms connect the Fijian individual to a dense social network comprised of kinship, historical, regional, and mythical relations. Complicated protocols for ritual exchange maintain mutually beneficial channels of reciprocity among a variety of social groups. Exchange of food or items of traditional value (*iyau*) such as mats, bark cloth, whale's teeth, *yaqona*, and drums of kerosene begins with individual contributions to the kin group so that the *mataqwali* may in turn collectively present goods for exchange to another group. For example, if members of a *mataqwali* plan to attend a funeral, they will arrange a meeting beforehand for the purpose of bringing personal contributions to the group's eventual presentation. The collectively presented goods will, in turn, be distributed among the members of the recipient group and will probably be recycled in a similar chain of exchange events during a subsequent traditional formal function (*ogaoga*). Other traditional goods, food, or *yaqona* will be presented by this group to the original donor group in immediate reciprocation.

The demonstration of respect (*varokorokotaki*) for chiefly or senior authority and for Fijian custom (*na itovo vavisi*) is a central feature of the core values governing behavior and bodily demeanor. Etiquette guides a subordination of personal needs to those of the community, manifest in the lavish hospitality extended to guests (*vulagi*) of the household or community and in self-effacing bodily postures and gestures. Public censure coupled with supernatural sanctions reinforce these norms.

Core Fijian values emanate from the concept *vakaturaga*, which encompasses qualities of chiefly behavior (Ravuvu 1987:320). Several associated personal behaviors are essential in forging an ethos of "share and care" — "a cultural norm which in turn elicits co-operation and thus unity between any interacting social groups" (259). These idealized modes of relating to the community — translated loosely as "helping," "consideration of others," "loving one another," "togetherness," and "being of the same spirit" — foster community solidarity (Ravuvu 1988:8) and are cultivated at the expense of autonomy and independence.[14]

The predominant relational emphasis in the prescriptions for ideal behavior disfavors personal achivements such as education or physical attractiveness as goals in actualizing the self. Youngsters are, in fact, admonished for pride in academic achievements; humility is a virtue, "while the quintessence of bad manners is to presume beyond one's station" (Toren 1990:183). Self-aggrandizement not only is antithetical to traditional values, but is also perceived as inviting vulnerability to supernatural retribution.[15] The pivotal existential quest of the Fijian is to engage with others via multiple established channels of serving, caring, and material exchange. Cultivation of the self is ideally achieved through the cultivation of social relationships.

The intensive investment in community projects is exemplified in the narrative related to me by Liku, a young, married woman from a chiefly family. Because of her leadership position in the community and, in this instance, in the church's young people's group (*Matavitokani*), she had been approached several years earlier to lead a fundraising effort (*holi*).[16] The request came at a time when Liku had almost no personal financial resources.[17] She described her reaction:

I really smiled at that [their invitation to open the *holi*]; I said "Hai! What made them think of me? I have no money, nothing!" [But they said,] "Never mind that."[18]

But she respected the legitimacy of their request and, after discussing the predicament with her mother and grandfather, accepted the invitation. Around the same time she unexpectedly received a F$700[19] refund from the government for taxes she had overpaid on her income as a schoolteacher. This was an unprecedented amount of money for her to receive as a lump sum. She had also applied for and received a loan of F$500 from the Life Insurance Corporation of India — another surprise. She used F$300 to buy groceries and to contribute to the construction of her grandfather's chiefly *were levu* (traditional Fijian house), planning to donate the balance to the fundraiser. Although kin are conventionally mobilized to assist an individual in this sort of situation, she was amused that her grandfather and mother, unaware of her windfall, were worrying about the size of the contribution. Finally, a young cousin took her aside:

Vasiti was so angry with me . . . [She said,] "Liku, what is wrong with you! Offer some *yaqona* to the *mataqwali*; ask the *mataqwali* to follow you when you open the *holi*. They should help you, they should give money." Me, I replied, "Why is that?" [She countered,] "For shame! The *mataqwali's* going to help out."

Having turned over her entire net worth, the newly acquired F\$900, in the *holi*, she recalled the event with obvious pride:

I'm always happy about it, my actions toward these people, never mind myself. I never want to be . . . greedy . . . I always care about other people.

Notably, Liku did not frame her large donation as a personal sacrifice; rather, she focused on the prestige the large gift had conferred on herself and her family.

The actions manifesting a sense of duty to one's family, children, *mataqwali*, village, church, or traditions earn the approbation of the ever-watching villagers. The person who achieves the epithet "good woman" (*lewa vina*) or "good man" (*seigwane vina*) is the one who is actively, selflessly, and visibly engaged in "carrying the responsibilities of the land on his shoulders" (*dagia na ogaoga ni vanua*).

One of the multiple ways in which selflessness is expressed and achieved in the course of daily activities is by respect (*varohorokotaki*) for authority, which is based on gender, seniority, and rank (that is, chiefly versus commoner).[20] Even individuals whose social position accords them legitimate authority rarely make important decisions without conferring with their kin group. Within a household, a woman is answerable to her brothers, uncles, cousins, or father if unmarried, and not only to her husband, but to his entire *mataqwali* if married. She is considered integral to his *mataqwali's* productive and reproductive resources, although her actual and prospective contributions to the *mataqwali's* endeavors are generally regulated by her husband. He, in turn, must guide his domestic decisions in accordance with the direction of his *mataqwali's* elders. The choice of a marriage partner ideally conforms to the interests of forging an alliance or bringing resources to the group. In some ways, a husband is not the master of his own marriage but a middleman in the management of newly acquired productive and reproductive resources embodied in his wife.

Other social units are similarly bound to hierarchical authority. Fijian kinship relations are structured as a segmentary patrilineage. Households (*vuwere*) are ideally comprised of a couple with their sons,

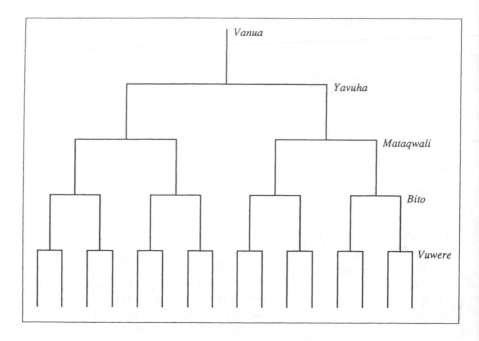

Figure 1.3. Schematized kinship structure in Nadroga.

daughters-in-law, and grandchildren. These *vuwere* are clustered into *bito*, which encompass a larger number of kin. The *bito* are in turn included within *mataqwali*, a still larger network of kin who consider themselves very closely related. These *mataqwali* are then grouped into *yavuha*, which compose a *vanua* (Figure 1.3). Although the latter two groups are reckoned also as kin groups, the unit usually mobilized for the purpose of collective action is either the *mataqwali* or the village (*rara*). For activities within a village, the *mataqwali* are organized separately for complementary functions. On the other hand, if the entire village takes part in a distant event, the various *mataqwali* may pool their efforts or contributions toward a common goal.

Respect for chiefly or senior authority is demonstrated in the strict etiquette governing interpersonal relations. Children are socialized to effect a "timid and self-effacing deportment" in the company of their elders (Toren 1990:183). The order in which bowls of *yaqona* are served or people are invited to eat recognizes and honors the status of the various participants in a gathering. Routine deference is bodily expressed by characteristic postures struck in the presence of others or in the performance of specific activities; for example, a person should crouch at the threshold of any household while awaiting an invitation to enter. More important, a person endeavors always to keep his or her head below the level of others' heads and not to reach or move above the head of another or above the sacred *yaqona* bowl.[21] If circumstances require that a person reach for something, permission is requested first, and after sitting down, this person should *hobo*, or clap with cupped hands, to show respect. Since it is nearly impossible to maneuver in a small area without passing through these spaces, one symbolically stoops while doing so.[22] After one shakes hands with a person of very high chiefly rank, tradition mandates sitting on the ground immediately afterwards and clapping as a sign of respect.

Kinship and Reciprocal Exchange: The Ties That Bind

The Fijian kinship universe is an intricate web fortified by numerous named, non-kin relationships. Personal positioning in Fijian society is secured and enhanced by the density and quality of the social network in which one is embedded.[23] The importance accorded to kin ties is linguistically marked in modes of address that substitute the name of the kin or other type of relationship for the individual name, emphasizing the connection between the individuals rather than the individuals themselves. Moreover, as a sign of respect, in very formal discourse one is referred to in the third person not by personal name but as the "son of so-and-so," or, on parenting offspring, the "father of so-and-so." For example, the chief of Nahigatoka Village, on the birth of his first grandchildren, was henceforth referred to as "the grandfather of the twins."

Use of the kinship system to represent genealogical and affinal relationships is in some ways secondary to its use for social manipulation. This is reminiscent of the "plasticity" of Polynesian kinship Firth described among the Tikopia (1936:485–87). He understood Tikopian kinship as an organizing principle for social cooperation which allowed that "its bonds serve as channels of communication for the members of the society" (484). Indeed, Fijians make an effort to be inclusive in determining kin relationships, assigning nearly everyone within their local area to some "vague category of extended kin" (Quain 1948:74). Two events recorded in my field journal illustrate the malleability of kinship reckoning in Fiji:

A married woman condemned her cousin-sister for a romantic liaison with her uncle, although their genealogical relationship was a social fiction and the two were near the same age. The informant complained that long ago, she herself had dated a fellow villager was her cross-cousin (*tavale*) and hence an appropriate romantic interest. Her mother, however, had objected to the liaison, finding genealogic evidence that the man was simultaneously her uncle and her cousin. Any further romantic relationship was forbidden.

A young woman from a distant village eloped with a man and took up residence in his village. His mother questioned the woman regarding her lineage to ascertain her chiefly connections and the appropriateness of the match. This session revealed that the couple's grandmothers had actually been sisters who eventually moved to locations distant from the respective villages where each of the couple had been raised, a fact previously unknown to the couple because of a series of shifted residences and broken relationships. By Fijian kinship reckoning, this effectively made the two lovers brother and sister, a relationship normally vested with stringent avoidance *tabus*. Since the two were already in love and the match was a mutually advantageous one, their actual relationship was overlooked.

In Fiji, both the relational and the organizational properties of the kinship structure are exploited for social interplay. The grounding of personal identity in regional and kinship networks is well demonstrated in the linguistic conventions used in making the acquaintance of a stranger. Standard questions posed in initiating a conversation refer explicitly to the quality and density of respective kinship networks. For example, two persons who meet may first ascertain what geographic area and family the other is from by asking, "You are a man/woman of what place?" Then they may mutually inquire, "Your parents are alive and well?" or "How many brothers and sisters do you have?" Within a short time, the two are likely to have negotiated a mutually acceptable named relationship based on distant kin, regional, or namesake ties that will govern the tenor of their subsequent interactions. Once this relationship is settled, the two will probably address each other by their relational rather than their given names.

An instance of this negotiation is recorded in my field notes:

When my research assistant and I traveled to the distant Wauosi Village, she seemed uneasy about staying in an unfamiliar village. In our previous site, Bemana, we had been hosted by her mother's half-sister, and our stay in the village had been a virtual celebration of the kinship ties that proliferated from this single relationship. After we presented our *hevuhevu* [*yaqona* offering to request entry and acceptance into a village], she shyly responded to our new hostess' questions regarding her kin. After a couple of well-directed background questions, the two identified a distant genealogical relationship, to their quite perceptible relief. Our hostess reassured the subdivisional nurse who had accompanied us to this village as the sister of a woman who had married into the village that our stay with her would be welcomed. "*Kua ni leqwa!* [Don't worry]," she enjoined, "we are related."

In the event that a kin relationship cannot be conjured from the meeting, the respective parties will invoke one of many other relationships that associate them in some way. For instance, they may be mutual namesakes (*Yaca*)[24] or their respective regional ancestral spirits (*vu*) may have been friends and so, by syllogism, they are *tauvu* and address each other as *Tau*. Other designated relationships linking persons native to Nadroga to those belonging to *mataqwali* in other particular provinces are *Naita*, *Dreu*, *Maseki*, and *Kai*.

Although kin relationships are often exploited to access care or resources in a particular social situation in rather mundane ways, social security and personal well-being fundamentally lie in kinship ties. Just as in other societies in which the lot of the orphan or the bachelor is viewed as "repugnant and even contemptible" (Lévi-Strauss 1985:46), Fijians who are bereft of kinship ties are pitied for their marginality, though efforts are still made to accommodate them within the community. While cross-cousin (*tavale*) marriage is culturally prescribed (if not practiced), a preference for exogamy is preserved in legend and in present-day disapproval of marrying within one's own village.[25] In Nadroga this practice is referred to as *qalu kania*, which implicitly compares the social foolishness of marrying within one's social unit to making the labor-intensive delicacy *qalu* and then eating it oneself in lieu of sharing it.[26] Food considered this special must be shared as an expression and affirmation of social alliance. In sum, marriage, like the sharing of food, is meant to enlarge the social universe by greasing the channels of exchange or engaging others in reciprocal exchange relationships.

Although some current interracial hostility exists between ethnic Fijians and Fiji Indians, Fijian protocol organized around receiving and entertaining *vulagi* suggests a traditional predilection to engage and incorporate those from outside the immediate social sphere. Claude Lévi-Strauss argues that outsiders are treated as valuable assets in cases in which "the foreigner enjoys the prestige of exoticism and, by his presence, embodies the opportunity of widening social ties" (Lévi-Strauss 1985:7). Despite their frequent bewilderment over European customs (*itovo*) or their criticism of the *itovo* of people from distant regions, Fijians are quite eager to create ties to distant groups and places through contact with *vulagi* who travel through their village. Elaborate rituals formally introduce an outsider into a new kin or village community. The initial welcome entails reciprocal presentations of *yaqona* in the *hevuhevu* and *matakarawa* ceremonies.[27] Thereafter, in some circumstances, the guest is honored with bounteous displays of food offerings and gifts and is often graciously attended to during a *magisi*. If the visit is an extended one, the guest's request for departure (*yaqona ni tatau*) and offering of thanks (*vavinavina*), both framed within presentations of *yaqona*, are reciprocated with a farewell feast or *yaqona* presentation (*vitalatala*) and often a pile of gifts with the feast (*bili ni mua*). Finally, in the absence of their departed guest, the hosts will convene to offer a special bowl of *yaqona* to commemorate the visit.

In addition to the complex array of kin and other named relationships that effectively enmesh Fijians in a network of social reward and obligation, social distance is negotiated through a variety of exchange relationships that cross-cut geographic and intergenerational distance. Reciprocal exchange is a ubiquitous feature of Fijian life; indebtedness continually accrues among namesakes, households, kin groups, or other particular affiliates mobilized to contribute labor, food, or material wealth to another group. However, traditional material wealth (*iyau*) — in the form of whale's teeth (*tabua*), *yaqona*, drums of kerosene, mats, painted barkcloth, or bolts of fabric — is rarely reckoned in terms of accumulation because its primary value is for exchange. Upon receipt, it is redistributed along with raw or cooked foodstuffs according to exchange protocol within the group to which it has been presented. Ultimately, the elements of traditional material wealth will resurface time and time again to be exchanged. For example, the marriage of a woman into her husband's village is celebrated with feasting and the exchange of *iyau*. During her married years, descendants of her mother's family of origin, or *kovana*, might visit with food gifts from time to time to pay their respect to her. Upon her death, each *mataqwali* in the village into which she has married contributes items to present at her funeral in addition to cooking for the many guests who will arrive. The collected drums of kerosene, *tabua*, mats, and barkcloth are subsequently redistributed among her *kovana*. Once having accepted these same items, her *kovana* will eventually, in turn, contribute them to their own *mataqwali's* effort at collecting *iyau* for presentation at other *ogaoga*, such as baptisms, weddings, or funerals.

Accumulation of *iyau* is generally transient; what endure are the social ties that are reaffirmed with each exchange and the prestige conferred upon both the recipient and the giver in enacting it. Marcel Mauss has cautioned against viewing such exchanges as economically instrumental; these practices are not motivated by utilitarian goals:

On the contrary, it is something other than utility which makes goods circulate in these multifarious and fairly enlightened societies. Clans, age groups and sexes, in view of the many relationships ensuing from contacts between them, are in a state of perpetual economic effervescence which has little about it that is materialistic; it is much less prosaic than our sale and purchase, hire of services and speculations. (Mauss 1967:70)

The primary purpose in the accumulation of any exchanged *iyau* is simply to equip the group to enter into their next exchange, thereby guaranteeing maintenance of social ties. Indeed, Fijians are explicit that their exchange practices are economically deleterious. They bemoan their inability to save money or accrue resources because of their perpetual obligations to contribute personal resources to the group. There are no net material gains in the enterprise, only social gains.[28]

Even when exchanges are not formal, there are mechanisms to remind one that he or she is always accountable to the whims and needs of others within a certain defined relational network. Fijians are loath to refuse requests, no matter how personally cumbersome. This is especially true of relationships between *tavale* and *tauvu*. Some of these transactions are greeted with acknowledged ambivalence, yet in theory the binding moral obligation to give supersedes any perceived personal sacrifice, or, more accurately, should militate against even experiencing it as a sacrifice. Exchange on this level is facilitated by the convention of *kerekere*, which frames a request as something which cannot be easily refused.[29] Fijians exercise *kerekere* with some degree of restraint, but all in all, favors, personal time, household goods, and food circulate from person to person and group to group, making the notion of ownership relative. One young woman explained that within the community "there isn't anything that belongs to you that really belongs to you — actually, that belongs to your uncle, to your auntie, to your cousins or anybody."

Some ownership, such as land rights and village structures, is explicitly communal (although these may be held in the name of the village chief, who acts for the collective). Other property may nominally belong to an individual, household, or clan, but the hold on these items is tenuous at best. In contrast, certain possessions are linguistically marked or culturally designated as inalienable. For instance, a *tadratadra* — a pile of mats and bark paintings presented to someone to mark an important occasion and on which they must sit — may not be taken away from an individual.[30]

Social intimacy is also approximated, though in a rather stereotyped way, through joking discourse (*viwaletaki*), which is ubiquitous in social relations and invoked with particular frequency in *tavale* and *tauvu* relationships. Fijian humor centers on allusions loaded with double-entendre that confuse the *mataqwali*'s *cavu* (roughly translatable as totem) with the personal genitals of its members. On occasion one is also subject to good-natured teasing based on social deviance, such as a propensity to drink too much *yaqona* or to be effeminate if male. The allusions to *cavu* are illustrated in exchanges like the following:

An elderly man was seen in the local outpatient department for a minor illness complaint. When a young woman inquired what the doctor had prescribed for therapy, the man replied that surgery had been proposed. The perplexed woman returned, "Surgery on what?" To this, the old man replied with a chuckle, "My *vudi* [his *mataqwali* totem, or representation of genitals] has to be cut!"

In other instances, a stranger may be greeted in a new village with joking about respective *cavu*. For example, once, after bathing in a river in Bemana Village, my hostess and I passed a group of men who rhetorically inquired where we were coming from. My friend whispered that I should reply, "We have just finished rinsing our *ivi* [the Tahitian chestnut, which is both a seasonal delicacy and the particular *cavu* of Bemana villagers]," a comment which was greeted with uproarious laughter from the men. This pervasive sexual pseudofamiliarity, which is also reflected in the fairly common greeting, "*Barewa*" ("Is it possible . . . [for us to sleep together]"), is juxtaposed with certain stringent avoidance tabus that govern a limited number of relationships.[31] In either case, Fijians engage in an extremely codified discourse that constructs or reaffirms their social positioning vis-à-vis the other with either stereotyped humor or respect.

In conclusion, Fijian experience must be contextualized as a continuous exercise in actualizing, cultivating, and maintaining the individual's connections to the social world. This process of mobilizing relational bonds, however, should not be seen as necessarily goal-oriented · though in some cases it may be quite calculated—but as a way of being. In this mode of accomplishing both quotidian and ritual tasks, individuals continually cast themselves as agents of the *mataqwali* or the community. Attributes that in Western ideology stamp the individual as unique or posit the individual and the community as polarized nodes are forgone in the interest of emphasizing the individual's multiple connections to the community, whether in conforming to codified behavior, in deference to the hierarchy of social groups in which one is nested, or in active accountability to others for exchange of resources and services. The following chapters detail the primacy of relational ties to and within the community in a variety of contexts that ultimately forge the experience of self and body in Fijian culture.

Chapter 2
Body Imagery, Ideals, and Cultivation: Discourses on Alienation and Integration

How are the various meanings that are projected onto and expressed through individual bodies socially mediated? How does the social inscribe its values onto the body, and to what extent is the individual a willing versus a hapless accomplice to the act of inscription? What legitimation is granted to the use of the body as an instrument of the social order or, alternatively, as a vehicle for personal expression of talents or affiliation with a certain community? This chapter addresses these questions by beginning to examine how the appropriation of the body as either a personal or collective entity bears on embodied experience, and the ways in which the body betrays, portrays, constrains, imprisons, or releases the self.

Core cultural values are clearly encoded in aesthetic ideals for body shape (see Douglas 1970; Suleiman 1985). Especially in the West, these ideals are constructed, homogenized, and reified in the media (see Bordo 1993). In Fijian society, too, there appears to be a consensual ideal with respect to the aesthetics of bodily form, with admiration of a particular shape corresponding to positive sentiments about what the shape encodes or suggests. What seems to differentiate the Westerner from the Fijian, therefore, is not the ability to construct and admire an ideal, nor the ability to identify the core values reflected in it, but rather, as we shall see in the pages that follow, the interest and investment in attaining the ideal by cultivating, nurturing, and disciplining the body.

The Cultural Construction of Bodily Aesthetics

The corporeal form registers the personal and social history that forges it, its contours remarkably malleable to efforts to remold or embellish them. At the most fundamental level, the body conforms to affirm its membership in a particular community. Claude Lévi-Strauss has observed that

all cultures leave their mark on the human body: through styles of costume, hair, and ornament, through physical mutilation, and through gestures, they mimic differences comparable to those that can exist between races, and by favoring certain physical types, they stabilize and perhaps even spread them. (Lévi-Strauss 1985:17)

This tendency may be more marked in societies in which solidarity is fostered, in which "the proper duty of man is to resemble his companions, to realize in himself all the traits of the collective type which are then confounded, much more than today, with human type" (Durkheim 1933:403). Indeed, social positioning solidly in the interior or at the margins of a group may be manipulated through either endorsement or disregard of consensual standards of body presentation.

Identification with a particular subcultural ethos is achieved through visibly cultivating the body — through dress, exercise, diet, or hairstyle, for example — in ways commensurate with the moral priorities of the community. In other words, core cultural or subcultural values are encoded in body habitus and participation in bodily conformity. Pierre Bourdieu has argued that "taste" is expressed primarily through the body.

Taste, a class culture turned into nature, that is, *embodied*, helps to shape the class body. It is an incorporated principle of classification which governs all forms of incorporation, choosing and modifying everything that the body ingests and digests and assimilates, physiologically. It follows that the body is the most indisputable materialization of class taste, which it manifests in several ways. It does this first in the seemingly most natural features of the body, the dimensions (volume, height, weight) and shapes (round or square, stiff or supple, straight or curved) of its visible forms, which express in countless ways a whole relation to the body, i.e., a way of treating it, caring for it, feeding it, maintaining it, which reveals the deepest dispositions of the habitus. (Bourdieu 1984:190)

Ideal types representing these core values, whether they be beauty, fertility, or self-restraint, are reflected in art and, more recently, in popular media. The shifting aesthetics of the body are documented in paleontological figurines and antiquarian sculptures depicting stylized obese, pregnant-like females (Bruch 1973:9) and traced through Renaissance to modern art as bodies are unclothed and reclothed and their dimensions fashioned according to current tastes. A number of studies document the evolving American cultural preference for a slender, tubular female form as embodied by such women as winners of beauty pageants and centerfolds of erotic magazines (Garner et al. 1980; Wiseman et al. 1992),[1] or pictured in women's magazines (Silverstein,

Peterson, and Perdue 1986; Silverstein et al. 1986). The media reifies and routinizes cultural predilections, making them widely accessible as a lexicon of the body (see Bordo 1993).

How, then, are body shape ideals constructed and endorsed? How is social positioning negotiated and legitimated through the emulation or rejection of such consensual standards? Bourdieu argues that appearance is adjusted to reflect "social markers" within a "system of distinctive signs which they constitute and which is itself homologous with the system of social positions" (Bourdieu 1984:192). This system is organized according to an economy of cultural capital; that is, desirability is relative to accessibility to various forms or practices that can be characterized as "rare" or "vulgar" (176). Specifically, Bourdieu notes that material constraints have shifted such that both cuisine and bodily form now reflect social distinction by rejection of "coarseness and fatness in favor of slimness" (185).

Likewise, Margaret Mackenzie notes that "restraint in eating and effort in exercise may become symbols of social prestige" in a context of abundance (Mackenzie 1985:175). On the other hand, in environments characterized by vulnerability to scarcity, such as in the South Pacific, prestige is more likely to be reflected in evidence of access to food resources. As an example Mackenzie cites the formidable stature of Tongan royalty as a cultural symbol of prosperity "in a context where only a king can control enough food resources and labor supply to eat enough and do no physical labor so that he becomes fat" (176). She concludes that since body fat is one of the few social markers accessible to individual control, it has great appeal as a target of manipulation in the achievement of social prestige (185).

Body shape as a marker for female beauty has evolved in the West throughout the twentieth century for a variety of reasons. From 1900 to 1920, medico-actuarial standards for weight were constructed to promote a leaner body as healthier (Brumberg 1988:233–34). During the 1920s American beauty culture was institutionalized through the fashion, modeling, and cosmetics industries and the advent of beauty contests and motion pictures (231). Through advertising, women were encouraged to study themselves visually and to compare their own appearance with those of others (Lasch 1979:167–68; Bordo 1993:25). Commercial production of ready-to-wear clothing standardized and emphasized garment sizes, thereby providing a comparative measure for women's bodies (Brumberg 1988:240). Around the same time, home economics promoted a scientific approach to food and eating, enabling measurement of caloric intake (236–37). As a result, dieting and the cultivation of the body have evolved as legitimate social pursuits as well as lucrative industries.

Although slimness as a marker of social prestige would seem to be equally attainable by all socioeconomic classes, popular perception associates slimness with wealth in the United States (see Ritenbaugh 1982). For example, aristocratic looks were associated with a romanticized image of tuberculosis early in this century (Sontag 1979:28). In the 1950s several sociological surveys demonstrated a dramatically higher than average prevalence of obesity in lower socioeconomic class girls and women (Bruch 1973:19). Moreover, the early literature on the epidemiology of eating disorders identified high socioeconomic status as a risk factor for developing anorexia nervosa (Garfinkel and Garner 1983:3). With an estimated 36 to 43 percent of the United States population overweight or obese (Gray 1989:9), weight control remains a fruitful arena for manipulation of social image.

A wealth of literature documents the ongoing pursuit of a slender body in the United States and Europe. The media continue to supply the public with idealized body types as (usually impractical) targets for emulation; health clubs have transformed exercise from an activity to a commodity; and the population continues to digest a proliferation of dieting literature and technologies. A 1985 study showed that a majority of women and a near-majority of men surveyed indicated dissatisfaction with their weight (Cash 1990:61). A recent survey of fifty college undergraduates found that a staggering 91 percent of the females and 30 percent of males wished to reduce their weight, and that 57 percent of the females and 15 percent of the males were actively dieting (Becker 1988). Investigators in another study have concluded that, irrespective of their body weight, most young women will, at some point, wish to be thinner and diet to lose more than three kilograms (Abraham et al. 1983:225). Finally, another study documents that more than one-fifth of a general population sample of adult women have symptoms of disordered eating (Cooper et al. 1984).

It has become fashionable to link this cultural preoccupation with body shape and dieting with the increasing prevalence of eating disorders (Bruch 1973; Brumberg 1989; Schwartz et al. 1983; Mackenzie 1985; B. Turner 1984; Bordo 1993).[2] While there has been debate over whether these disorders represent extreme behavior on the dieting continuum or distinct psychopathologies (Garner et al. 1984:255; Pope and Hudson 1984), cultural critics argue that these psychopathologies and their widespread behavioral analogues are a "crystallization" of Western culture (Bordo 1993).

The bodily disparagement and wish to control weight and appetite that are phenomenologically highlighted in eating disorders engender body alienation. Feminist and cultural critics have drawn appropriate attention to the objectification of the female body and the promotion of ideal body types through the media and consumerism; these are indeed implicated in some of the tragic manifestations of the consumerist-driven manipulation of body shape and weight.

The Alienation of the Self from the Body in Western Discourse

John Shade's physical appearance was so little in keeping with the harmonies hiving in the man, that one felt inclined to dismiss it as a coarse disguise or passing fashion . . . His misshapen body, that gray mop of abundant hair, the yellow nails of his pudgy fingers, the bags under his lusterless eyes, were only intelligible if regarded as the waste products eliminated from his intrinsic self by the same forces of perfection which purified and chiseled his verse. He was his own cancellation.

—Vladimir Nabokov, *Pale Fire*

The thematic disjuncture between the essence of self and an incongruent exterior surfaces in literature (with legends of princes appearing as toads) and in the common knowledge that "books are not judged by their covers." The discourse on Western embodied experience has noted the possibility of extreme objectification of the body and the often concomitant alienation of body from self (see Shilling 1993:200, B. Turner 1992:40). The literature on illness experience documents the possibilities of profound estrangement from the body. Pain can threaten the "taken-for-granted quality of the lifeworld" (Good 1992:41) and deconstruct the self's relation to the body when, "as a locus of pain, the body takes on agency over and against the self" (39). Illness or disability may cost the "unreflective harmony" of the body (Zegans 1987:30) when the body begins to "invade" one's thoughts (Murphy 1987:13). The experience of the self as *separate from* the body is evident in statements such as "he felt as if he no longer inhabited his body" (Zegans 1987:30), and "Gradually, my thoughts became disembodied, and I began to think of myself as if a part of me were perched over the headboard, watching the rest; it was as if it were happening to somebody else" (Murphy 1987:5). Alternatively, the self is portrayed as *trapped within* the body, as in "the entombment of my mind in inert protoplasm" (29). In either case, the connection between self and body is disintegrated and the two are cast as adversaries. Emily Martin has extensively documented the separation of self from body in her work on the female body. Self is separated from physical sensation—an experience fostered by anesthetic technology and the biomedical tendency to dehumanize its clinical subjects—in verbal imagery such as *"Your self is separate from your body," "Your body is something your self has to adjust to or cope with,"* and *"Your body needs to be controlled by your self"* (Martin 1987:77; italics in original).

Although this estrangement of self from bodily sensation is fore-grounded during an illness episode or its biomedical management, the alienation of the self from the body is by no means restricted to gyneco-logic or general illness contexts. It also emerges in popular experiential discourse in such references as "a woman trapped in a man's body" or "a thin person trapped in a fat person's body." Similarly, obese persons have often been found to conceptualize themselves as living a "double life in which the body or outer appearance represents a false self as opposed to the true, hidden, inner one" (Millman 1981:186).

On the other hand, physical stigmata are publicly read as indicators of the self in the body. Frustration about the disjunction between the self and body image is commonly experienced with respect to the body's shape or the body's needs. Obesity in our society is profoundly stigma-tizing (Bruch 1973:99; Mackenzie 1985).[3] Hilde Bruch observes:

Fat people tend to talk about their bodies as external to themselves. They do not feel identified with this bothersome and ugly thing they are condemned to carry through life, and in which they feel confined or imprisoned. (1973:102)

Moreover, obese persons may identify with only their head or face as their "core 'self'" (Millman 1981:94). As a result, the "probability of experiencing the body with unease, embarrassment, timidity grows with the disparity between the ideal body and the real body, the dream body and the 'looking-glass self' reflected in the reactions of others" (Bour-dieu 1984:207).

With the increasing divergence between cultural standards and actual bodies (Garner et al. 1980), embodied experience risks intrinsic alien-ation. For example, the elaboration of dieting technology and discourse has contributed to the experience of hunger "as an alien invader" ex-trinsic to self (Bordo 1993:146).[4] Restricting the appetite becomes an exercise in self-control and diet is recast as an arena of moral choices. One young American woman observed, "If I said I was 'good' today, [my husband] knows just what I mean, . . . it means how I ate" (Becker 1986:9). Another American woman reflected on the preoccupation with diet among college friends:

Some people would say that they think about food all the time, that all they do is they think about . . . y'know — they go to breakfast and then between breakfast and lunch all they are thinking about is . . . what they ate at breakfast and how they're going to burn it off, and how much or how little they're going to eat at lunch . . . you know it's hard to study when . . . the only thing you're really concerned with is . . . what to eat and what not to eat and how much to exercise, and y'know, constantly counting calories and it can get really frustrating because it's hard, like I said, it's hard to keep up with your studies when . . . the thoughts of food are the predominant thoughts in your mind. (1986:10)

In these instances appetite is formulated as conflicting with the goals and desires of the self. The legacy of mind-body dualism lends itself to the description and experience of the body as alien, limiting, and the enemy, themes echoed in the anorectic's body imagery (Bordo 1993:144–49).

Working on the Body: The Cult of Cultivation

The discourse on embodied experience of the self in the West contrasts images of the body "to be escaped" on the one hand and "to be worked on" on the other. In the latter case, the body becomes a disguise, a costume, or a representational schema for the inner self. Erving Goffman likens this presentation of self to a performance structured in accordance with various public symbols (1959:1). The individual makes use of a repertoire of "expressive equipment" in conveying a particular image by manipulating these symbols. For example, "As part of a personal front we may include: insignia of office or rank; clothing; sex, age, and racial characteristics; size and looks; posture; speech patterns; facial expression; bodily gestures; and the like" (24). For a variety of reasons, body shape rivals the above categories as a dominant, preferred symbol in the presentation and representation of the self.

Christopher Lasch traces the evolution of self-cultivation in American culture from its roots in the Puritan ethic of devotion to the social community. In the eighteenth century, the self became an object of cultivation with respect to mind and character. Finally, in the early 1900s, appearance was emphasized as a window to the person (Lasch 1979:105–67). This development has culminated in the "self-absorption" that "defines the moral climate of contemporary society" (61) and is reflected in the emphasis of the visual presentation of persons and in the concomitant manipulation of the visual images, so that life is focused on "seeming" rather than "being" (see Bourdieu 1984:200). This "mechanical reproduction of culture, the proliferation of visual and audial images in the 'society of the spectacle'" lends contemporary experience the quality of "a hall of mirrors" (Lasch 1979:96–97).

The promotion of the self through a particular image referrable to public symbols may well have begun at the turn of the century with the romanticizing of tuberculosis (Sontag 1979:28). What has ensued is the public projection of the self through the manipulation of body imagery. That is, precisely because the body is "a site of enormous symbolic work and symbolic production," it becomes "an environment we practice on and also practice with" (B. Turner 1984:190). In this sense, bodies reflect self-image and character through symbols. For example, an obese or "unrestrained" body may translate to a statement about "unrestrained morality" (197). Indeed, obesity has become a dominant symbol for "moral shortcomings in self-discipline" (Mackenzie 1985:175). In turn, self-image is built upon the body, and a "sense of adequacy, shame, or worth often arises from a sense of the comparative value of the body" and dissatisfaction with their body image may lead people to reconfigure their appearance (Zegans 1987:42).

As Bryan Turner observes, "we labor on, in and with bodies" (1984: 190). The self constructs a particular public image by choosing from a field of bodily symbols that may equate obesity with indulgence, laziness, or sheer ineptitude in managing self-presentation; thinness with embodied restraint; and toned musculature with disciplined work on the body. The body and its desires are formulated as entities to struggle against in our efforts to sculpt and inscribe our virtues in their contours. In short, bodies exist not only to live in and think with, but also to struggle against in forging a personal identity.

Where is the appeal in the intensive labor on the body, the suppression of its desires, and the manipulation of its shape? The legitimation of and interest in cultivating bodily space is rendered meaningful against the backdrop of the basic tenets of the Western experience of selfhood. Where there is cultural validation of expression of autonomy through the body and authorization of a congruity of body with identity, bodily cultivation is permitted and even celebrated.

Effecting autonomy through the discipline of the body has been evident in the discourse on body and gender. Feminists and religious scholars have noted that women, historically constrained by patriarchic authority, have otherwise sought autonomy and personal control through the use of their bodies, particularly with respect to dietary restraint. In medieval Europe, fasting was a chief avenue of self-expression for women, so that "by means of food, women controlled themselves and their world" (Bynum 1985:10). The extreme dietary abstinence of several female saints is well-documented in Rudolph Bell's work on "holy anorexics," who exercised control over their lives by refusal of food. Bell writes:

Over this invasion of their bodies these women retain but one choice — whether to bring a bowl to their lips or a fork to their mouths — and they choose to say no. (Bell 1985:115)

Both Clare of Assisi and Catherine of Siena refused to eat as a religio-culturally validated means of demonstrating autonomy; it was "a positive expression of self by a woman in response to the world that attempted to dominate her" (178).

Similarly, anorectics' refusal to eat is often contextualized as a bid for control against a parent's will. And a chief means of establishing autonomy in contemporary Western society remains control over personal bodily maintenance (Minuchin et al. 1978, B. Turner 1984:191; Bordo 1993:178–79). The power in the refusal to eat lies in its eventual manifestation in flesh. Within the context of "holy" and contemporary anorexia, the battle for self-determination is realized through manipulation of the body. Thus these women — tragically and ironically — become accomplices to the objectification of their own bodies.

The reflexive cultivation of the self and body in Western society is rooted in the formulation of "oneself as the ethical subject of one's actions" with the eventual promotion of the care of the self (Foucault 1988:84). Michel Foucault has written:

It also took the form of an attitude, a mode of behavior; it became instilled in ways of living; it evolved into procedures, practices, and formulas that people reflected on, devloped, perfected, and taught. It thus came to constitute a social practice, giving rise to relationships between individuals, to exchanges and communications, and at times even to institutions. And it gave rise, finally, to a certain mode of knowledge and to the elaboration of a science. (1988:45)

Drawing from Foucault, Bryan Turner argues that "the emergence of the detailed, disciplined control of the body in a matrix of social settings" spawned the development of the ethic of a "sober, disciplined and rational life style in capitalism" (1982:256–57). He locates bodily cultivation in this context, writing that "contemporary anxieties about obesity and dieting, slimming and anorexia, eating and allergy are part of the extension of rational calculation over the body and employment of science in the apparatus of social control" (267). He further writes:

The new self is a visible self and the body, suitably decorated and presented, came to symbolize overtly the status of the personal self. Identity became embodied in external performance. (B. Turner 1984: 202)

Hence the commodification of the body within late capitalist, consumerist culture engenders a vested interest in its cultivation (see also Bordo 1993:15).

The body has increasingly become a forum for the staging of the self; the self commandeers this presentation by methods subject to the symbolic significance the society imputes to body shape. Social success is contingent on a careful construction of a particular image — especially on the cultivation of "successful bodies, which have been trained, disciplined and orchestrated to enhance our personal value" (B. Turner 1984:111). Health has become associated with various practices on the body: aerobic exercise, a scrupulously formulated diet, the ingestion of multivitamins and megavitamins, and so forth. In essence, health is an "achieved" status, with each individual "expected to 'work hard' at being strong, fit and healthy" (Scheper-Hughes and Lock 1987:22). Work on the body is displayed through the wearing of "workout" clothing and in health clubs that choreograph exercise as a public performance. The cultural validation of this ethic of intensive investment in the body as the primary expression of the self has transmogrified the goal of work on the body from the end product of health or aesthetic form to the display of its cultivation.

The modes of bodily cultivation have proliferated through the various industries designed to transform the body's appearance. Cosmetic technologies (particularly targeted at women) have evolved from disguising and highlighting facial features to actually reconfiguring bodies through breast augmentation and reduction, liposuction, and collagen injections. The intensity and extremity of this investment in resculpting the body are testimony that "no price is too great, no process too repulsive, no operation too painful for the woman who would be beautiful" (Millman 1981:117; see also Fallon 1990:97). In short, vanity has been transformed into a virtue in a culture in which "creation of the self" is the "highest form of creativity" (Lasch 1979:168).

In many ways, cultivation of bodily space has become the preeminent mode of self cultivation in contemporary Western society. This stems from the commodification and objectification of the body within consumerist late-capitalist culture, thus legitimating and encouraging work upon it. Foucault has maintained that in the West the relation of the self to the body is rooted in the larger societal institutions that seek to discipline and control bodies en masse, the body being a social substance that is "manipulated, shaped, trained, which obeys, responds, becomes skilful and increases its forces" (1979:136). Anthony Giddens has argued, however, that in high modernity the body is reflexively appropriated as part of the "project of the self," and is not exclusively subject to institutional forces disciplining it. That is, the body and the self "become intimately coordinated within the reflexive project of self-identity" (Giddens 1991:218).

Foucault argued that in the development of " 'the cultivation of the self' . . . the relations of oneself to oneself were intensified and valorized" (1988:43). In the post-traditional world, we have become increasingly "responsible for the design of our own bodies" (Giddens 1991:102). The mutual identification and congruity of self with body has permitted the representational use of the body to flourish in this context. Hence, the use of the body as a vehicle for self-expression is facilitated by its objectification in consumerist culture, core values supporting individuation and autonomy, and the authorization of use of the body as personal space. This latter dimension is essential to determining whether the body is personally or socially cultivated. In fact, in comparing the cultivation of bodily space in the West and in Fiji, a key issue which emerges is not *how*, but *by and for whom* the body is cultivated. One's authority and interest in reflexively cultivating one's personal body hinge on the cultural validation of personal agency and identity with respect to the body. This, in turn, is linked to the experience of self vis-à-vis a community.

The Western cultivation of the personal body requires that personal excellence and identity can be represented (or misrepresented) by manipulation of bodily symbols indexing aptitude and discipline. Moreover, this cultivation presupposes that the self has jurisdiction over the body for the purpose of communication, and that the body represents a *personal* as opposed to a *community* resource for expression. On the other hand, in the context of an intensified degree of embeddedness in social relations (and perhaps less in one's body) cultivation of the body is not legitimated as an exclusively personal enterprise.

In the ethnographic data below we will begin to explore how it is that the relation of the self to the body is mediated through the relation of the self to the community. The remainder of this chapter discusses the bodily cultivation through attention to weight and appetite in the Fijian context. Subsequently, we will explore the salience of body shape as a marker of social connectedness rather than of personal identity.

The Body and the Self in Fiji: The Ethnographic Data on Body Shape Preferences

Given the historical flux of Western preferences for body shape, it seems intuitive that there will also be cross-cultural variability in aesthetic ideals for body shape and weight. Moreover, we suppose that these preferences might reflect core cultural values somehow encoded in body shapes themselves. We further conjecture that attention to body shape and interest in cultivating the body reflect social processes, stemming from the political economy, gender relations, or the cultural construction and social conditioning of the self.

Anecdotal evidence in the ethnographic literature suggests a tremendous variability in bodily aesthetics, including body shape.[5] In a study in which Kenyan and British subjects were shown cartoon drawings of gradated female shapes (varying with respect to body fat), Kenyans perceived endomorphic female shapes more positively than the British did (Furnham and Alibhai 1983).[6] Researchers attributed the Kenyans' more positive valuation of obese female figures to their association of body fat with sufficient food in a land of scarce resources.

Similarly, ethnographers in the South Pacific have noted the association of social status with physical stature (see Johnson 1981:327; Macken-zie 1985; Shore 1989); specifically, chiefly *mana*, or power, "is expressed in images of abundance" in Polynesia (Shore 1989:138). The corpulence of high-ranking women in traditional Samoan, Tongan, New Zealand, and Tikopian society is associated with "forms of societal and cosmic regeneration" inherent in the symbolism of "sacred maidens" (156–59). Moreover, in these societies the relative vulnerability to food shortage also makes prestige unlikely to be symbolized in dietary restraint (Mac-kenzie 1985).

Given its geographic and cultural proximity to Western Polynesia, it might be conjectured that there are similarities in aesthetic ideals for body shapes in Fiji. Indeed, largeness is highly valued in a variety of contexts, including body size. The Fijians' explicit attentiveness to fluctuations in weight and body shape is often registered in insults asso-ciating weight loss and thinness with social neglect or deprivation and compliments relating a robust form with healthy vigor and social con-nectedness. However, while there seems to be a consensual preference for particular ideal physical attributes in Fiji, there is a striking absence of interest in attaining these as a personal goal. Moreover, given the close attention directed toward others' body shapes and sizes reflected in constant commentary, there is a paradoxical denial of interest in cul-tivating one's own shape to approximate the ideal. Both the cultural ideals and the attitude toward them are discussed in the following pages.

Attitudes Toward and Assessment of Self and Body Shape: The Survey Data

In order to establish a basis on which to compare perceptions of ideal body shapes among Fijians with those of other cultures, Fijians in four Nadroga villages, including Nahigatoka, were surveyed about their atti-tudes toward body shape and work on the body.[7] In an eight-page ques-tionnaire administered to 129 adult men and 172 adult women (see Appendix B, Figure B-1), respondents were asked in their native lan-guage about attitudes toward their own bodies and toward body shapes in general. The questionnaire consisted of four major sections regard-ing: (1) baseline demographic information, (2) dietary behavior and attitudes, (3) attitudes toward male and female body shapes, and (4) the relative importance of various personal attributes. Section 3 asked re-spondents to evaluate 24 randomly presented cartoon drawings of men and women (12 of each gender) ranging from very thin to obese shapes in approximately even gradations, adapted from Furnham and Alibhai (1983) with modification of hairstyles to resemble traditional Fijian hair (Figures 2.1, B-1). Participants were asked to rate these shapes on a

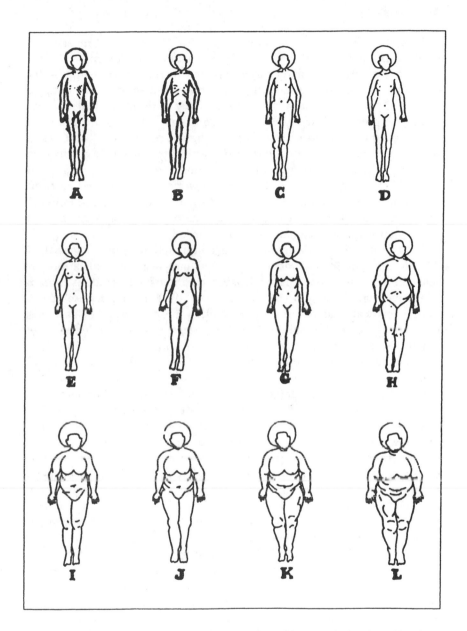

Figure 2.1. Gradated female body shapes (adapted by permission from Furnham and Alibhai 1983).

scale from 1 to 7 (1 being the most positive, 7 being the most negative) on the basis of selected polarized attributes: for example, attractive/unattractive, well taken care of/poorly taken care of, eating well/eating poorly, healthy/unhealthy, thoughtful/selfish, happy/unhappy, respected/despised, and wealthy/poor. They were then asked whether the figure presented hypothetically ought to gain, lose, or maintain his or her weight. In addition to rating each figure, respondents were asked to rate themselves according to the same attributes on a scale of 1 to 7. In order to help them expand on their responses, they were also asked to select from a compiled set of shapes in answering a number of questions including, "Which shape looks best?" "Which shape do you resemble?" and "Which shape would you like to resemble?" Each respondent's own weight status was also calculated and recorded.[8]

A total of 301 questionnaires were completed in four villages. Distributions, frequencies, and some Chi square tests of association for selected variables were analyzed using the Statistical Analysis System (SAS) package, Version 6 (SAS Institute 1990). For the purpose of creating statistically adequate sample sizes, some categories of variables were collapsed in the analysis. Further specifics of the survey sample, details about the development and administration of the questionnaire, and selected statistical representations are presented in Appendices B and C.

While the survey collected men's and women's responses to both male and female shapes, data presentation and interpretation focus on female responses to female shapes for two reasons. First, because most studies on body image and dieting behavior focus on female attitudes and behaviors, there are few comparative data by which to evaluate male responses or responses to male shapes in Fiji. Second, and more important, because of methodologic difficulties inherent to cross-gender interviewing in Fiji, ethnographic interview data, which make the survey data meaningful and interpretable, were collected primarily from women. Although selfhood and embodied experience are implicitly gendered, this analysis will bracket the important categories of gender and age in order to narrow its focus on the impact of the relation of self to society on embodied experience within the general cultural ideology. Many facets of daily experience and routine in Fiji are gender-segregated, suggesting that the differences in male and female attitudes toward bodies and in embodied experience will provide a fruitful area for further investigation. On the other hand, whereas the data presented in this analysis largely reflect Fijian women's experience and attitudes, there are grounds to believe that many of the important elements of cultural notions of selfhood and attitudes toward body shapes described here are generalizable to both sexes.[9]

The first important result revealed by the study was the extremely high prevalence of overweight and obesity among Fijian as compared with American adults (Figures 2.2 and 2.3), with a striking two-thirds of Fijian adults (both males and females) categorized as overweight or obese.[10] Despite falling into the latter categories, many obese and overweight Fijian women apparently perceived their own weight as appropriate or under a desirable weight, with 54 percent of obese female respondents indicating they felt they should maintain their weight and around 72 percent of overweight women answering they felt they should maintain their present weight. In addition, 17 percent of obese women and 8 percent of overweight women responded that they wished actually to gain weight.[11]

The survey investigated whether there was a consensual preference for a particular body shape, as well as what attributes might be associated with various degrees of thinness and obesity. The findings are partially presented in Figures C-1 through C-13 in Appendix C. Briefly, Fijian women rated the medium weight range female shapes (Figure 2.1, D through G) as the more attractive; the most attractive shape selected was F (the mid-range shape). Since the body shape drawings used in this survey were similar to those used in Adrian Furnham's and Naznin Alibhai's 1983 study of British and Kenyan attitudes toward body shape, a tentative intercultural comparison of evaluations of the various shapes is possible. Matching the responses of the Fijian, British, and Kenyan subjects side by side reveals striking cross-cultural consistency in identifying a similar cluster of medium weight range shapes as most attractive (Figure 2.4). By the same token, all groups rated extremely thin or obese shapes as relatively unattractive. However, Fijians and Kenyans were more tolerant of the overweight to obese figures, rating figures G through L relatively more positively than did the British women.

One might speculate that exposure to Western institutions and values may have influenced the Fijians' selection of an ideal form, accounting for the similarity to British preferences. The available data, however, do not support such a hypothesis. Regardless of a respondent's age or the relative distance of his or her village from an urban area, attractiveness ratings were consistent across the full range of body shapes, with all the demographic groups responding most favorably to the mid-range weight shape, F (Figures C-14 and C-15). Moreover, men and women showed no appreciable differences in their assessments of either female or male shapes (Figures C-16 and C-17).

Despite giving relatively low attractiveness ratings for the range of overweight and obese shapes, Fijian women associated them with the very positively valued high quality of care (*viqwaravi*). They perceived that the thinner figures (A, B, and C) were poorly cared for relative

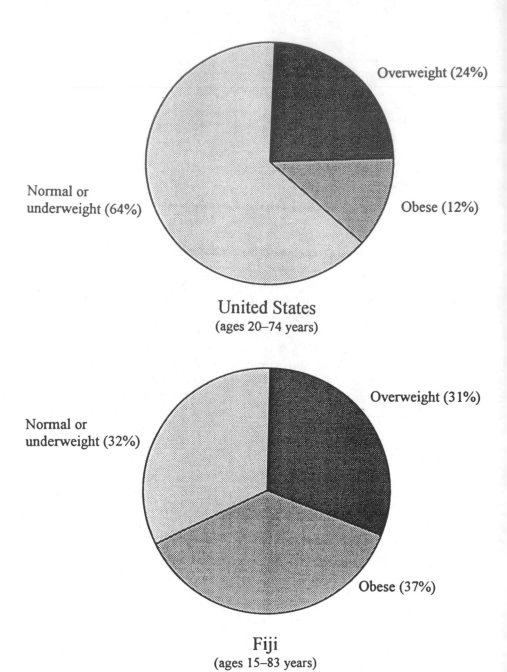

Overweight (24%)

Normal or
underweight (64%)

Obese (12%)

United States
(ages 20–74 years)

Overweight (31%)

Normal or
underweight (32%)

Obese (37%)

Fiji
(ages 15–83 years)

Figure 2.2. Prevalence of overweight and obesity among females in the United States
and Fiji (U.S. data from Gray 1989:9).

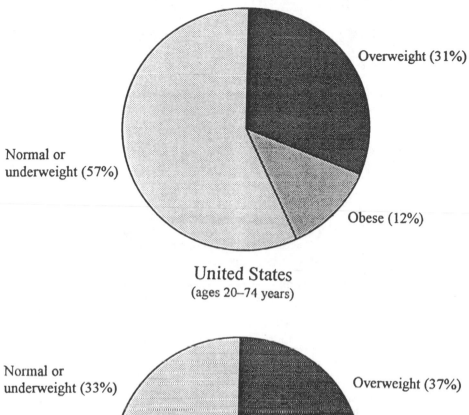

United States
(ages 20–74 years)

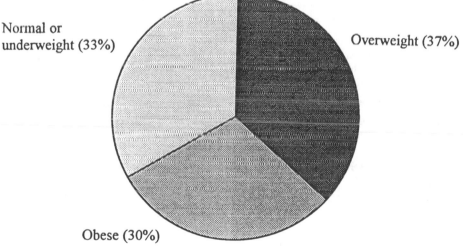

Fiji
(ages 15–84 years)

Figure 2.3. Prevalence of overweight and obesity among males in the United States and Fiji (U.S. data from Gray 1989:9).

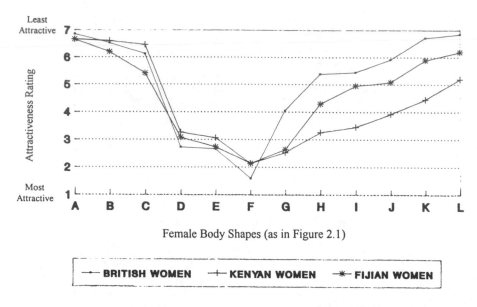

Figure 2.4. Cross-cultural comparison of women's mean attractiveness ratings of female body shapes (data presentation format and data for British and Kenyan respondents from Furnham and Alibhai 1983).

to the medium and overweight range figures. In fact, their responses indicated an inverse relationship between thinness and quality of care among the thinnest shapes, A through C. Perceived quality of care was consistently high in the medium weight to very obese shapes, with the modal response for this attribute rated as the highest level quality of care for each figure. The shapes garnering the highest percentage of responses that reflected the opinion that they enjoyed the optimal quality of care were F, K, and L, the latter two being the most obese (Figures C-1–C-13, C-18, C-19). Hence, the survey responses demonstrate a strong local tendency to associate *viqwaravi*, or care, with weight, which is elaborated on in Chapter 3. This finding also suggests that inferring an "ideal shape" solely on the basis of an attractiveness rating may be somewhat misguided since other shapes may be positively valued with respect to other criteria. It is also possible that respondents interpreted "attractiveness" as referring to sexual attractiveness — that is, how young women and men might view each other during the courtship phase of their lives. Since sexual attractiveness is ostensibly most relevant during young adulthood, the participants may have been biased toward selecting more youthful-appearing shapes (hence the medium weight ones) in answering this question.

Perhaps the most intriguing result of the survey surfaces in respondents' assessments of whether these figures hypothetically ought to gain, maintain, or lose weight. Although it was hypothesized[12] that respondents would strongly favor the gain or reduction in weight necessary to achieve a more ideal form, the responses were more moderate than expected. While, on average, the respondents did tend to favor a weight change in the direction toward the "attractive ideal," there was a surprising lack of consensus as to whether a given figure ought to add or subtract weight. Despite the mean group tendency to favor a change in weight toward the ideal, there was a striking degree of tolerance for the shapes as presented. In fact, for shapes C through I, which include all but the extremely thin and obese shapes, the modal response was that the figure should maintain her present weight (see Figures C-1 through C-13). Thus these data suggest that, in contrast to the stronger Western drive to cultivate the body's shape to approximate a culturally constituted aesthetic ideal, Fijians display relative complacency about the need to manipulate body shape.

When asked to consider their own body shape rather than the hypothetical ones, the majority of Fijian women responded that they did not wish to modulate their weight appreciably. This tendency held for those who fell into a normal body weight, overweight, and obese range (Figure 2.5), and held even for adolescent and young adult females (Figure 2.6) — a group especially invested in weight-control behaviors in America (see Moore 1988:1114). Moreover, women were asked to choose which shape they most resembled, and then which they would most like to resemble. Twenty-nine percent of the women sampled matched their perceived own body shape with the shape they would like to be and an additional 40 percent selected a shape only one gradation different from their perceived shape. Furthermore, there was no association between the desire to change one's diet and the degree of difference between the self-perceived shape and the desired shape (Figure 2.7), further substantiating Fijian women's relative lack of interest in formulating attainment of an ideal shape as a personal goal.

The majority of Fijian women sampled rated themselves positively with respect to attractiveness, along with describing themselves as relatively well cared for (Figure C-13). In contrast to study data from the United States demonstrating that women who perceive themselves as thin have the most positive self-image (Powers and Erickson 1986:37) and that obese girls show significantly more dissatisfaction with their weight and figure than do non-obese girls (Wadden et al. 1989:89), self-perception of attractiveness in Fijian women did not vary appreciably by weight category (Figure 2.8). In fact, the obese group displayed the lowest percentage of self-perceived unattractiveness.

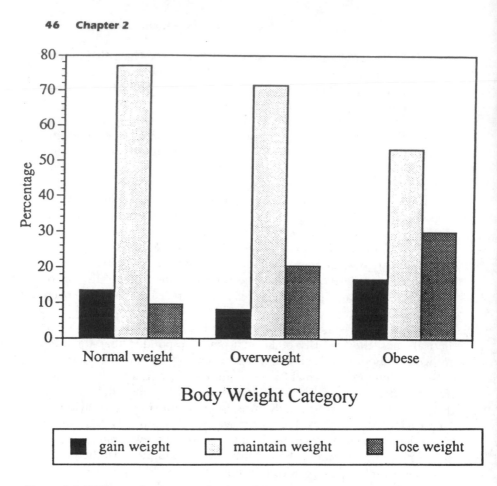

Figure 2.5. Desire to change or maintain weight among Fijian women, by weight category.

In summary, the results of this survey suggest that Fijian women enjoy a positive self-image irrespective of their weight status. Despite the clustering of opinion of what constitutes an aesthetically pleasing shape, Fijian women are relatively unmotivated to discipline their bodies and appetites in order to attain a desired shape. By contrast with Western women, whose self-image is heavily contingent on body image — and, specifically, a thinner body — Fijian women tend to be relatively unconcerned with their weight status, even when it diverges considerably from the perceived ideal. In short, they are both complacent and comfortable with respect to their bodies.

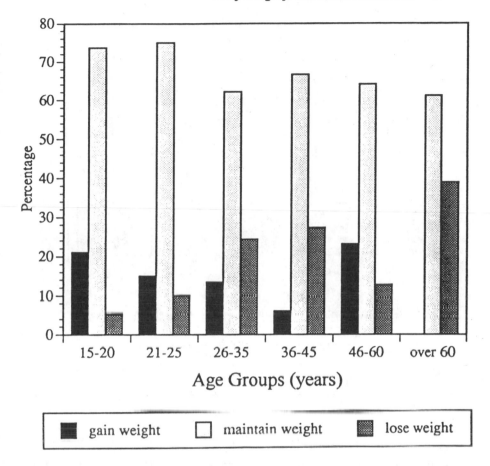

Figure 2.6. Desire to change or maintain weight among Fijian women, by age group.

Field Observations and Ethnographic Interviewing

The questionnaire was in some ways only a crude instrument for eliciting attitudes toward body shape. In particular, the use of cartoon drawings is of questionable validity. First, it is not clear that responses evoked by cartoon drawings accurately reflect attitudes toward corresponding human forms. Second, this method focuses on only one parameter of body shape, that of relative weight and adipose tissue. There is no provision to assess attitudes, for example, toward degrees of muscle tone, posture, height, or proportion (see Feldman et al. 1988). Nonetheless, the data do suggest consensus regarding ideal shapes and provide an objective measure to corroborate information obtained from both partici-

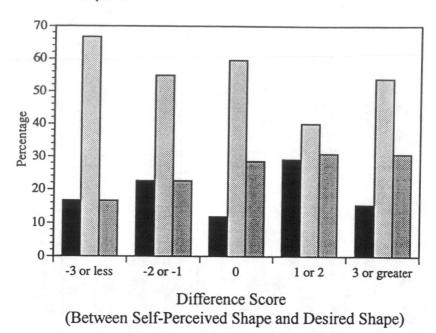

Difference Score
(Between Self-Perceived Shape and Desired Shape)

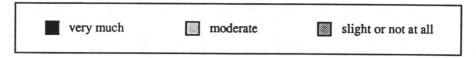

Figure 2.7. Desire to change diet among Fijian women according to the degree of difference between self-perceived body shape and desired shape. Difference score is calculated by the number of gradations of shape between the self-perceived shape and the desired shape (e.g., a difference score of –1 implies the respondent wishes to resemble a shape one gradation larger than she perceives herself to be, a difference score of 1 implies she wishes to resemble a shape one gradation smaller, a score of 0 indicates there is no discrepancy between her self-perceived and desired shape).

pant observation and responses elicited during formal interviews. While the survey data help to make interview data collected from a relatively small number of subjects more generalizable, the in-depth interviews relate meaning to opinion and validate conclusions based on findings from the objective responses.

Open-ended interviews were conducted in either the Nadroga dialect or English and tape-recorded; the majority took place after I had spent a full year at the field site. In Nahigatoka, formal interviews included twelve women and two men, and ranged in duration from a half hour to more than six hours over several sessions. Additional interviews

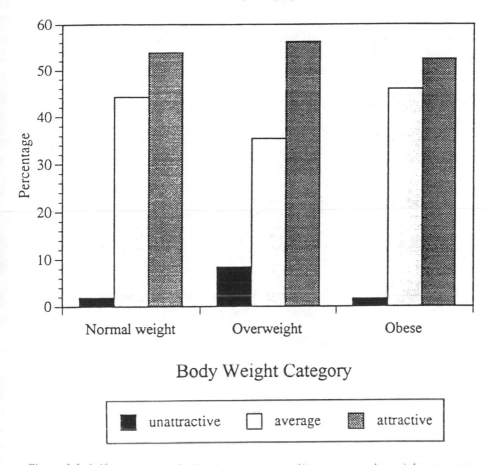

Figure 2.8. Self-perception of attractiveness among Fijian women, by weight category.

were held with some of the respondents to the questionnaire in the four villages surveyed and with female students at the University of the South Pacific, including four Fijians and several from a variety of Pacific island ethnic backgrounds, including Samoan, Tongan, Cook Island, ni-Vanuatu, and Solomon Island. Interviews in Nahigatoka generally took place in the household where I or the respondent was living, sometimes while we were engaged in preparing a meal or drinking *yaqona*. Frequently, there were others present who listened to, commented on, or joined the interview in progress. Although it seemed initially that the presence of others might bias the designated respondent, it gradually became quite clear that an exclusive one-on-one interview, being more than a bit unnatural in the context of village life, was likely to introduce a different kind of bias to the interview material. Since much opinion is formulated through dialogue, interviewing Fijians alongside their participating family or peers produces responses which reflect attitudes germane to the context in which they develop.

Narrative Data: The Discourse on Body Shape

The cultural preference for robust body shape is convincingly substantiated in frequent and quotidian discourse equating size with health, strength, and social connectedness. Fijians make two general types of comments about body size. The first type refers to an individual's shape as a fixed attribute. The second refers to the relative changes in an individual's shape, and is often accompanied by conjecture about the reasons for the change. As discussed in the next chapter, the second type of remark almost always refers to an individual's relational status in his or her social field.

The language of insults, compliments, and concern is replete with open references to body shape and weight change, drawing attention either to an aesthetically pleasing form or to obesity and excessive thinness. For example, Fijians often greet acquaintances by remarking that they appear *colacola vina*, which literally means "healthy" but also connotes robust appearance with respect to weight. There are also frequent explicit remarks on the appearance and general shape of others. For example, when favorably impressed, Fijians describe a person as *jubu vina* (well-formed), which generally refers to a full, though not obese, form.[13]

Fijians specifically associate ideal shape with physical characteristics suggesting strength or the ability to work hard: someone who is *kaikai* (strong) is one who looks able to "do all sorts of work." Fijians believe that hard physical labor necessitates eating large quantities of food. For example, one young man who was interviewed said that men notice the shape of women before anything else "because you can see in the shape of a person . . . the ability to work hard." He continued that men are more inclined to consider the shape of a woman's body than her face. "[Men] want them to be . . . women who are *jubu vina*; if they see that they are *jubu vina*, the second thing they look at is the behavior."

A cardinal feature of physical attractiveness in a Fijian woman is the shape of her calves (*bosi la*), which, somewhat eroticized, tend to be concealed from public display after marriage.[14] As this same young man explained: "Men, when they're just looking, they are going to look at you . . . and they are going to look at your legs, your calves. Seeing the calf is like seeing the whole body; . . . lots of times you can just see the leg and know the entire build of the body." The shape of a strong calf is associated with the woman's ability to work. He pointed out that when men notice a particularly well-shaped leg, they will think, "this woman here, she can work . . . she can work hard." A young woman agreed that men were particularly attracted to a well-shaped calf: "If it's, uh, really nice and fat, that, that to them is attractive." A young woman from Nadroga studying at the University of the South Pacific remarked, "I always admire boys who have big calves, even women too . . . and I always wish to have big calves." She went on to describe meeting a student from Germany whose legs she admired. Learning that the German woman had developed her calves by skiing, she had felt envious and recalled saying to herself, "I wish that . . . we can ski in Fiji, so we can go for skiing so I can have big calves like [hers]." Another student reported routinely admonishing her sister to eat more and gain weight because "it doesn't look nice when you've got skinny legs."[15]

Whereas Fijians explicitly admire robust forms, they are equally vocal in criticizing extreme obesity, although their perception of what constitutes overweight and obesity does not correspond to Western medico-actuarial standards. Since evidence of physical strength is central to judging the aesthetics of female figures, it stands to reason that an overly obese form is undesirable. One woman explained that women who were too big were considered unappealing and probably unable to work hard. A man corroborated that "those women who are large . . . they won't work much, they will just lie around." In fact, as often as insulting remarks designate the overly thin, the obese are referred to tauntingly as *kese levu* ("big belly").

As one woman pointed out, however, there is a broad range of acceptable forms:

It's only when you are really too big that people make [a] joke of it . . . and if you are really too thin, people make fun of it: oh, look at that one, she's so skinny; oh, look at that fat lady, she's so big.

That is, despite the stated preferences for well-shaped calves and, in general, for persons who are *jubu vina*, body aesthetics are not narrowly defined. This fact was emphasized to me by the village chief. He repeatedly commented that he wished me to grow fat during a meal we ate together, so I asked whether this was because Fijian men preferred big women. With a twinkle in his eye, the eighty-year-old man replied, "No, they like all kinds of women."

Overall, despite the expressed admiration for particular shapes, there is a striking disinterest in attaining these ideals as a personal goal as evidenced in the analysis of the survey responses. This relatively passive stance with respect to manipulation of body shape and weight is even more remarkable given the frequency of comments directed toward others' shapes. Nevertheless, several women did express a desire to change their figure, either to gain or lose weight or to add bulk, although they phrased these concerns vaguely. Some acknowledged that exposure to Western movies and magazines had inspired their wish to reduce their size and thereby distinguished themselves from women who were older or who stayed in the village (whom they saw as more traditional in their preferences for larger bodies). For example, a university student from Nadroga traced her ideas about maintaining her weight to her exposure to the Westernized, urban population in Suva. She abandoned any dieting while in her home village, however, explaining:

When I go to the village, I just eat anything that comes, and I eat any amount, I do what they do, I don't care about anything; it's only when I come back to Suva then I want to go on a diet and go for running and all that.

She also admitted that on her return to school her peers would routinely comment on her appearance, with remarks such as "Hey, you have gone fat. What have you been doing to yourself?"

One young village woman had also recently begun to worry about her weight, having been prodded by her peers; nonetheless, she seemed somewhat ambivalent about her plans for weight loss. She admitted, "I am cutting down on my diet a little . . . I don't really do it a lot, I just do it a little bit." She had previously been entirely unconcerned about her weight, and enjoyed "eating whatever," until her friends began to comment, "You've gotten way too big" or "You're really huge!" While she acknowledged that her friends had correctly recognized that she had become quite overweight, she defended herself in saying that women "who are too thin look horrible."

On the other hand, women oriented to traditional village life do not, in general, formulate weight loss or reshaping the body as a personal goal for two main reasons. The first has to do with local understanding of personal agency vis-à-vis the body, and the second relates to the emphasis on expressing community, but not personal, identity through the body. Not only are Fijians traditionally not self-reflexive in choosing to mediate identity through work on the body, but they also do not conceive of the body as malleable. This is in contradistinction to modern contexts in which individuals "negotiate lifestyle choices among a diversity of options" (Giddens 1991:5). The acceptance with which Fijians experience their bodies is similar to that of the Tahitians as described by Robert Levy: he describes a man's resignation that he cannot be thinner, as he would like to be, since he is unable to alter his desire to eat a great amount of food. Indeed, in this context too, "[T]he self is not conceptually something one can change; it is what it is" (1973:222–24).

A Fijian university student revealed her sentiments that she had no personal control over her body in her self-effacing comments about her appearance. After responding to a questionnaire about attitudes toward body shape she commented, "Oh, I know I'm very unattractive . . . just look at me, I am not very attractive." When pressed to elaborate she explained that she admired slim women with large calves and full hair, whereas she had thin calves, felt she was overweight, and had short hair. But she countered this with the observation,

I don't think about myself a lot . . . I think only people who are beautiful or attractive, they, they think about themselves a lot; us people, who are unattractive, we don't think a lot about ourselves . . . we just think that's the way we are, just leave it like that . . . I just say that's the way it is; I just have to leave it like that. I never care whether people think I'm attractive or not.

She pointed out that the only time she gives her weight any thought is when she is weighed. Even when she realized she had gained a great deal recently, she denied worrying about reducing. She insisted, "I never think about my body . . . only sometimes." While fully acknowledging that she admired others' figures and especially their fuller hair, she flatly denied any interest in modifying her features. For example, she described her hair as never growing: "I don't like it . . . but I have to like it . . . it's just there because God made me so and I have to accept it; . . . I like it this way and yet I hate it."

Fijians also indicate that while there may be a brief period of interest in appearance, eventually women yield to other priorities that include attention to their roles in caring for their extended families and contributing to their community. A middle-aged midwife speculated that the younger generation, particularly those of marriageable age, thought more about their figures than older women. As for her peer group, she observed, "We don't care much about our figures." As an illustration, she compared her observations of how Fijian versus Indian mothers felt about breast-feeding. Whereas she perceived Indian women were typically concerned that their breasts would sag as a result of breast-feeding their babies, she noted that nursing Fijian mothers generally dispense with wearing bras for ease in breast-feeding. "With us," she said, "it doesn't matter [whether] your breasts [are] hanging down . . . we don't care, that doesn't matter."

The women interviewed revealed that regardless of their feelings about their body shape, Fijians rarely modify their diet in an effort to gain or lose weight. One woman described her family's reaction to her restricting her diet when she returned from the university to the village. She remarked that she usually ate a lot at home because

My mother, if she sees that I am eating less, then she will always comment, but if I say that I want to lose weight then, they'll say that I'm not that fat . . . because out there, back in the village, they're not very much concerned about your body shape . . . they'll just tell you, just eat as much as you can, 'cause if you go back to town, you won't eat this kind of food.

Meals are characterized by an abundance of food and often a variety of dishes. Most people rest after a meal, and after a large Sunday dinner it is not unusual to observe young women unfastening their skirt waistbands when uncomfortably full. Special feast foods and any delicacies such as fish or fruit are consumed with little restraint. One informant remarked that regardless how overweight people are

they don't care about their diet. Although they're big like this house, they still eat . . . and they don't know that eating too much doesn't help. The more food is there, the more they eat; [. . . if there are] plenty [of] mangoes, there, the more they see the mangoes, the more they eat.

Another woman concurred that there was little conscious management of diet based on its nutritive value. In earlier times, she explained, "there was no balanced diet,"[16] and likewise today "we eat according to what we can afford to get." People "eat what they feel like eating, for the taste . . . they eat as much as they can, according to their taste." Indicating her mother as an example, a woman explained "She might like mangoes better than oranges, so during mango season, she'll eat *as much* as she could." Her mother added, "With us we can eat dozens and dozens [of one fruit] . . . that's how we eat, we don't balance out our diet."

Paying inordinate attention to one's appearance is actively discouraged within villages. Women seen as attempting to dress or make themselves up so as to attract men are chided for being *qamuqamu* (flirtatious in a pejorative sense), while those who wear a great deal of makeup or dress in pants are sometimes accused of being like a *kabawaqa* (literally, one who climbs after ships—in other words, a prostitute). In a church play performed in Nahigatoka Village, for example, the women portraying ne'er-do-well sorts painted themselves with rouge in marked distinction to the female cast members who wore no makeup.

While some degree of vanity is apparently forgivable when a single woman is looking for a husband, after marriage she is expected to focus on her household duties instead of her appearance. According to one young women,

Sexual competition is not strong after one gets married, eh? . . . after you get married, we think that person likes you that way, I mean the one you're married to, and you shouldn't be doing other things to attract other people.

Echoing this sentiment on the impropriety of vanity after marriage, another woman exclaimed, "[If] you've already got a husband, what would you want to attract a husband for?" Indeed, Fijians believe that women who spend inordinate time enhancing their appearance by fixing their hair, scenting themselves, or dressing finely may, by their actions, entice certain spirits to molest them (Herr 1981:344).

There are specific tabus preventing women from attending to appearance in the postpartum period. A woman described the strictness with which the tabus are observed:

The mother-in-law, if she sees the daughter-in-law combing, trying to comb her hair, just after she has given birth, a month, two, three or even four, five months, six months, combing, trying to comb her hair and straighten up her hair and look in the mirror like that, she'll growl at her . . . she'll tell her off . . . That's why . . . just before they give birth, the pregnant women, they cut their hair short, very short.

Refraining from combing or cutting hair, in addition to avoiding exertion, protects postpartum women from developing *na tadoka ni vasucu*, a Fijian syndrome of postpartum complications, although one woman claimed that this tabu means to keep a woman from attracting her husband, ostensibly to reinforce the strict postpartum tabu against sexual intercourse for up to one year. One woman elaborated, "We give birth and we don't comb our hair . . . [we] aren't ashamed because that is the [correct] behavior for a Fijian woman." She pointed out that "we want to be strong" and when "we comb our hair [in the postpartum period] we are weak."

As a rule, Fijians do not wish to distinguish themselves by a unique appearance. Although traditional dress did change radically over a century ago with the missionaries' influence, clothing styles have since remained fairly stable, with women continuing to wear long garments to cover their legs. The traditional hairstyle, the *hui ni ga* ("duck's tail"), is still preferred as well. While women do occasionally experiment with some alternative styles, including shorter haircuts and Western-style skirts and dresses, wearing trousers is actively discouraged. Moreover, both men and women are required to demonstrate respect in their comportment by adhering to traditional norms of dress at formal ritual occasions.

Social pressures encourage compliance to traditional codes of behavior and appearance in Fijian society. On the other hand, conformity to community standards of appearance results not only from prescribed, locally acceptable modes of attire and appearance, but also from limited self-reflectiveness concerning appearance. In this context, the body is not a source of individual differentiation, but a medium of community participation and identification.

Summary

In support of the hypothesis that core cultural values may be encoded in body shape ideals there is abundant evidence suggesting that, at least in some European and North American cultures, the body has become a vehicle for public projection of personal qualities expressed through visible and tangible work on the body. Body shape and appearance are commonly manipulated to construct an image. In fact, there is not only permission to develop the body as a means of representing personal identity, this is often the expectation as well. This intensive cultivation of the body, permitted by its objectification and culturally sanctioned self-reflexivity, sometimes precipitates an adversarial relationship between self and body, and the extreme personal identification with the body may render situatedness in the body socially isolating.

Fijians likewise express an admiration for certain valued features associated with body shapes, apparent in their virtually constant assesment and commentary on bodily forms. The language of insults, meanwhile, reveals a distaste for overly obese or thin persons. Idealized features such as large calves or a "well-formed" body are associated with the perceptions that the person has the ability to work hard and has been well cared for. The survey data on attitudes toward gradated body shapes demonstrate a striking association between being cared for and body weight. The clear preference for a robust form (sometimes corresponding to overweight in the West) consistently emerges in discourse relating to body shape. What distinguishes the Fijian attitude toward the body is the relative absence of self-reflexive interest in matching an ideal. One does not assiduously cultivate his or her own body to project a particular image because the body identifies one with a community more than with a self image.

The Western cultivation of the body is partially motivated by the possibility of representing personal status and accomplishments through this medium. By comparison, in Fiji the cultivation of one's own body is not socially legitimated as a means of distinguishing oneself. Still, despite this relatively passive stance toward the body, commentary on body shape — how one is formed, whether one has lost or gained weight — is central to everyday discourse in Fijian villages. As we shall see in the next chapter, this unremitting attention to body shape and to appetite is a master idiom of care and nurturance within a social network. What is thereby encoded in and read from the form and changes of the body is the social positioning of individuals, consequent to how each has been nurtured or neglected in his or her social universe. Collective care, then, is recognized in the body's physical form.

Chapter 3
Nurturing and Food Exchange:
An Ethos of Care

Fijians seem to be more complacent than Westerners about the culti-vation of the body's shapes and spaces. Although they express admira-tion for aesthetically pleasing forms and a clear preference for robust shapes, they make little or no effort to attain the culturally defined ideal in their own bodies. Paradoxically, remarks drawing attention to size and changes in others' bodily forms are unremitting; greetings, jokes, and insults abound with references to weight loss or gain or to unusual body size.

The relative lack of interest in cultivating one's body is grounded in the understanding that personal achievements are indexed not by bodily shape or by the disciplining of the body, but by one's connectedness with and performance of care in the social matrix of the family, the *mataqwali*, and the village. In part, the adequacy of this performance is judged by competence in providing and serving food within and outside the household unit. This competence is manifested in acts of service to and for others, encompassed in the concepts of care — *vikawaitaki, viqwa-ravi,* and *vilomani* — and coupled with appropriate demeanor, including *varokorokotaki* (respectful behavior and knowing one's relative social posi-tion). Although a shared understanding of correct behavior (*itovo vina*) extends to all social contexts, this *itovo vina* is most frequently and visibly operationalized in the procuring and sharing of food resources. The cumulative efforts of the caregivers are embodied in the morphology of their charges. Thus the Fijian body reflects the achievements of its care-takers. A body is the responsibility of the micro-community that feeds and cares for it; consequently, crafting its form is the province of the community rather than of the self. And because the individual body is the locus of vested efforts of its community, the individual's own efforts are directed back toward the community.

An essential corollary of the notion that the personal body is the community's province is that, just as shape encodes one's capacity and propensity to serve the community (for example, by indicating who is likely to work hard), it also reveals the community's investment in and ability to care for its members. As such, body shape is an indicator not only of relevant personal abilities but also of one's connectedness to the social network and one's powers to nourish and esteem. Children and guests are often targeted for extraordinary efforts in care, since their weight gain or robust forms will be credited to the caretaker's social prowess. The hyperbolic cultivation of chiefly bodies as a collective representation of their communities (see Shore 1989:156–59) can also be understood within this conceptual framework. Since there is an explicit association between caring in the sense of feeding (*viqwaravi*) and weight and body shape, commentary on *viqwaravi* and its manifestations in body morphology become parallel discourses on nurturing and negligence.

Food Symbolism in Social Relationships

The symbolic role of food — its substance, cultivation, distribution, and exchange — is central to the regulation and negotiation of social relationships in South Pacific cultures (Ravuvu 1983; Meigs 1984; J. Turner 1984; Pollock 1985; Kahn 1986; Toren 1990; Mageo 1989; Ravuvu 1991). In Fiji, reciprocal exchange is embellished with food prestations and feasts that are complex orchestrations of collective mobilization of labor and resources. These events fundamentally structure village life, and provide a means for community reflexivity about the status and strength of important relationships.

Food prestations and *magisi*, formal feasts given to demarcate a social exchange or transition, are invariably discussed in great detail when participants return to their home villages or households. People who were unable to attend eagerly await the accounts of returning *mataqwali* or village members. Reminiscences about an especially memorable *magisi* and exclamations about the lavishness of the occasion invariably focus on the abundance of food and the quality of its presentation. The latter is determined by the variety and size of foods offered and their relative prestige (determined by whether they are delicacies unique to a locality or season, or totem foods). In the wake of such occasions, the extensive commentary and retelling (*talanoa*) about foods and the *viqwaravi* assess the success or failure of the event.

Food is consumed with expressive relish, often in quantities that necessitate resting after finishing the meal. Fijians take pleasure in gustatory satisfaction and especially look forward to tasting seasonal or local delicacies in host villages. In fact, delicacies and totemic foods are important goods of exchange between members of different villages regardless whether a formal *magisi* is being given. Hosts give regional delicacies to guests to take to their home villages, and travelers take them as offerings to their hosts. Such gifts are enthusiastically received and rapidly distributed among family and peers. My field notes record an example of the social management of *cigana*, the regional fish delicacy of Nahigatoka:

> In mid-May the first sighting of *cigana* in the river basin caused excitement throughout Nahigatoka. This favorite local delicacy had not been sighted for five or six years. Their migration through the area lasted for several weeks, during which women periodically boarded boats or waded in the river to scoop large quantities into their nets. These fishing expeditions, which were rapidly organized when a sighting of a school was made, had a celebratory air. According to tradition, the *cigana* are a "gift" to the village and as such may not be gathered to sell, but only to share. . . . In our household, the excess fish were frozen to serve to guests or packaged and distributed to the doctors at the local hospital and to some shopkeepers in town.

Food gifts that circulated to our household in Nahigatoka during the year included Tahitian chestnuts, fruit bats, a sea turtle, and eels.

In addition to seasonal or local foods, many *mataqwali* or villages have totemic foods (*icavu*), which are either brought to them as gifts or are designated for their exclusive pleasure at a social gathering.[1] For example, one woman related that if she were to find a snake, the *icavu* of a neighboring village, she would surely take it there to present. She explained that one's *icavu* is one's special food to eat; one also expects that others will treat it with respect.

> On an expedition to a valley village, my research assistant and I were offered a plate of freshwater prawns. When I had finished eating, Mere asked that I pass her my plate. She then consumed the heads of the prawns which I had left uneaten, explaining that it upset her that I had not eaten her *icavu* with respect by finishing them in their entirety. The hostess, who was looking on, agreed on the importance of eating an *icavu* "nicely."[2]

Anthropologists have long noted the totem's role in forging solidarity through commensality (Goody 1982:10–12). For example, in the New Guinea Highlands shared substance through food consumption is instrumental in forging a "locality ideology" that supplements a kinship ideology (A. Strathern 1973:26–29). In their capacity for "embodiment of ideas and relations," Claude Lévi-Straus maintained that totems are understood as "good to think" as opposed to "good to eat." The totemic "image is projected, not received; it does not derive its substance from without" (Lévi-Strauss 1963:31, 104). In Fiji, too, the *icavu* is an emblem of collective identity. In the Fijian case, it appears that *icavu* are both "good to think" and "good to eat" — not in the traditional functionalist sense, but as items that are delicious precisely because of their special relationship to the group, which simultaneously allows recognition and celebration of collective identity of one group in the process of being hosted and fed (*viqwaravi* and *vikawaitaki*) by another. An analogous mutual affirmation of a social relationship occurs with designation of particular foods as "belonging" to the respective parties in the *veibatiki* relationship. In eastern Viti Levu, when a *mataqwali* are *bati*, or warriors of a chiefly *mataqwali* (and thus the two stand in the *veibatiki* relationship to each other), there are specific foods that the one group may not eat in the presence of the other (see also Ravuvu 1983:34 and 1991:632). If a feast is given at which both groups are present, the food (for example, fish) will be reserved for its designated group. Transgressors of this tabu are said to choke on the bones of the forbidden food. Thus the parallel food restrictions designated by the *veibatiki* relationship concretize social relationships as do the exchange of *icavu* and other foods.[3]

Finally, there are special foods that are by virtue of their rarity, flavor, or symbolic associations considered to be prestigious additions to a food prestation. These include pigs and sometimes cattle or turtles. In addition, yams and taro are regarded as choice ceremonial foods for a *magisi*. Although desserts are rarely served, *qalu* (caramelized, pounded cassava with coconut cream that is also known as *vakalolo*) is considered a festive addition to the fare. When these foods are prepared, custom requires that, in addition to serving them to the designated guests, the first offering must be made to the village chief. Similarly, if a large animal is slaughtered or any of these prestige foods prepared, it would be unthinkable not to distribute these items in some way.[4] As we shall see, food distribution is axiomatic even in the most mundane contexts.

Yet another ceremonial exchange of designated food gifts occurs during the first fruits ceremonies (*ihevu*). This ritual offering of the first harvest of yams and other *cawa dina* to the church and to the village chief takes place in early March, coinciding with the first harvest. Although in Nahigatoka most offerings are made at the altar of the church, concomitant offerings are still made to village chiefs in many other Nadroga villages. The presentation of yams is a "potent symbol of solidarity" and an "eloquent expression of differentiation within an encompassing unity," for the crops are presented to the chief as the representative of the ancestors and ancestral deity (*vu*) (J. Turner 1984:133, 139). The tandem presentation to the church pays homage to the adopted Christian deity, *na Kalou*. This exchange is thought to solidify the relationship between the villagers and their spiritual benefactors, hence guaranteeing a prosperous supply of food in the coming year (141–42).

Viqwaravi on a Grand Scale: *Magisi*

Fijian social relationships are fundamentally mediated and affirmed through the exchange and distribution of food. In his remarks on pot-latch in Melanesia, Marcel Mauss cited Maurice Leenhardt's work in New Caledonia, where persons conceived of their feasts as:

the movement of the needle which sews together the parts of our reed roofs, making of them a single roof, one single word. (Leenhardt quoted in Mauss 1967:19)

Indeed, in Fiji, where it is a "basic tenet . . . that ceremonial exchange is, in and of itself, a life enhancing activity" (J. Turner 1984:133), no important transaction is completed without a *magisi*, or feast, the most formal means of making food prestations and enacting *viqwaravi*.[5] In his analysis of Fijian ceremonies, Asesela Ravuvu concludes that ritual offer-ings of food and drink display "one's care and concern for the life and well-being of one's guests" (Ravuvu 1987:238, 307).

Transitional life events are marked with at least one large feast. *Magisi* also accompany virtually every important occasion, such as the arrival of a guest, the celebration for a new job, or a winning sports team. In addition, any invitation to a group to come to offer donations (such as for the construction of a community hall or church) requires several ceremonies marking the receipt of the support and culminating in a *magisi*. *Magisi* occur with such frequency that the members of a *mata-qwali* seem to be nearly constantly planning to either hold or attend one. As a result, preparation for such events verges on a routine ac-tivity. Depending on the scope of a *magisi*, it may also demand collective participation by all households in a *mataqwali* or in the village. Each household is expected to donate either cash, *cawa dina*, or cooked food. In addition, women are expected to congregate to prepare foods com-munally (for example, to butcher meat, chop vegetables, or peel root crops) and to serve their guests. A family's social standing partially rests on its ability to grow "the right edible crops" so that it can make the "right contributions" at feasts (Pollock 1985:201).

Typically the *magisi* is a festive event with bountiful quantities of *cawa dina* offered with a variety of traditional delicacies and dishes. The rich flavors and textures and the abundant portions contribute to the partici-pants' conviviality. The area reserved for guests is decorated with woven palm fronds and hibiscus blooms. Great platters, piled high with baked or boiled taro, yams, sweet potatoes, and plantains, are placed at inter-vals along stretches of cloth. Roast pig, chicken, and turtle are set out with fish, crab, and prawns cooked in coconut cream and usually beef

cooked in taro leaves, chop suey, and curries. The meal may be sweet-
ened with passion fruit juice or ripened bananas with coconut. Women
from the host village fill platters with *cawa dina* and other foods and
move among their guests, urging them to eat more. Other women fan
the food to chase the flies and, when their guests assure them they can
eat no more, bring them water bowls to wash with.

Inviting another village or *mataqwali* to donate money (*holi*) incurs
not only the immediate obligation to offer them *yaqona* and a *magisi*, but
also the enduring obligation to attend and support their future fundraising endeavors. The following account of reciprocal prestations between
two villages illustrates the *magisi*'s role in social exchange.

In Yavulo Village, also situated in the Jubuniwai area, construction of a new
community hall and church began with the new year. In March, after news of
the construction reached the Nahigatoka villagers, a *visiko* (formal visit) was immediately organized. The men from the various *mataqwali* met to determine what
each could manage to bring to the exchange, while the women decided that
each household would contribute baked goods to help the Yavulo villagers feed
the carpenters working there. On the appointed day the Nahigatoka villagers
gathered at the Yavulo-Nahigatoka boundary, each bearing their respective food
gifts. The men formed a line with large stems of plantains and led a live cow
to present to their waiting neighbors. The women followed them to offer their
cakes, puddings, and scones. After the goods were presented, the women of
Nahigatoka assisted the Yavulo women in the *viqwaravi* of the carpenters. When
the carpenters had been served, the two villages partook of the food as well.

Several days later, villagers from Nahigatoka who were *vahu* Yavulo (that is,
had mothers born in *mataqwali* from Yavulo) organized a surprise presentation
of goods for the carpenters' tea (*holi ti*). Again each woman baked something
as her contribution, taking it with her to present collectively so as to relieve the
Yavulo women of their daily obligation to serve afternoon tea to their guests,
the carpenters.

Months went by before the community hall and church were completed for
use and the chief of Nahigatoka was invited to open the structure officially. For
this occasion, the members of his *mataqwali* were again mobilized to make their
donations toward a cash gift that the chief would present at the opening.[6] Over
F$1,000 was collected and presented with the requisite *yaqona* and *tabua*. Im-
mediately after accepting the offerings, the Yavulo villagers countered with a
reciprocal offering of *yaqona, tabua,* and *iyau*—in this case, piles of mats. After
this, tea was served by the Yavulo women, who reversed the earlier roles and enacted the *viqwaravi* toward the Nahigatoka group. After the opening ceremony
of the structure was completed, a *magisi* was presented to honor the guests from
Nahigatoka. Again, the Yavulo women tended to their guests' needs during the
repast, and the Nahigatoka people in turn praised the flavor and variety of the
foods they were served. Following their return to Nahigatoka, another food gift,
consisting of a roasted boar with cooked breadfruit, arrived from Yavulo. As
onlookers stood by exclaiming on the magnificent size of the boar, the chief directed the men of his household to divide the carcass into portions to distribute
to the members of the *mataqwali* who had contributed to his cash gift.

Thus over the period of one year there was a reciprocal flow of food gifts as a token of the mutual obligation of the two villages to care for and support the enterprises of the other. The Nahigatoka participants recollected the event both in terms of their satisfaction with their contributions and their delight in the reciprocal offering of the *magisi.*

The particulars of such feasts serve as a measure of the relative mutual esteem between the two groups. A woman from a chiefly family in Nahigatoka who often is called on to participate in such events explained, "We are ashamed . . . if our contribution is only slight; it shames us"; on the other hand, she indicated her village had felt proud after the ceremonies in Yavulo because "we gave well." She described their corresponding evaluation of the performance of the Yavulo villagers:

We'll say, "Wow! Look at those people from Yavulo, they really made us a huge offering of mats, they gave us huge *tabua,* they gave us a huge amount of food . . . [they gave us] the boar!"

She further explained that through the performance of this exchange, both participating groups affirmed their satisfaction with their neighboring village and renewed their implicit promise to take care of the other in a manner befitting their relationship. If the reciprocal gift had been judged inadequate, the Nahigatoka villagers would have been disappointed and disgraced. As this woman put it, "we would have said, 'Gee, these people, they don't respect us.' " Fortunately, this event had pleased both groups. She emphasized that paramount in the evaluation of this event is the presentation of the feast:

The important thing, [is] the *magisi,* [whether it's a] large amount of food. If the food is meager, if something like that happens, [we'll exclaim,] "Oh! What are these people doing? The amount of food they presented is very small!" [It should be that] the amount of food is huge!

The language of praise centers specifically on the intrinsic qualities of the food offerings. She continued:

All the people, they were eating and they were commenting "Wow, the fish, how much there is! Wow, the chicken! Wow, the boar! . . . the amount of food is really something that this village made!" That is what they noticed. They will really notice, they'll say, "Wow, the amount of varieties of food!"

If there is great variety, and especially if a pig is presented, "it shows their *kawaitakinia* [their caring] for us . . . they arranged that we eat well." On the other hand, a *magisi* judged to be the result of an inferior effort because of only a small amount of food will be sure to draw critical

The art of eating and drinking remains one of the few areas in which the working classes explicitly challenge the legitimate art of living. In the face of the new ethic of sobriety for the sake of slimness, which is most recognized at the highest levels of the social hierarchy, peasants and especially industrial workers maintain an ethic of convivial indulgence. A bon vivant is not just someone who enjoys eating and drinking; he is someone capable of entering into the generous and familiar — that is, both simple and free — relationship that is encouraged and symbolized by eating and drinking together, in a conviviality which sweeps away restraints and reticence. (1984:179)

Bourdieu postulates that this conviviality in eating is a form of "being-in-the-present" which is "an affirmation of solidarity with others" (1984: 183). Moreover, he contends that the mode of consumption of food, among other things, distinguishes the working classes, "who give priority to being," from the middle classes, "where the concern for 'seeming' arises" (200).

Andrew Strathern also has shown in his work in New Guinea that the sharing of food cements social bonds and in fact mediates between locality and kinship to affiliate individuals with the community in which they live and eat. He writes:

Food creates substance, just as procreation does, and forms an excellent symbol both for the creation of identity out of residence and for the value of nurturance, growth, comfort and solidarity which are associated primarily with parenthood. (1973:29)

Although Fijians indisputably regard feasting as an affirmation of solidarity, and take explicit experiential pleasure in the event, they derive substantial gratification from the adequate performance of the *magisi.* Thus, the presentation of the feast must achieve a conviviality through the conspicuous and abundant display of foods and the abandon with which guests are urged to partake. In retrospective evaluation of the *magisi*, it is always the way in which *viqwaravi* and *vikawaitaki* were enacted that accords lasting value. Food is, of course, perishable; what endures is the capacity to mobilize and regenerate the social relationships that supply the goods.

Kana Valevu: The Rhetoric of Care

Food and the food quest are central to most of our traditional social and economic activities. No ceremonial function is considered complete without a presentation of food or *magi[s]i.* A function is considered good, apart from other things, if there is more than enough food for everyone attending. It is shameful if people go hungry. (Ravuvu 1983:41–42)

The ubiquitous Fijian concern with the collective performance of *vika-waitaki* as a means of creating a public image can be compared with the cultivation of the body as a projection of the self in Western cultures. In fact, a similar interest in cultivation of bodies is evident in the language and performance of *vikawaitaki, viqwaravi,* and *vilomani* in the micro-cosmic workings of the household. The discourse on nurturing both reflects and creates the quotidian world of the Fijian.

There is a primary cultural preoccupation with hunger and the distri-bution of food throughout Melanesia and Polynesia (Meigs 1984; Kahn 1986; Shore 1982; Mageo 1989), reflected in a language of insults elabo-rated to lambaste both those who are hungry and those who do not share food. Bronislaw Malinowski reported that in the Trobriand Islands the most degrading comment one could make on another's condition was to call him "hungry":

Accumulated food to them is a good thing — its absence is not only something to be dreaded, but something to be ashamed of. There is no greater insult than to tell a man that he has no food, *gala kam,* "no food thine"; or that he is hungry, *kam malu,* "thy hunger." No one would ever ask for food, or eat in a strange place, or accept food unless in obedience to traditional usage. (Young 1979:69)

Condemnation of those who do not share food complements this dis-course. For example, in Papua New Guinea, "people are judged 'good' or 'bad' according to whether they share or hoard food," and " 'to be stingy' " is tantamount to not sharing food (Kahn 1986:37). In Tongan, the word *kaipo* pejoratively designates those who do not share food, and in Fiji, one of the most cutting insults is to accuse one of being *kanakana lo,* or eating secretly.

Conversely, feeding is the "quintessentially positive act" in the Eastern Highlands of New Guinea; moreover, "a good person is, almost by defini-tion, one who feeds others generously" (Meigs 1984:41). In Papua New Guinea generosity, which represents the highest social value, is framed in terms of sharing food. Miriam Kahn writes:

Any food that appears in public must be shared with as many people as see it. The Wamiran assumption is that the onlooker feels hungry and, if not given any food, would feel slighted and jealous. As a woman explained to me, "We are not like white people, we share our food. If we are eating and someone sees us, we have to offer the food to that person. (1986:41)

As we have already seen in the context of the Fijian *magisi,* "the sharing of food becomes the dominant symbol of solidarity" (J. Turner 1984:133). Feeding and food sharing in the household are the chief means of conceiving and maintaining social relations and organizing domestic activity in Fiji. Allusions to hunger and to generosity with food must be understood as metacommunications on the reciprocity of care (*viqwaravi*) in the social milieu. In other words, the disparagement of hunger must be heard as moral commentary on the person who can neither provide food for himself or others nor obtain it through his affiliation with a community that feeds its members well.

The positive valuation of *mataqwali* and village members who can work hard has been discussed in Chapter 2; moreover, we have seen that personal attributes—specifically those of strength and the ability to work hard—are to some extent indexed in body shape. Conversely, inferences based on the appearance of the body are also made explicit in the associations between thinness and deprivation (material and social) or thinness and laziness. One woman explained why the word *layahewa*, "skinny legs," was an insult:

With us, eh, if someone is . . . skinny, it doesn't look nice to us. That shows that she doesn't eat well; . . . "She's very skinny . . . that one, it could be [she is not] eating well, that's why she is so skinny."

This woman added that the suspicion that one is "not eating well" leads to an assumption that "most probably they don't have enough to eat" or "they're lazy to plant; they have land but they don't plant." A household reduced to eating bread because of a dearth of *cawa dina* is widely perceived as *beci* (disgraceful), and people will criticize the inadequacies of its chief provider in comments such as, "What will he feed his wife? His wife has no *cawa*." So an explicit association is made between the propensity to work, the ability to work, and the way in which these are reflected in care within the household.

While people perceived as lazy farmers and poor providers are openly criticized, those seen as greedy with respect to hoarding or hiding food are considered more despicable. These people are accused of being *kanakana lo*, "one who eats secretly." As the following episode shows, this is a particularly caustic insult:

One Sunday morning during the cold season, Liku and I were eating our breakfast. We had bolted the door and closed the window against an especially brisk wind blowing off the stormy South Pacific. Liku and her namesake had already been cross with each other earlier that day; moreover, we were late in getting to the cookhouse to help the other women prepare the noonday meal. Liku's namesake stepped out of the cookhouse, probably to check on our whereabouts, when she saw that we had closed our door during our meal. She shouted that we were *kanakana lo* and returned to the cookhouse. Liku retorted, "*Kanakana lo ca?*" ("How can you say we are *kanakana lo?*") and appeared close to tears. She complained that the closed door and windows were a measure against the weather and insisted that we refrain from helping that morning with the cooking and from joining the household members in the midday meal. Liku and her namesake continued to feud for an additional couple of days, eventually naming and resolving a number of conflicts that had been brewing in their strained relationship.

In this instance, the insult issued a statement regarding a number of conflicts; it was a metaphor for unacceptable social behaviors. Our apparent failure to share food and to participate in meal preparation evoked the accusation that we were *kanakana lo*, to which Liku insisted we respond by the ultimate antisocial act: not joining the household in its meal.

The Fijians' moral imperative to share food and meals extends to impoverished distant relatives. One woman described how her household regularly supplied relatives with food: "They don't usually ask [for food]; it's just the feeling that comes out from us, that we should look after them because they don't have any plantation." The impulse to share food is deeply ingrained. Some young women explained to me that not to offer food to someone else in your presence is unimaginable; they made statements like "I always want to share my food; . . . if my friend comes along, I always share it . . . I love sharing my food" or "I never keep anything for me, and I always, you know, give it [food] away." This ethic reflects and reinforces the sense that members of the community are enmeshed in a network of care. People are expected to look after one another's needs, particularly if someone is unfortunate enough to be in need of food. One villager framed this as a frequent moral dilemma about sacrificing already scarce resources:

So even when we are eating . . . and then if somebody just came and passed in front of our house, and we used to call them to come and eat. And even sometimes we, you know, if you don't have enough, but still we call people to come and eat . . . That's part of our culture . . . That is why we, now when we are big like this, it is, even me, I feel really bad if we don't share anything to anybody, if I'm eating something . . . if I don't give it, I feel bad.

Indeed, whenever a household serves food, its members must open their doors and windows, so that in essence the meal is publicly displayed. Moreover, those who are eating or serving the meal keep a watchful eye on the doorway for passersby. Everyone who passes within earshot, whether kinsman or stranger, is invited in to partake of the meal (see also Toren 1990:57).[8] The standard greetings issuing forth from each household at mealtimes are "Come and eat!" (*La mai kana!*), "Have some tea!" (*Homu ti!*), "Have your noonday meal" (*Vahigalevu*), "There's food here" (*Na kana okwe*), and "There's cassava here" (*Na tavioka okwe*). The invitations are axiomatic and somewhat rhetorical; although people are genuinely welcome to enter the household and eat, they usually continue on to where they were expected for a meal. One woman laughed as she recalled an incident when she invited a passerby for food that was not yet cooked. She said she had invited him as a reflex and had fully expected him to decline. She recalled:

The food wasn't even cooked, but this guy was walking outside and I called, "Come and have lunch!" My mother said, "If he came, what would he come and eat?" and I said, "Oh, who said he is gonna come, he's gonna say '*vinaka* [no, thank you]'"... He said, "*Vinaka.*"

Just as there is a vested interest in creating an impression of abundance at the *magisi*, householders are equally concerned that their food supply meet extraneous demands. This is reflected in their habit of cooking extraordinarily excessive quantities of food, especially root crops, which are later fed to the pigs if uneaten by household members and guests. Heaps of plantains, yams, taro, and/or cassava are peeled and boiled for routine meals, but rarely finished. A woman observed that "in some homes, food is a problem, that is disgraceful ... the most important thing is that we have enough food" either to feed to one's family or to contribute to *mataqwali* functions. She continued that to fall short of food during a meal constitutes the ultimate social disgrace:

[If there] is not enough for us, the members of the household are going to be ashamed that there is too little food ... we should eat, we should be *bori vina* (well-sated), never mind if there are leftovers ... if only because it should never happen that we eat just a little ... that we still feel hungry, yet the food is finished ... that would make us ashamed.

This is standard practice throughout Fiji, since it would prove "embarrassing to the host to find there was not enough food to feed everyone who entered the house during mealtime" (Ravuvu 1983:41). Moreover, since an inadequate food supply reflects poorly on the entire family, "the image of the group or even the village will be marred if visitors are not well hosted and fed" (41). On the occasion of unexpected visitors that might strain otherwise limited resources, it is customary for *mataqwali* members and even other villagers to contribute *cawa dina* and cooked *ilava* to the household where guests are being hosted. This practice, called *kabekabe*, occurs commonly since there are frequently a number of guests in the census of any given village. For example, if a visiting preacher comes to the local church, if a woman has just delivered a baby, or if relatives arrive from a distant locale, their meals will be furnished in the household in which they are staying, but augmented by contributions from other villagers.[9] These food offerings become elements in the reciprocal exchange typifying community etiquette. During any given

meal, attention is then divided between incorporating outsiders and seeing to the needs of persons eating. The following narrative describes the
essential dynamics of *viqwaravi* at an Easter Sunday dinner; although
this was not exactly a typical meal, given the holiday, the enactment of
dining etiquette was by no means extraordinary:

The women clustered in the cookhouse to begin the labor-intensive preparations for the special meal. Liku and Atelaite sliced beans and carrots and
chopped chicken and garlic as their grandmother peeled the taro for the meal.
We took turns at the gas stove and a makeshift wood fire outside, as the *cawa
dina* boiled over the open fire in the cookhouse. When the cooking was finished
we changed our clothes to attend the village church service. On our way back to
our household, Liku and I exchanged invitations with another friend to dine at
the respective households; having each mutually politely declined, we returned
to finish setting out the food. We helped set plates along the length of a cloth
placed on mats in the main room. The chief and a guest were summoned as
yaqona was mixed, and Liku and Jita placed platters of steaming *cawa dina* on the
cloth and filled bowls with chop suey, curried pork, and roasted chicken that
had been freshly killed.
    While the men continued to drink *yaqona,* our guest from out of town was
asked to come to eat. I was directed to take the chief's special plate to him so
he could begin his meal as well. Some of the children sat at the mat to eat while
women of the older two generations sat by the pots to tend to serving. A villager
arrived to give something to Liku and was immediately asked in for dinner but
declined the invitation and left. We passed the various dishes to the chief and
our guest, bidding them to make their selections first. As we were enjoying the
meal, a neighbor brought a plate of two fish in coconut cream and another plate
with two yams, two plantains, and a large taro root. This gift was to thank us
for our morning *kabekabe* to their meal for the visiting minister. Liku accepted it
and filled a bowl with chop suey and piled some *cawa dina* (two yams and two
taro roots — nearly identical with the visitor's offering) onto a plate for her in
exchange. We thanked her for her *kabekabe,* and she left to tend to her guest
at home. In the interim, Tai Pita, a mentally ill man who shifted from home to
home in Nahigatoka, wandered in and was immediately seated at the food. Tai
Mosese inspected a particularly appetizing yam in front of him; he leaned over
to a small boy next to him and proposed that they divide and share it.
    Later in the afternoon, the cloth was spread again with the warmed dishes and
the *bulagi* (leftover *cawa dina*). Tai Vani described the food she had sent home
with our guest, and several minutes later Jita re-listed the items she had helped
her pack for him. Via asked me if I had eaten sufficiently at noon while we ate.
A child arrived at the open door carrying the pudding that had been awarded
to our *mataqwali* in the choir competition. It was immediately sliced into portions and taken away to be distributed to the other member households. As we
finished our meal, Tai Pita was spotted outdoors and called to come in and have
his supper, which he happily did.

This meal allowed the orchestration of food exchange within the
household to extend into the community. Outsiders were incorporated
into the event with several invitations to join the core household. Guests
were fed, the *kabekabe* was reciprocated, and in the evening the women

who had participated in the *viqwaravi* were able to reflect contentedly on what foods they had sent home with their main guest.

A central feature of the *viqwaravi* of a meal is the verbal commentary maintained by the hosts and servers, encouraging people to eat as much as possible. Thus the rhetorical instruction and conversation during the meal complements the requisite invitations issued from the cookhouse to passersby. While men, children, and guests enjoy their meal, the women keep a vigilant watch on everyone's plates. They urge "Eat a lot" (*Kana valevu*), "Eat some more" (*Kana tale*), or "There's still more food" (*E hi vo na cawa*); alternately they express disappointment with the meager amount the guest has eaten: "You haven't eaten much" (*O tasi kana valevu*) or "Quit eating like a nurse" (*Kua ni kana vanasi*).[10] A particularly assiduous host or hostess will insist, "Eat a great deal, so that you may become fat!" (*Kana valevu, mo urouro!*). This request is also meant quite literally, besides being a matter of politeness.

One afternoon Tai Mosese was reprimanded by another member of the household for having been unnecessarily cross with me. He evidently felt remorseful and personally came to inform me that my dinner was ready in the cookhouse. During our meal together, he was unusually attentive to and solicitous about my needs. As I began to eat my soup, he repeated several apologies for the inadequacy of the meal. He assured me that he had gone to a great deal of effort to look for fish, but that the market had had none. I replied that the soup was fine, but he continued to brood. A few moments later, he continued, "Alas, you are eating so poorly." I again insisted I liked the soup and finished my bowl as proof. No sooner was my bowl empty, than he directed one of the women serving to fetch me another. When I protested that I was full, he complained that I never ate enough and declared his wish that I "eat lots and become fat" (*kana valevu mo qe urouro*). I pointed out that I had already made a good start by gaining five kilograms during my stay in Nahigatoka, and he looked pleased. A few hours later, his granddaughter arrived home and also criticized his earlier behavior toward me. This prompted him to seek me out again to urge me to "become fat."[11]

Tai Mosese's apologies for the midday meal were his attempts to reconcile our differences expressed in the idiom of feeding me. Rhetorical apologies exaggerating the inadequacies of the meal are also part of the armamentarium of the decorous host or hostess. Remarks such as "It is terrible that there is no pig to give" or "How awful that we have no milk for your tea" are routine accompaniments to mealtime commentary.

The Rhetoric of *Vikawaitaki*: Core Value or Ambivalence?

To a degree, the axiomatic encouragement to eat well is requisite to performing one's role as a host and affirms one's grounding in the moral context of village life. Nevertheless, this mealtime commentary is no mere palaver, as Fijians are genuinely disappointed if their guests do not appear to eat with gusto (see also Ravuvu 1983:32; Gatty n.d.).

A. Irving Hallowell cautions against assuming that "food-sharing is an indication that the individual has become so closely identified with other members of the group that there is an inseparable coalescence of interests"; indeed, often it constitutes an "act of self-defense against possible aggression" or sorcery (Hallowell 1967:102–3). Kahn's work in the New Guinea Highlands suggests that generosity with respect to sharing one's food, though an explicit virtue, is nonetheless exercised with restraint and ambivalence. For example, a person may elect to remain hungry in order not to expose food "because the person did not want (or have enough) to give any to the visitors" (Kahn 1986:40). Furthermore, "ravenous appetite, or the lack of control over it," is causative of misfortune to the extent that persons have a vested interest in controlling their appetites. Kahn interprets this preoccupation with appetite control as a defense against greed, revealing a concern with reaching a balance between deprivation and gluttony (40–41). Jeannette Mageo notes that in Samoan society "oral aggressiveness" (in speech and eating) is tantamount to a lack of "subordination of the subjective self" while "oral restraint" is associated with integrity (Mageo 1989:416). Bradd Shore has also illuminated the Samoan emphasis on containment of private desire by societal prescriptions (1982:185).

Given Fiji's cultural and geographic proximity to both New Guinea and Samoa, can a similar analysis to the Fijians' absolute requirement to appear generous with their food be applied? While food sharing in Fiji seems to occur in the context of the ethos of expressing care, it is true that there is noticeable ambivalence in narratives about the potency of food gifts. In fact, unsolicited food from strangers generates a good deal of distrust, which is recontextualized in the interpretation of untoward illnesses and deaths. There is also recurrent, if not consistent, dream imagery of food as poison. If someone's death is attributed to unnatural means, a seer (*daurairai*) is consulted to ascertain the immediate cause of death.[12] Although greater attention is focused on which person or spirit is to blame, also frequently implicated is a food — usually brought from a stranger or a household known to enlist spiritual assistance in revenge — that has poisoned the afflicted individual. One woman, after relating the story of a man who had died after eating a cursed eel, recalled that her father had also been poisoned with some bananas.

He was given some bananas, from another house, it was when he went to our village, and uh, after awhile, he . . . he just, man! Something happened to his stomach, eh? It was so painful, that he got these, uh, what are they called, the

bubbles coming on his mouth . . . and he just started praying and it finished . . .
Another person, he also ate the bananas, he, he just went to some place, I mean
he was riding on a horse, and then he fell, and he broke his leg.

Others reported that any food offerings considered suspicious would be
accepted and then set aside: "Whatever food they bring; we put it away,
we never eat it," said one woman. Another recalled an incident when a
villager who otherwise never visited her grandparents' household sent a
suspicious gift of food:

The grandchildren, they made pancakes, and they brought pancakes right for
my grandmother; but they don't usually come at home, those kids, and then uh,
we already knew that the grandfather is like that, eh? I think if she had eaten
the pancakes, same time [she would have been poisoned].

In dreams food is also a potent agent of spirits, and in this context
offerings must be declined. A university student related her aunt's catastrophic illness, which had been portended by an offering of food in
a dream.

Like it has happened to my auntie, like, a man comes bringing food and says,
"Your mother sent me to bring this to you." . . . And then she says, "No, if my
mother wanted me to have anything she'd bring it herself; she wouldn't send
anybody to bring it to me." And he tries to force her to eat it, and she doesn't,
they just argued, and she wakes up. Well, that . . . she didn't know . . . but the
next day, she . . . was blind, that auntie of mine . . . she became blind.

Food is the agent of empowerment—whether as a potion or a poison—in several contexts. For example, some savvy women reported that
love potions can be concocted as food offerings to the target of one's
affections. Food perhaps approaches the limits of its potency when prepared by a woman who is concealing a pregnancy. While her effects on
food are inadvertent, they are quite toxic and potentially lethal to the
infirm and the young.[13] In all these cases, control and exchange of food
confers power within the social milieu. Certainly, this can do nothing
but augment the incentive to display generosity with food in the conventional ways described above. However, performance of *viqwaravi* appears
to be consciously governed by a vested interest in appearing competent
in the arena of caregiving.

Notwithstanding the requirement to share food, Fijians must occasionally find sharing limited resources in conflict with the more pragmatic
concern in providing for the immediate household. Moreover, an unusual number of guests to care for may prove taxing, as reflected in the
exasperated comment of a woman while fixing a plate of dinner to send
to a postpartum mother: "We are tired of all the *kabekabe*." The same

woman ever so subtly indicated that she found her duty for *viqwaravi* burdensome with regard to a man who, by virtue of his homelessness and apparent mental illness,[14] became a perpetual guest at our meals.

I first made Tai Pita's acquaintance on returning from a field trip. I was surprised to find a rather disheveled man apparently measuring the dimensions of the cookhouse and then our porch without any meter-stick. Although most members of the household ignored the odd behavior, a woman reported to me that he had recently attacked someone with a knife. We were having our morning tea in the cookhouse so that the household could debrief us about their relatives in Vatulele when Tai Pita appeared at the door and was beckoned in. He was seated at the table and served a meal with no comment but the invitation to come in and have tea. As he made somewhat of a spectacle of himself in spooning great quantities of sugar into his tea and slicing an entire loaf of bread crosswise for his portion, I looked quizzically at Tai Vani, who rolled her eyes in mixed amusement and annoyance. Tai Pita frequently took meals with us during the next several months. Another household member later explained, "We say, 'Let him come in, let him eat, no matter if that's the way he is, or if he is sick in the head.'"

Tai Pita's recurrent presence at our meals suggests that although there may be practical limits to tolerating the requirement to welcome guests, there are scarcely ideological limits to it. Certainly, the conventional obligation to feed any stray visitors may engender some ambivalence, but this is rarely expressed and virtually never acted upon. To the contrary, in most instances people take obvious pleasure in their role of *viqwaravi*. In the context of food exchange, ambivalence about giving food rarely competes with the powerful social sanctions to maintain an open, generous household.

The occasional Fijian ambivalence about receiving food cannot be compared with the Samoan struggle to subordinate the self through oral restraint (Mageo 1989) or with Kahn's portrayal of the New Guinea Highlanders as struggling to conceal their greed in exhibitions of generosity (1986). Fijians may be equally eager to display their generosity conspicuously, if not by the sheer superfluousness of foods at a *magisi*, then in the record of their vigilance in monitoring the social environment for opportunities to display care. Although it may seem plausible that Fijians are also countering "selfish" impulses by an elaboration of the rhetoric of caring, the alternative (and more likely) possibility is that this ideology and its enactment make the core value of *vikawaitaki* explicit.

Clearly food sharing in Fiji is not entirely unfettered by ambivalence. This is not altogether surprising in view of the environmental disasters that have threatened the food supply. But more importantly, the ambivalence woven into narratives about sharing food underscores the deep terror of the possible unraveling of human relationships. However, the moral requirement to share food is far more than a defense against a putative inner greed; rather, it is an affirmation of the fundamental interconnectedness of human lives and the core cultural value of *vikawaitaki*. Our insistence on seeing nothing but the ambivalence inherent in sharing only reflects our own cultural preoccupation with independence and devaluation of care (see Tronto 1993:157–62), and reveals our privileging of personal needs over and at the expense of social ones. The explicitness and primacy of *vikawaitaki* in Fijian society reflect not a defense against a conflicting personal agenda, but an affirmation of the existential condition for being-in-the-world [15] as fundamental interdependence. Care, food, and exchange — all ultimately manifest in bodies — are constitutive of the meaning and security in human relationships in Fiji.

The Discourse on Nurturing

The preceding sections have revealed that the creation, maintenance, and evaluation of social relationships are founded on the reciprocal exchange of care, alternately conceived of as *vikawaitaki*, *vilomani*, and *viqwaravi*. Moreover, the social standing of a particular community or *mataqwali* rests on its perpetual performance of care, which is concretized in a variety of ways. The key elements in enacting care involve both feeding the household and maintaining at least the illusion of the ability to feed the wider community. Care is evident in the quality of food exchange (the quantity of yams, the size of the boar, and so on) and also in the robust physiques of one's charges. Indeed, commentary on care exploits the metaphorical significance of body shape for discourses on both nurturing and negligence. This metaphorical significance derives from ethnonutritional theories that explicitly link the consumption of a large amount of food with the energy to work and with a bodily form that is *jubu vina* (described in Chapter 2).

Feeding visitors is an explicit expression of *vikawaitaki*.[16] Fijians who travel from their home village to a distant one anticipate the local delicacies to which they might be treated. On their return home, they will be debriefed with questions about the foods tasted and the *vikawaitaki* of the distant host villagers. If the hosts are inattentive to their guests' comfort and enjoyment, the travelers will convey this to their audience in condescending remarks; if on the other hand the care is judged superb (which occurs in an overwhelming majority of cases), the returned travelers will give glowing and detailed descriptions.

The degree of *vikawaitaki* evident during a *magisi* or a small-scale meal implicitly reflects the tenor of the relation between the guest and host groups. One Nahigatoka woman explained that the visible effort to provide plentiful and appetizing food demonstrates "how they *kawaitakinia ketatou* (care for us)." She elaborated on this by drawing from our experience as guests on a recent field trip to her relatives' village on the island of Vatulele. Of her uncle's household's agenda in hosting us, she commented:

They always really try to manage that we eat well because they know that as soon as we return here, the people are going to ask, "Did you all eat well there? Did you eat a lot of fish? Did they go diving in the sea for your fish?" And then Tai Mosese is going to say, "Did Apisa go fishing for your fish? Did he dive a lot?" If we said, "No, we had no fish to eat!" [Tai Mosese would say], "Tch! What were they doing? They were lazy!"

True enough, our stay in Lomanikaya Village on Vatulele had been marked with delicious and abundant fresh ocean fish both fried and cooked with coconut cream. The men in the household had gone spear-fishing daily to provide these meals and to present us with smoked *vai* (stingray) as a special gift for Tai Vani because it was her *icavu*. Tai Vani and Tai Mosese greeted us with their habitual questions about what we had eaten while away from Nahigatoka. "I don't know, did you eat a lot of fish?" Tai Mosese wondered. Liku, Mere, and I were pressed to reiterate culinary descriptions over and over as other householders eagerly asked for news of their Vatulele kin.

Liku summed up her impressions of the critical importance of the performance of care as follows:

Yes, we always demonstrate our [caring] . . . if a guest comes to us, we endeavor to provide what he likes . . . it is essential that we cook well, that we please him, this is because, when he returns to his home, we don't want him to sit there and say that we didn't *kawaitakinia*.

She added that showing this care is particularly important among *viwekani*, kin related by blood. For one thing, the debt would surely be repaid: "one day we will be guests in their homes" and "[if we did not care for them appropriately] they won't *kawaitakinia* about us," she observed. Moreover, being perceived as "people who never show *vikawaitaki*," would likely strain social relations, she added. The global sense of duty in demonstrating *vikawaitaki* is of paramount importance in Fijian life and social relations. She referred to core Fijian values in explaining that

Fijian life is like that . . . the important elements in Fijian living . . . the most important thing, *me tu vilomani, na vikawaitaki, me tu vidokai* [that we care about one another, that we care for one another, that we respect one another] . . . the most important things are our caring about, taking care of, and respecting one another.

This explanation reflects her notion of the reasons for maintaining the community as Fijians know it. "We help each other, we support each other"; no matter what problems arise "we help one another, we *vika-waitaki*."

Fijians are concerned that their efforts to nurture their guests will be rewarded with the recognition of the adequacy of their *vikawaitaki* and *viqwaravi*. These efforts are not only reflected in the descriptions of the meals the hosts prepared, they are also manifest in body morphology. Hence the recurrent commentary on body shape.

It is routine for hosts to direct their guests to eat well to avoid any possibility that their care be deemed negligent. A university student recalled her relatives' insistence that she eat well while staying with them. If a person is too thin, she reasoned, people "think you, aren't being looked after well." Her recent stay in her aunt's village had elicited constant pleas for her to eat more. "They say to eat more [because] when you go back home, they see that, you know, that you've . . . we have been feeding you well." A student from Lau noted that trips to her island were occasions to enjoy the abundance of food. She felt that her family was concerned that she appear well cared for when she returned to Suva. She explained,

I think they might think that if you come back, if you come back to Suva, then you'll become skinny, lose weight and all that. They might say, "Oh . . . you went to the village and they didn't feed you nicely," and all that.

This implication would be particularly disgraceful if another household had assumed care and had appeared negligent. For example, a woman from a Nadroga village stated,

They'll be very, very proud, if you put on weight and really look healthy before you go back to your parents; and if you go back to your parents skinny, you know, there are a lot of reasons behind it, eh? And maybe they'll think that your parents won't want to send you back to them, and then like maybe they'll think that they'll never feed you properly.

When a woman marries, her husband's family is charged with her care. In one household, a young woman's pregnancy precipitated a great deal of concern that she eat well. An in-law's preoccupation with maintaining her robust shape was heightened as their *mataqwali* planned their visit (*vakavanua*) to the young bride's natal village to consolidate the marriage. The young woman confided that she felt "forced" to eat a lot; she added, "They want me to eat a lot . . . because of the baby."[17] Just before the *vakavanua* the in-law, on watching her eat, urged, "You must eat a lot, you should get large like Make [a rather large new bride in the *mataqwali*]." In essence, he articulated his desire that she embody the cumulative effects of their nurturing.

The in-law's concern that the young woman's body form should reflect their *mataqwali's* effective nurturing was paralleled by her own family's concerns about her well-being in her new village, which was also evident in their commentary on her body shape. Her sister exclaimed, "*Sa lila,* you're so thin!" on seeing her. Likewise, when she visited her parents later in her pregnancy, they immediately remarked on her weight loss. Their reflexive response was to feed her, and she recalled consuming sausage with a half-dozen eggs in that first meal at home.

Given the explicit associations with nurturance and *vikawaitaki* of invitations to eat, the comments indicating a host's wish to fatten his guest, and the protests that a guest is not eating well enough, the commentary during mealtimes is an idiom of care. That is, encouragements like "Eat well" (*Kana valevu*) or "You should become fat" (*Mo urouro*) express concern for well-being by mobilizing a complex set of symbols relating care to food exchange and body morphology. This rhetoric is also used to make social amends, and is pressed to its limits in achieving the ultimate goal of the intensive care of an individual: that he should become fat. However, despite such hearty encouragement, Fijians do not find obesity in and of itself particularly appealing. Nurturing, rather than the actual cultivation of body shape, is the ostensible goal of this ethos in practice.

Finally, these attempts to demonstrate care through concrete changes in body morphology were also illustrated by the diligent care of pigs in our household. Given its ritual importance in exchange for an important *magisi*, a pig's size is explicitly related to the prestige of the offering. In my journal I noted that

> One of the village women had assumed responsibility for the care of her husband's pig during his extended absence from our village. The animal grew to be so large that her household decided to roast it for the Christmas dinner, lest it die from its obesity. Just before preparations to kill and butcher the animal, its proud owner asked me to photograph it so she could show her husband (away for an extended period) how well it had grown in response to her diligent nurturing.

In this case the ultimate reward for the laborious cultivation of the pig is to be recognized for the masterful cultivation of form — whether this results in an enormous pig or gigantic yam — for an offering to the community.

"Going Thin": Critical Commentary on Negligence in Care

Fijians monitor changes in body morphology within their network of care with great vigilance. Any evidence of weight loss is assumed to reflect a disruption in connectedness to the social milieu or gross negligence on the part of the caretakers. The common phrase "going thin" (*e luju hara ga elala*) generally identifies a perceived weight loss as a social loss.

For example, a woman drew my attention to a friend of hers who had recently broken up with her boyfriend. She described her as *lila* and took her "going thin" as evidence of her broken heart. In another instance two women described the appearance of a young man who had stayed in their village during his vacation from the university. After several months in Nahigatoka he had been called home because his mother had suddenly become ill. When his Nahigatoka hostess chanced to meet him in Suva only a week or two later, her initial reaction was "*Isa!* Esala has gone thin!"[18] In her view his appearance reflected not only his worries about his mother but also the absence of a caretaker.

Fijians are especially attentive to changes in children's weight, either remarking on a gain in a self-congratulatory way or equating a loss with neglect on the part of the caretaker.[19] If a child is adopted or his or her parents separated, it is common for two Fijian households to share the duties of childraising. In one household in Nahigatoka, frustration with custody disputes was often articulated as a critique of the other household's abilities to take care of the children. In one particularly contentious situation, a two-year-old boy was taken by his father without permission from his mother's house to his father's village. When the child was returned by the police after six days, the family's outrage at the incident was framed in repeated references to the neglect of the child in the hands of his father's household. His aunt exclaimed that "he really lost weight." Another told me that his first words on his return were a request for food; yet another relative corroborated the child's state of hunger on arrival. His great-grandmother lamented, "His body is so thin" (*E mama elala*), and her husband repeated, "He has gone thin" (*A luju elala*).

In the same vein, commentary on the weight status and growth of a two-and-one-half-year-old girl, Kini, implied negligence in her care during a brief visit to her mother's village. Her paternal grandmother explicitly related the child's failure to thrive to neglect by the mother's family.

[She lost a bit of weight there] but, uh, soon after one or two days, she picked up again, eh? I think it's the way they feed her, because no one cares, eh? And the mother goes to work, she's just left, and I think we've noticed that we've come across a few times that she has been left alone . . . She can't feed herself, eh? . . . So, most probably that's why she's losing, eh? . . . When she comes back here after one or two days, she picks up quickly, eh? Everybody pays attention, eh? . . . I don't think she's happy there. If she's there, after one or two days, she'll start asking, crying that she wants to come back here . . . Every time she comes back, she's really [lost] weight.

Similarly, Kini's aunt in Nahigatoka criticized her care in the other village by speculating that they had failed to provide her with milk. Even Kini's four-year-old sister added, "Kini, I'm big, just look at my stomach," and then said that her sister had "gone thin." Her Nahigatoka relatives claimed the child's body approached a "malnutrition case." In the ensuing weeks they regularly noted their progress in fattening her as an implicit substantiation of their superior abilities as caretakers.

A critique of social neglect is often framed as a comparison of skills in caring. The following edited narrative recounts a woman's achievement in rescuing her adopted child from malnutrition. In it, she contrasts her skills in *viqwaravi* with the moral and practical failings of the biological mother and uses the core symbols relating care and body shape in an effort to demonstrate her personal achievement (embodied in her adopted daughter) and to legitimate her custody of the child.

[Vasenaca explained that since she had two sons, she had wanted a daughter as well. Three years ago, her cousin's wife became pregnant while nursing her infant daughter, then only a few months old.] The mother became pregnant again, that is what caused her baby to go thin. Because of, we always say, she was *vadabe*.[20] She was *vadabe* that way, and the mother's breasts became empty because she was still nursing when the husband came to his wife and wanted her again . . . This child [had] fever, this child had diarrhea, she was a good girl but . . . she had diarrhea! She was thin! She was suffering from what you doctors call malnutrition. And that child's body became thin . . . The nurse told her, "Quit nursing her." At that time I came to the village, the mother was in her eighth month of pregnancy . . . Oh . . . if you could see her picture, I took a picture of her . . . of her malnutrition illness, the *thin* neck! . . . her bloated belly, tiny legs, tiny arms.

The mother took her to the grandmother; she took her there for the baby to stay for awhile . . . those people ate late, they didn't feed her until after twelve o'clock, or sometimes they just had cassava for their tea, and the children just had cassava for their tea, too.[21] In a case like this, it is important that the child is well fed. After this, the child did not regain her health, [she was still] sick. So they brought her here, they brought her to her auntie . . . to be with those people. They didn't take care of her, she was just sick. I was the third person [they brought the baby to].

It was really something, my *lomania* [concern], eh? I went there, I brought her back; I told them, "I'll bring her home with me, I'll stay with her, and she will be mine." Now there is a girl in our house, eh? Then I took care of that child . . . Today . . . she is just like Titilia [a healthy little girl in the household] she has gotten big, she's at home — my third child.

The child's life was in my hands, it was such a severe illness. We went to the hospital, we stayed there . . . Her condition was such that as soon as she ate, she passed her food; I was taking care of her . . . and sometimes, as soon as I gave her food, it made her go to the bathroom. I gave it all my strength. [Vasenaca described her experience with the growth chart in the Maternal and Child Health Clinic.] This child never moved up on the chart. [Finally the nurse told her:] "Vasenaca, she is starting to move up the chart; feed her well, *qwaravi vina* [take good care of her]." Well, I bought her milk . . . I started her on milk again, I bought her eggs, she ate eggs, I went fishing, I brought her *malaya* [a fish caught in the Sigatoka River], I cooked it with taro leaves for her to eat; I paid attention to her food so the nurse couldn't say that she was suffering from eating poorly, from malnutrition.[22]

And today you can't tell that she once suffered from malnutrition. [At that time] I took her picture, so that when she is grown up, she won't be rude to me. When she is grown, I will show her herself in the photo; I'll say, "I took care of you at the time your body was like this, your father's family didn't know you, I was the one who bought your clothes." I mustered all my strength to chase her illness away.

In her narrative, Vasenaca establishes the legitimacy of her relationship with her adopted child in the description of how she heroically rescued the child from malnutrition. She openly criticizes how the infant's health was initially compromised by her parents' sexual indiscretion, and later by her grandmother's and aunt's failure to nurture her. She then juxtaposes this with the account of her success in restoring the child to an acceptable weight. The changes wrought in the child's body by her nurturing cement the connection between the two. Even if custody should be challenged, Vasenaca's snapshot documents her claim to the child through her transformation of the child's body.

The Preoccupation with *Macake*: The Fear of an Appetite Disorder

Because maintaining a child's weight has such pragmatic and symbolic importance, Fijians carefully monitor the appetites of their charges. Loss of appetite is not only the pathognomonic symptom for the culturally elaborated syndrome *macake*,[24] but it is also considered a primary marker heralding more serious illnesses.[24] Appetite is conceived of and negotiated as the key variable in restoring health. The following case illustrates both how an illness episode was construed as an appetite disturbance and how care was organized around restoring the patient's strength through feeding.

Seini, age twelve, developed a skin infection around her left eye along with a high fever a week before Christmas Day. She was taken to the outpatient clinic and started on penicillin injections for the infection. By Christmas Eve the swelling around her eye appeared to be resolving, but her temperature was hovering around 102 degrees — information that concerned me but evidently not my hosts when I was enlisted in the child's care. As the adults discussed her condition in the cookhouse, it was apparent that their primary concern was her failure to eat. Hence her care was organized around preparing foods to tempt her appetite. When she continued to refuse food, however, the tensions associated with her refractory illness escalated. Her frustrated aunt, whose efforts to feed her had been to no avail, shouted, "Leave her alone then; she wants to die that way!"[25] Tai Vani, the child's grandmother, suggested that they treat the appetite disturbance with medicine for *macake*. The two discussed the alternative therapies and settled on the one considered to be most potent, a traditional preparation called *drala*.

Seini's aunt left the cookhouse and returned shortly with the *drala* she had gathered. Tai Vani prepared the medicine and took it to her granddaughter. Her initial invitation to drink the *drala* was gentle. The child, however, refused and provoked her grandmother to inquire, "Do you want to die?" She insisted that she take the *drala* so that she could eat and "strengthen her body." She pleaded further that the child's body had already "gone thin." The child continued to refuse, to the consternation of the relatives who had gathered. Tai Vani was later to confide that this was not a disease of the appetite but a *baca ni vadinadinaya* — a disease of stubbornness. All the women in the room joined in their criticism of the child's refusal to eat. They addressed her with questions such as "Do you want to die?" and then complained to one another of their frustration that "she won't say what she wants to eat." After Tai Vani was finally able to persuade Seini to drink the *drala*, she did begin to eat, and the vigilance was relaxed with the return of her appetite.[26]

Within a short time the child became critically ill and was admitted to the hospital with presumed meningitis.[27] At this juncture the family redirected its efforts toward organizing shifts of relatives to sleep with her in the hospital and to cook her food. Following the acute period of her illness, her recovery was appraised by the family in terms of what foods, and how much, she was able to consume.

Although this episode involved an unusual disease, the monitoring of Seini's appetite as the chief indicator of the severity of her illness and the subsequent organization of her care around restoring her appetite typifies culturally sound *viqwaravi*. During my stay, two women in our household suffering from *kune bura*, a condition characterized by poor appetite and vomiting during the first trimester of pregnancy, were hospitalized for intravenous nutrition and rehydration because the family was alarmed by their inability to eat.

Although poor appetite sometimes heralds the onset of an illness, it is more often attributed to *macake*. *Macake* is a syndrome characterized by a poor appetite for *cawa dina* and other nourishing foods, and a craving for sweet ones. The syndrome typically includes a whitish coating on the tongue, sores in the mouth, a change in urine color, inflamed gums, a runny nose, and fever — the latter two being more common in pediatric cases.[28] This illness is endemic among young children and also quite prevalent in the adult population.

Episodes of *macake* are precipitated by excessive consumption of sweets, and Fijians link its rising incidence to the introduction of Western foods. *Macake* was experienced as a craving for sugary foods by a university student who had lived in Suva her entire life: "I just want to keep eating . . . biscuits, keep on drinking Coke . . . all the junk food possible . . . then you just don't feel good with yourself."[29] The preoccupation with *macake*, however, is focused less on the quality of the diet than on its implications for lack of interest in eating. A man described *macake* as the sensation that "one's inside doesn't want to eat; one just doesn't feel like eating." A woman described the experience as "our insides don't want . . . to be eating food; they don't know the taste." This lapse in appetite leads to the most worrisome feature of *macake*: it causes children "to go thin."

Macake, an illness unfamiliar to Western biomedical nosology, can be understood as an elaboration of the Fijian interest in body morphology regardless whether we can map it onto Western-based physiologic realities (see Good and Good 1982:141–46). Although the diagnosis and therapy of *macake* is ostensibly pragmatic, the constant surveillance for its symptoms and the regular prophylactic dosing of *dranu*, or traditional herbal therapies, are important means of enacting *vikawaitaki* and *viqwaravi*. The slightest diminution in appetite raises a suspicion of *macake* and prompts the administration of one of several *dranu* therapies to forestall further loss of appetite.[30] One mother explained how she administered *macake* medication (*wai ni macake*) monthly or even fortnightly to her children, "no matter if they are healthy or not." This regular, prophylactic dosing is ubiquitous; it is the community standard of care.

Although sweets are directly implicated in the pathogenesis of *macake*, parents rarely withhold them from their children.[31] This preference for administering *dranu* in lieu of withholding food is entirely consistent with the Fijian equation of feeding to nurturing. The widespread administration of *dranu* not just for *macake* but for a vast range of minor ailments is a natural extension of *vikawaitaki* and the nurturing of bodies. The preparation and administration of *dranu* is only one way to exploit the diagnosis of *macake* as an idiom of care. Perhaps more significantly, *macake* generates the requirement to maintain careful attention to changes in appetite and body shape as possible indicators of distress in the body or the social world.[32] The guarding and monitoring of the appetite are fundamentally integrative, since treatment of *macake* both practically and symbolically enmeshes the afflicted individual in a network of care.

Conclusion

The Fijians' apparent complacency about cultivating the body initially seems quite paradoxical. If Fijians are not concerned with manipulating their "self-image" through the body, why has a corpus of rhetorical instructions to nourish — even to fatten — one's guests developed? And why has commentary on the body proliferated into parallel discourses on nurturing and negligence?

In Fiji the cultivation of bodies is legitimated as a collective rather than a personal endeavor. Indeed, the community is embodied through its work on its members' bodies. The measure of its success relates to a complex set of symbols referencing the core value of *vikawaitaki* and condensed in the body's morphology. Care, then, is concretized in anatomic space. The display of core cultural values through the medium of personal bodies is a primary expression of the ethos of care within the social body. Thus, the body is the showplace of its caretaking community.

Social relationships in Fiji are fundamentally mediated through the exchange and distribution of food. Care, or *vikawaitaki*, is manifested in food exchange and feeding, and subsequently in bodily form. Whether occurring within the microcosmic regulation of domestic food production and distribution or formalized in the grand-scale food prestations such as *magisi*, the ethos of care is reaffirmed in the quotidian life of the villagers. The cumulative effects of this collective *viqwaravi* are indexed in the body morphologies of those under the community's care.

Fijians have not only elaborated a variety of idiomatic expressions to stimulate the appetite, they have also institutionalized vigilance over the appetite through their monitoring for and treatment of *macake*. Moreover, Fijians make frequent and direct comments speculating on the etiology of weight changes. This attentiveness to changes in weight and appetite can also be understood as attempts to enmesh the individual in the community.

The effective performance of *vikawaitaki* is the quintessence of virtue and marks the body with the record of its success. That body shape is an explicit marker of groundedness in a network of care underscores that the labor on its form is a collective activity. The interest in cultivating bodies must be understood in terms of the individual's relation to his or her community and the community's appropriation of and representation in the individual's body.

Chapter 4
Disclosure and Exposure:
The Body and Its Secrets Revealed

E sega ni vaka na cavu ni dalo matua me laurai.
(You cannot hide the hole from which the mature taro is pulled.)
—Fijian proverb

The preceding chapter presented evidence of Fijians' extraordinary vigilance in monitoring bodies for information about their social connectedness. In the process, responsibility for cultivating the personal body is removed from the sphere of the individual to that of the collective. The community's moral qualities are symbolically condensed in bodies, which record and reflect the care vested in them. To the extent that a body indicates something of an individual's character, it does so largely in terms of this person's capacity to redirect nurturance to the community.

This chapter examines the social monitoring of bodies for confirmation of their participation in the regeneration of the community. It also continues to challenge the exclusive relationship of self to the body that is the backdrop of Western embodied experience by showing how, in Fiji, bodily information transcends exclusively personal experience and awareness and infiltrates the collective by relocating in other bodies and in the cosmos.

This transcendence is most evident in the popular narratives concerning the disclosure of pregnancy that reveal the potency and toxicity of bodily secrets that ultimately escape the confines of personal knowledge. Both the body and the disembodied self, or *yalo*, are conceived of as intimately entrenched in the collective. The reciprocal exclusive identity of body with self is disconfirmed, and both the body and the *yalo* are bound to the collective. We will see here that ultimately the body neither contains secrets nor circumscribes experience. To be sure, there is a tension in balancing a personal agenda with moral obligation to the collective demonstrated and then erased by these narratives, as the lore confirms the impossibility of secrets.[1]

Surveillance in the Village: The Collective Gaze

Chapter 3 described how Fijians relate bodily morphology to how effectively the community is nurturing its members. Body forms also indicate whether individuals are, in turn, sustaining the community. A robust form is considered pleasing because of its perceived ability to engage in the rigorous daily labor of village life. But since such robustness indicates only the capacity to perform these tasks, the community must monitor behavior as well as form. This surveillance is partially accomplished by a pervasive and encompassing visual attentiveness in the village.

The small size and tight organization of physical space in the village allows the community's gaze to penetrate into the household and observe the activities of its occupants, thus obliterating privacy[2] (see Levy 1973:175; Shore 1982:179). Both the layout of the Fijian village and the architectural design of its homes contribute to this fishbowl effect. In Nahigatoka, for example, households are arranged close together, away from the village plantation plots. The community hall, where a villager remains on duty during the daytime to collect a toll from cars entering the village, and where people congregate to discuss village business or to drink *yaqona* late into the evenings, is centrally located on the road entering the village. In this way villagers can monitor the itinerary and business of their neighbors: who has been fishing, who has purchased fish at the market, who has bought a cow, who has hired a carrier to transport it, or what guests have come to visit and share meals.

Many households have separate buildings for sleeping, cooking, and latrines; thus individuals' movements through the household space are visible to those outside it. Moreover, both etiquette and the oppresive heat require that doors and windows be kept open during the daytime, except in inclement weather. These factors also render household arguments public. On several occasions I observed people hurrying outdoors so as better to eavesdrop on the quarrels of their neighbors.

Especially effective in maintaining the aura of surveillance is the rapid and diffuse dissemination of information within the community. If not heard as firsthand information, anything of interest is circulated as *talanoa* within the *yaqona* circle, where events are reconstructed, opinions discussed, and gossip offered time and time again. Fijian gossip (*kwekwe*) amounts to a moral critique of behavior and is fueled by the conflicts of interpersonal or intergenerational interests in the community. In particular, elders and any other villagers who have not lived in urban areas are critical of changes that mark a departure from tradition, especially changing customs in dress and decorum. A student recalled having been admonished along these lines, having been told:

If you are in town, you dress like the people in town, but as soon as you step in the village, step [inside] at the gate, you just leave everything there. When you come inside here, remember that you belong to this village, to act like, you know, somebody in the village, and you just have to live up to the standard that we expect of you.

Another student said that most of her childhood friends had married out of her village. When she appeared less than enthusiastic at attending village functions in order to help, the older women had harsh words for her behavior. She related, "They said I didn't help them out, I was lazy, I didn't know how to cook." "You should start learning what to do," they urged; "Whenever a communal thing like this is done you have to come and help out."[3] This woman added that she was careful to conform to village standards now, explaining that,

People in the village, they're so, they're so observant, eh? very observant of what you're doing . . . if you stay in the village and you, I mean, you behave well, they'll start talking about you . . . but if you are a bad person they'll start gossiping about you.

This surveillance and gossip about the activities and mishaps of community members center on moral behavior and the individual's obligations to the *mataqwali* or village. Commentary about men reviews their participation in community events and their diligence on the plantation; similarly, women are appraised for their conscientiousness in fulfilling their various domestic and village duties.

"Just Wasting the Cassava": The Imperative to Reproduce

Attention to reproduction epitomizes moral surveillance in the community. Regeneration of the *mataqwali* is of paramount concern in Fiji. Fijians explicitly acknowledge their ambitions to create a large family in hopes of augmenting their human resources for cultivating the crops, nurturing the household, and contributing to village endeavors (see Ravuvu 1978:32).

Since Fijians are (ideally) patrilocal and exogamous with respect to *mataqwali* and village, on marriage daughters generally leave their natal household and village. At this time they are charged with the care of members of their husband's family while retaining the obligation to contribute to their natal *mataqwali*'s ceremonial functions. For this reason, although Fijians are loving and indulgent parents to both sons and daughters — male children are clearly preferred.[4] Because parents depend on their children for support and care in their old age, in anticipation of this need those who have no sons often seek to adopt or incorporate male children into their families. Although marriages are also clearly instrumental in forging social alliances, the explicitly stated goal is to produce progeny for the *mataqwali*.[5] These core priorities are revealed in the formal ceremonial proceedings between two *mataqwali* regarding the transfer of two women; one group addressed the other with the following statements:

May nothing divide us
May your habitations be darkened [be crowded with people]
May your progeny be increased wherever you are
May your mutual [host] chiefs who have ceremonially received
you this morning be alive and healthy. (Ravuvu 1987:107)

In another verbal exchange, a chief expressed his wish to the visiting group that "our daughters will bear like plantains for thee to have more offspring" (ibid.:101).

The transfer of property during marriage consummates the social alliance between the respective *mataqwali* of the bride and groom. Although it is a reciprocal exchange, the groom's *mataqwali* and village make a proportionally larger offering, securing their rights to the offspring of the marriage.[6] On the occasion of a marriage an entire village is mobilized to prepare the requisite *magisi*. One woman explained why it was only proper that the whole village perform the *viqwaravi*:

We all help out because that is the *dola* ["opening"] of the woman . . . that woman, she will come here and do the work of the village, she will come here and produce descendants.

An elopement with a man is considered a theft of sorts and incurs the obligation on the part of the groom to offer restitution in the form of a ritual atonement (*horo*) (Sahlins 1962:178).

When a woman enters her husband's village at the time of her marriage, her sexual and fertility history is subject to scrutiny by her groom's *mataqwali*. According to tradition, on her wedding night, members of the *mataqwali* await evidence confirming or disconfirming the bride's virginity based on whether the barkcloth the couple uses for their inaugural sexual coupling becomes stained with her blood. The news of a blood-stained barkcloth is rapidly communicated to the bride's family, which then celebrates. On the other hand, if the evidence suggests that the bride is sexually experienced, news is conveyed to her kinsmen in such a way as to disgrace them (Quain 1948:339–40). In Nadroga, the prestigious roast pig is presented to the bride's *mataqwali* as a symbol of esteem during the *magisi* celebrating the marriage. The respectful means of serving them roast pig is by presenting it headfirst; however, if the bride is revealed not to be a virgin, the animal's presentation is reversed to expose a gaping hole which has been carved in its perineum. The social stigma suffered and shared by the respective kin groups is graphic and public. The symbolically enfleshed relocation of a bodily moral transgression enhances the social transparency of bodies.

As soon as a young bride is established in her new residence, speculation begins about whether she is already pregnant or whether she might become pregnant in the near future.[7] Women in particular are attentive and wise to the early signs and symptoms heralding the more obvious stages of pregnancy.[8] A young woman explained,

For Fijians, oh, the old ladies, they're smart . . . they can tell when a woman is one month pregnant, or two months pregnant . . . by the look of the lady, eh? the pregnant woman, eh? they can tell. They said . . . in the early pregnancy, first month of pregnancy, second month, eh? they can tell by the look of the pregnant lady, she'll lose a lot of weight, eh? . . . They used to say that they automatically lose weight . . . they said when it comes . . . when the baby inside is getting, you know, more matured or bigger, fully formed, eh, they say that that's the time when she'll gain weight again . . . four months time, five months pregnant . . . they'll uh, regain their weight again . . . they'll get fatter that time. And also . . . another sign the old ladies can really tell that she's pregnant, by you know, they'll eat a lot of unripe fruits . . . like mangoes . . . they won't eat the ripe one, they prefer the unripe one . . . that's a sign of pregnancy.[9]

Again, weight and appetite are the key variables monitored.[10] Other women explained the changes as an initial weight loss noticeable in the face and in prominent clavicles; another woman observed that the legs, especially the calves, will become thin along with the neck, and in general "the bones will show." Later the hips and the breasts enlarge, and the complexion is thought to become fairer. A pregnant woman recounted an anecdote illustrating another woman's knowledge of her pregnancy in her second month before she had disclosed it, "Nanisi knew! . . . [She asked me,] 'Are you pregnant now?' Me, I was hiding it at the time . . . them, they knew about it." Another woman in the village agreed that others had suspected this same pregnancy early in its course. She recalled,

Even Lusiana, oh about how many months ago, was asking me, "Is that girl, pregnant?" I was saying no, and she said, "No, I think she's pregnant, because the face [is fairer and thinner]."

The widespread concern with who is pregnant has its parallel pre-occupation with who is not. As the rhetorical blessings in ceremonial discourse suggest and individual accounts confirm, Fijians are eager to maximize their family size. Failure to produce sons or, worse still, complete infertility often is taken as a manifestation of moral transgresion.[11] In fact, the prevalence of this view has hindered attempts to implement family planning in Fiji, as Mere Pulea explains: "A Fijian couple's standing in the community is said to be related closely to the size of their family. The father of a large family is described in terms of approbation: *tamata dodonu, tamata kalougata, tamata vutuniyau e na ka kece*, (a man is honest, fortunate, rich in everything). His children are considered the reward for respecting traditional beliefs" (Pulea 1986:68). One woman revealed her conflicted feelings about starting oral contraceptives[12] when she confided that, although she was not yet married to the man she lived with in Nahigatoka, if she did not become pregnant soon, other villagers were likely to criticize her for "wasting the cassava" (*kana vaosi na tavioka*).[13] She eventually discontinued her efforts to avoid pregnancy, whereupon she immediately conceived. Six months later she insisted she was no longer ambivalent about it. Just days before she had overheard a story of a mother-in-law telling her son's wife, "You should leave, there is no use for you because you have borne no children." She added, regarding her own pregnancy, "I'm happy because now they won't talk about me, [they won't say] that I'm wasting our *cawa*."

An older woman recalled her past anxieties about infertility when entering Nahigatoka upon her marriage. She told me that women of her generation "wanted to have children; . . . if [we had] not, we would have been ashamed." This woman, now having several grown children, had transferred her concerns to son's wife's apparent barrenness. She noted that this daughter-in-law and another new wife in the *mataqwali* were "wasting the cassava." She explained,

We really hate that [when women fail to produce children] . . . When a woman comes here, she should produce descendants . . . we always say, "Oh! that woman there is wasting the cassava [laughs]. All she's doing is just wasting cassava, she hasn't come here and produced descendants . . . she hasn't given a single child. We women of the *mataqwali*, we fill [the *mataqwali* with descendants], eh? It's no good if a woman has no children. We Fijians, we want women who come and produce progeny; that is what is good.

A series of special therapeutic baths had had no effect on her fertility,[14] and she pointed out that she and her family wished the woman would get pregnant like another new bride in the *mataqwali*. When a woman produces offspring for the *mataqwali* the "*iyau* [the items in the wedding exchange] have been useful."

Bodily Secrets Disclosed: Confession and *Yalo ni Cala*

Even when socio-moral transgressions escape the watchful surveillance of the community, a variety of socio-cosmic mechanisms serve to elicit relevant information and ultimately render the body transparent to the collective gaze. In Fiji, the confession of moral transgressions is an important means of translocating this information from the personal to the collective domain, thus neutralizing its potentially dangerous ramifications. Moreover, articulation of interpersonal conflict or of the untoward events in a premonitory dream is thought to dissolve, defuse, or forestall potential mishaps. In essence, transformation of emotion or social conflict into shared language leaches out its danger, protecting the community from mishap and the individual from moral isolation.[15]

For example, a woman who is having unusual difficulty delivering her infant in the late stages of labor is encouraged to "confess" the true father of the child.[16] That is, her protracted labor throws the paternity of the child into question and requires that she disclose the secret she may be harboring regarding this identity (Geraghty 1989). Another illness that plagues young brides, *cavucavu*, means literally "to call out" or "to confess." It consists of "pain in your genitals . . . when you urinate," and the sensation that afterward, "you still feel like urinating some more." It potentially afflicts sexually experienced women upon their marriage. On the other hand, "if virginity is safe-guarded . . . it cannot possibly affect [that woman]."[17] The only way to cure this particular disorder is to *cavucavu*, or confess, the names of the men with whom she has had sexual relations prior to her husband. One informant gave a detailed description of the ailment and its cure.

For example, if there is a *vulau* [maiden], [and] this *vulau* goes to the village of her husband, there is a sickness that can happen to this woman; we say she is like, for instance, Litia [a woman suspected of being promiscuous]. Litia has many "friends" . . . "boyfriends," that is, those who come to her to have intercourse, intercourse, one night, one boy, or one week, another person . . . there are times when a woman is like Litia, or there are times when she is a true virgin.

Her *vudi* [genitals] are going to hurt; she is going to urinate, and it will hurt; it will be hurting and they'll bring the medicine she should drink for this sickness, right? . . . But there have been far too many men that she has slept with. This particular sickness, [normally] it should not affect us older women, like those of us who are twenty-eight, twenty-nine, or thirty years old . . . yet, it can affect a woman like that. Or if, at the time she is married, or even in the time before she has a husband, and she pretends to be a true virgin, this sickness can affect her. After that, if they look for all the *dranu* for her to take to prevent it, those *dranu* will be useless. And then it will be [decided], "You had better tell her to *cavucavu*."

This *cavucavu* means that she must enumerate . . . one by one, the men she has been with. For instance, if the number is twenty, and she only says fifteen, she will not be cured. If she says eighteen, the illness continues, but if she admits to all twenty, then she will be cured, the pain will stop, and she will be healthy! But if she doesn't [confess completely], she will die with this illness, it is really possible to die with this illness![18]

In her discussion of Lauan nightmare experiences, Barbara Herr dismisses confession as an infrequent occurrence because of the extreme shame associated with "publicizing" sexual matters (Herr 1981:345).[19] However, in contrast to the exposure of a woman's virginity on the occasion of her wedding, the therapeutic effects of confessing appear to lie not in publicizing, but in simply disclosing the secret. The same informant who explained *cavucavu* to me also gave an example of a successful cure.

One woman, the elder sister of my best friend, . . . she was married and then afflicted with a case of *cavucavu*. She enumerated them, my dear; she named every single man that she had been with . . . That was a secret though, eh? The one who was taking care of her brought in the nurse; she came in and said to her, "*Cavucavu*, tell me."

Hence, in this case public disclosure is not essential to the cure; rather, the removal of the secret from the individual is all that is required. The key element in transforming the illness lies in turning the internalized and personal outward, by articulating experience, and spilling the words into interpersonal space.

An inevitable tension arises in the voluntary disclosure of personal moral transgressions; for example, a person may be disinclined to reveal an unwanted pregnancy or an extramarital affair for fear of punishment or criticism. Regardless of an indisposition to reveal intimate bodily secrets — specifically, a hidden pregnancy or an illicit sexual activity — under certain circumstances these very secrets are disclosed in the tacit confessions of *yalo ni bukese*, or disembodied selves, which wander from the body into the community to disclose secret pregnancies, or in the voices of *yalo ni cala*, spirits that enter and speak through villagers to indicate that adultery has occurred.[20]

In the event that an adulterous liaison remains unacceptably hidden, a *yalo ni cala*, self-appointed as a guardian of disclosure, may appear in order to assist the community in eliciting the information. The following is a firsthand account of how the voice of a *yalo ni cala* exposed a couple's adulterous affair:

In the village, there is a woman and man; her *yalo* . . . went wandering. With us Fijians, if a married man and a woman go around together [if there is an adulterous affair], their *yalo* are going to [be manifest] because of their *cala* [wrongdoing]. If someone eats a spirit [is possessed of a spirit],[21] it is also asked [of the spirit], "Hey! what kind of *yalo* is this? Maybe this is the *yalo* of a dead person, or maybe the *yalo* of a living person, or maybe it is a *yalo ni cala*, hmmm?" And then it will reply, "*Yaloooo ni cala.*" That's if a married man and woman go around together. If people go around together like that . . . one of their *yalo* [is going to be manifest], if not the *yalo* of the man, then the *yalo* of the woman.

One of my best friends — my very best friend — was going around with a married uncle of mine. . . . No one knew [about this]; I was the only one who knew because my uncle had told me. The woman didn't even know that I knew about their affair. . . . Afterward I heard that . . . it was said that one day . . . one spirit was eaten . . . in Raravayawa [the pseudonym of a village]; a spirit was eaten there, and what did it say? Well! They caught it.[22] And it said it was Elenoa [the woman who was having the affair]. After that, and then what happened? No, it pleaded, it cried, that they release it. After that, they released it, it still hadn't said a thing.

After that, one evening, we were drinking *yaqona*, we were actually drinking *yaqona* at Elenoa's house. Elenoa was there with us too. See here . . . Elenoa was sitting right there, and this *yalo* was eaten [by another member of the group]. We were drinking *yaqona* and at the time it was eaten, they caught it. It said, "I am Elenoa." Yes! Elenoa was sitting there! [laughs][23] Elenoa was sitting there, and she said, "My goodness, that spirit is lying! You people catch it, catch it! . . . Right now it is going to explain what kind of *yalo* it is, a *yalo ni cala*, a *yalo ni bukese* [*yalo* of a pregnancy], or a *yalo* of what." It was caught and asked what kind of *yalo* it was. It didn't speak, it was crying . . . that *yalo* that had been eaten was crying. It was asked again, "What kind of *yalo*?" [It replied,] "*Yalo ni cala.*" Here [Elenoa] was terribly ashamed because this spirit was delivering a true report . . . This woman [Elenoa] didn't say a thing . . . after that, they released the spirit.

Those two were wondering, eh? They denied [the truth of] this, because I was the only one who knew, not a single other person knew of this, only them and me. . . . And then my uncle came to me. He said, "Please, don't say anything, because I've got a wife" . . . the *mataqwali* would punish him with *na totono ni vanua* [a public whipping].[24]

In this anecdote, the guilty woman's *yalo*, or self essence, is embodied in another to reveal its bodily transgressions to witnesses. Consequently, the couple forfeit their privacy. In this instance, my informant took pity on her uncle lest he be publicly whipped, and refrained from divulging what she knew of the adulterous affair. Her complicity, however, did not prevent the ultimate disclosure of the adultery. Rather, this transgression was manifest in the public realm through (albeit involuntarily) the bodily medium of a community member possessed by the *yalo ni cala*.[25] Thus disclosure is, in some ways, inevitable; the body cannot contain its secrets. The *yalo* here demonstrates a primary allegiance to the community while tattling on its body. In essence, its affiliation with the community outweighs its attachment to the body in this case.

The Hidden Pregnancy: The Social World
Turned Upside Down

We have already seen several ways in which the community manifests its interest in monitoring and controlling the reproductive processes of its members, demanding access to intimate bodily information. Perhaps in no case so much as during a pregnancy, does the collective seek claim to knowledge of the body.

Ethnographic work elsewhere in Melanesia has substantiated the danger imputed to female fertility. For example, Annette Weiner has shown that in the Trobriand Islands female power is contained in the ability to regenerate human beings (Weiner 1976:228–29). Because of their potency in the cosmologic realm, "women represent sexuality and fertility but also danger" (193). In the Highlands of New Guinea as well, female reproductive powers are associated with contamination, potency, and danger; it is "implicit in the male view that the mere presence of certain categories of women destroys many cultural projects" (Meigs 1984:36). In eastern Polynesia there are similar cultural associations between women's reproductive powers and danger (Shore 1989:145–47; see also Levy 1973:158).

Likewise in Fiji, pregnancy is thought to confer extreme potency on a woman, rendering her dangerous in the social world. While this specific association of danger and potency with female fertility is indisputable elsewhere in Melanesia, in Fiji, it is the secrecy of a pregnancy, not the pregnancy itself, that most explicitly threatens the community.

We have seen how secrets are spilled into the public space, manifest in the whispered *cavucavu* or the parahuman voice of the *yalo ni cala*. In the case of an undisclosed pregnancy, the gravid body slowly reveals the presence of its hidden fetus under the watchful gaze of the community. Women across many cultures have devised clever means of concealing their pregnancies (Bok 1983:22), and Fijian women also have found ways of attempting to keep this secret by hiding their bodies from public scrutiny. But it is precisely such concealment of a pregnancy that in turn precipitates its extracorporeal revelation in the social world.

Theoretically, a pregnancy is good news. However, sometimes a couple may withhold information about their pregnancy for fear it will be cursed by people harboring a grudge against their family. Or, should a pregnant woman be unmarried or already the mother of a young infant (and therefore expected to abstain from intercourse), news of her condition may instead be greeted with ambivalence; accordingly, she may be reticent in announcing her pregnancy. In such instances, a *yalo ni bukese* (literally, a spirit of pregnancy), can separate from the pregnant body during sleep to evince the pregnancy.

For instance, a woman recounted having discovered she was pregnant while in boarding school far away from her home village. While she lay in the school infirmary, suffering from severe nausea and not yet having told her family the news, her *yalo* appeared to a woman near her home. This woman then sought out her mother to let her know that her *yalo* was wandering in the village; she guessed this was either because she was ill, or because she was pregnant. Worried about her daughter, the teenager's mother traveled to her boarding school to confirm she was indeed pregnant. In another anecdote, a person's *yalo* assumed the responsibility of disclosing news of her friend's pregnancy. One woman explained how, when her sister's friend had seen her sister's *yalo* knocking at her door late one night, they surmised that although it appeared to be a *yalo ni bukese*, it could not be her sister who was pregnant, but someone close to her, since her face was uncovered. A *yalo ni bukese* characteristically wanders about the village with a blanket over its head to indicate shame. When her sister and her friend approached a woman whom they suspected of being pregnant (by virtue of her being a close friend), she initially denied knowing she was pregnant; she gave birth, however, seven months later.

Inherent in the possibility that one's *yalo* will detach from the body to divulge secret information to the community, is the conceivability that the *yalo* is more identified or affiliated with its community than with its body. In other instances the body itself appears to be integrated into the collective. That is, the body is intimately connected to and regulated by the cosmos; thus, the unshared knowledge a pregnancy cannot be contained as a secret by the body. Even if a woman does not intend to conceal a pregnancy, it is common for an owl to cry from her house if the pregnancy is as yet unknown. After this, other villagers may approach her to confirm that she is pregnant by directly asking about it.

Fijians understand that a failure to disclose a pregnancy will ineluctably lead to a variety of untoward events. In the words of one woman:

If [a woman] is pregnant, if she's hiding her pregnancy, there'll be a sign . . . If she's baking a cake, that cake will not be cooked; . . . It will be half-done; if not, it will not rise, it will just go down, like that. If she's singing in a choir, they'll be singing . . . all of a sudden [the tune] will collapse. If that happens in a choir, somebody will be saying, the choirmaster, eh, "Hey, somebody . . . must own up, somebody is pregnant."

Another woman's testimonial described a similar effect in spoiling a fishing expedition:

Last year, some people in my village, they went fishing . . . and there was this woman who was hiding her pregnancy. They were fishing, they didn't catch any fish, and then after a while, they started thinking, someone must be pregnant, eh? and . . . that person must have just realized herself, and then she [left], and after [that] . . . then people start catching fish.

Similarly, an account from a woman who had recently returned from a sea voyage to an outer island is paraphrased below:

A group of women from Nahigatoka were returning from an organized visit to Vatulele to contribute toward the new church under construction there. They had boarded a mid-sized punt in fine weather for the thirty-kilometer journey to the main island. Some time later, their boat encountered rough winds and large waves, which prevented it from making any headway at all. The distressed captain made a plea to the passengers for the group's safety. He inquired whether any of the women might possibly be pregnant. A silent moment or two elapsed before a timid voice ventured, "I am." She was rebuked by the captain for her carelessness, which might have endangered all of them, while the other passengers criticized her for not carrying a stone to drop into the sea, which would have neutralized the secret.

A decision was made to cast some plantains overboard and continue the voyage.[26] After twenty more minutes, they were still unable to make progress against the wind and waves. The frustrated captain turned once again to his passengers and demanded whether yet another woman had failed to reveal her pregnancy. Finally, another woman broke the silence to reply that, indeed, she was pregnant as well. Upon this disclosure the rough weather subsided, and the boat reached its destination without further mishap.

Another woman, who had already heard the account, remarked that women boarding a boat like that ought always to "board with a stone" so the "boat can avoid problems" just in case anyone is pregnant. In another instance, a near plane crash, resulting in a forced landing was attributed to an unannounced pregnancy:

They were wondering . . . what was wrong [why the plane was forced to land again at Nausori]. And then [a woman on the plane] finally confessed that she was pregnant, and everybody was mad at her because, I mean, because of her unconfessed pregnancy, they all could have died.

Given the prevalence of firsthand accounts of the untoward consequences of undisclosed pregnancies, Fijian women are well aware that failure to share news of a pregnancy constitutes a breach of one of the most powerful social tabus in community life.[27] Secrecy, then, is a risky proposition, since it poses a danger to a woman's social universe.

Of particular concern are the other more concrete and dangerous embodied manifestations of nondisclosure. For example, Fijians explain that food can be contaminated by the very touch of a woman harboring a secret pregnancy and can subsequently prove particularly toxic to either her very young children or to the frail elderly.

A woman described an unfortunate event befalling a friend of hers:

This friend of mine, she was pregnant, she doesn't want to stay in her home because her mother might know, so she moved to a friend of hers.[28] . . . And then, the friend of hers, her grandmother was sick, she was just lying down there, and this friend of hers and [she] were preparing, cooking [laughs] the old woman's food. She was about, she was about four months pregnant; that [nondisclosure in the advanced pregnancy] is worse, she was still hiding her pregnancy, and all of a sudden that woman died. And when she died, her pregnancy came up, everybody was blaming her: "She's the one who made *Tai* [Grandmother] . . . die, because she was hiding her pregnancy."

She continued that a secret pregnancy is particularly toxic to the infirm. She explained that since she was charged with preparing her husband's grandfather's meals, her hypothetical failure to disclose her pregnancy could prove fatal to him. Indeed, several months later, having found herself pregnant, Tima wasted no time making it known, explaining that, "If Tai was sick, and I didn't tell them I was pregnant, Tai can die straight away."

Proper disclosure of a pregnancy requires informing senior members of the household through a formal presentation of *yaqona*; it is not sufficient that the father of the baby or other interested people know or guess through other means. Another woman's improperly disclosed pregnancy precipitated a prolonged crisis in her household as her family tried to make sense of an acute illness that struck her young son, Jioji.[29] The eighteen-month-old boy had become irritable over the course of a week. He was eating poorly and vomiting, and had noticeably lost weight. He subsequently fell ill with fever and, though fully immunized, developed the unmistakable rash of measles.[30] The boy's classificatory mother,[31] who had learned of his mother's pregnancy secondhand, expressed conflicted feelings about intervening. She offered the following interpretation of events. First she rationalized the child's fussiness by acknowledging that the child was likely to be sensitive to his mother's mood. Ever critical of her younger cousin-sister, she could not resist framing her as a negligent mother with comments on her success in feeding Jioji:

[He] knows through the love. It also affects the way [his mother] looks after Jioji . . . she doesn't seem to worry a lot about Jioji, like she used to . . . But when we came to hear that she is pregnant again, her . . . love for Jioji declined, eh? Jioji could see that; she went and she sat there and she never talked, eh? He didn't want to go to the mother . . . he was crying, crying, crying . . . She has been complaining that he is not eating his food properly, eh, he just tastes it and throws it away . . . I was advising her, "Don't worry about him not eating his food properly, because it was just the same when Eleni and Sala were little girls, eh? When they come to that age . . . after one year old . . . they like playing a lot . . . so they miss their meals and all, eh? So I was advising her not to worry a lot about it . . . but I didn't realize at first that she was already pregnant; when I came to know that she was pregnant, I said, "No wonder . . . this little boy is not eating his food properly."

When I pressed her to clarify her interpretation of the child's refusal to eat, she reasoned that the child had lost his appetite both because of the emotional estrangement from his mother and because of the "hidden" pregnancy as a force in itself.

And even the strength of the effect of what is inside there, makes him not feel like eating; like that, you know, he'll lose weight, he'll worry, too [32] . . . That was what I was telling you, eh? He can even die . . . because he'll be affected by that, because the mother is hiding, eh? . . . That's our belief . . . I think the measles is just an ordinary sickness that is going around . . . but, uh, the vomiting and crying a lot . . . being fussy . . . that's the effect of the pregnancy . . . It's so bad to . . . keep [a pregnancy] to yourself, eh? Like this one; Jioji has been sick for, all of last week he was sick, as soon as she feeds him, he kept vomiting. When he comes here, he eats a lot . . . he doesn't vomit here because someone else is feeding, eh? [He is] not sick like a sickness, eh? It's something that happened when he eats food.

She continued to criticize Jioji's mother's carelessness in feeding him. Again her focal attention on the feeding is typical of the discourse on negligence:

The most important thing is the one who is feeding them, that's the most important thing. If she knows she's pregnant, she should ask somebody to cook . . . then there won't be any effect on the baby. If she cooks the food . . . even though the baby doesn't know — the baby is very young, he doesn't know all this — but the strength of what is inside there, it affects [him] . . . She's the one who is touching the food, she shouldn't be touching the food at all . . . What we believe is that the right thing to do, whenever a woman is pregnant and has still got a very young baby who is just one, or not yet, less than a year old, the right thing to do is to let the other members . . . of the family know. And on top of that, she should stop straight away cooking the food for her baby . . . It's automatically affected from what is inside there . . . When he eats the food, it's just like, when it gets in the tummy, he'll start vomiting it out . . . See, Jioji was vomiting eh? . . . As soon as she gave the food to him . . . he started vomiting.

In her view, the mother was engaged in most egregious behavior: she was effectively poisoning her child.

Whenever she feeds the baby, the baby will keep on vomiting . . . You know the baby will even *lose weight* [dramatic emphasis], yes, he can die; it's very strong . . . If everybody knows . . . she's pregnant, it's all right; but if she's hiding it, keeping it to herself, and at the same time feeding and looking after her own baby . . .

that's very dangerous. Sometimes it kills the baby . . . many times, many cases it happens.

Finally, she had deliberated whether or not to intervene by informing the senior family members in order to protect the child from worsening.

I don't care what happens to her . . . I pity that little one . . . This morning . . . he was crying after me; . . . he'll lose a lot of weight . . . That's why I'm thinking of telling them . . . rather than the baby suffering; its very important to let the other members of the family know . . . When they know, he'll stop automatically; . . . he'll stop vomiting, he'll get back to normal again.

Jioji's mother, appropriately alarmed at her child's sickness, approached her sister-in-law to enlist her help in feeding her son. Still unwilling to divulge the news of her pregnancy formally, she hid from her grandmother's view and stopped cooking for the baby. She reasoned:

[My sister-in-law] should cook for him, [she] should feed him. . . . Because if I give him the food . . . he is eating a lot, but he is thin now, he won't grow . . . his weight will go down, even if he [eats a lot] he will just stay tiny.

Nevertheless, the child failed to recover and, faced with potential calamity, Jioji's mother finally formalized her disclosure in her third month of pregnancy. She recognized this as her moral obligation, since she was doing much of the cooking for the household.[33] In retrospect, she recalled that the situation had neared disaster:

Yes, Jioji went thin! You can notice it in the photo; . . . he looks terrible . . . because I was hiding [my pregnancy] and taking care of him . . . Children can go thin . . . or an elderly person can die.

She concluded her story by affirming that as soon as she had properly presented her news with *yaqona*, Jioji had become healthy.

Socio-moral transgressions (or, breaches of tabu) have ramifications in both the social and the cosmic realm in Melanesia and Polynesia (Koskinen 1968; Kirkpatrick 1977:325; Leenhardt 1979; Shore 1989:143). For example, in pre-Christian Tahiti, "*mana* and *tapu* (tabu) were important dimensions of social control"; *mana* in Tahiti still regulates appropriate human conduct through the agency of spirits (Levy 1973:156–57). Moreover, in pre-contract Polynesia, "Breaches of etiquette or chiefly protocol did not merely have social repercussions, but cosmic consequences as well" (Shore 1989:143). In present day Fiji, if a chief or spirit is offended, or an important *tabu* broken, misfortune may ensue regardless of any willful intervention of the offended chief or spirit.

That is, individual behavior and bodies are inextricably linked to cosmic forces (see Giddens 1991:109). The environmental manifestations of a hidden pregnancy in Fiji rely on the body's intimate location in the cosmic dimension. In his classic work, *Do Kamo*, Leenhardt describes the fusion of self, other, and cosmic identities in the traditional Canaque "cosmomorphic" view of the world in the context of which the Canaque "does not distinguish the world from his body" (1979:21). "The Melanesian projects himself into the world. He does not distinguish between its reality and his own psychic life, between his self and the world. He plays a quasi-cosmic role. His behavior is inspired by a kind of intimacy between the world and himself" (175).

In addition to cosmic "signs" and "mysterious insights" as important ways of knowing in ancient Polynesia (Koskinen 1968:13, 16), truth or knowledge was also experienced in the body (49). Likewise, in Fiji, in the instance of an undisclosed pregnancy, knowledge is available to others by various somatic cues, whether or not a woman deliberately chooses to reveal her condition. For example, a secretly pregnant woman contaminates food with her touch and the person eating it experiences illness. A woman hiding her pregnancy causes others' hair to fall out when she cuts it. And her mere glance at a nursing mother's breast can dry up the woman's milk. One woman explained:

If [a] pregnant woman sees the breast of the lactating mother, one [breast] can become shorter, or else, she might, uh . . . the milk just dries up . . . It happened to me when I was a kid . . . One woman . . . she was pregnant, . . . and she saw my mother's breast, and as a result, my mother's breast dried up: . . . My mother had to resort to powdered milk to feed me.

Another woman reported that her mother experiences an "itching breast" whenever a member of the family is pregnant. She considers the evidence compelling enough to prompt an interrogation of the daughters regarding the possibility of a hidden pregnancy:

She'll say, "Oh, someone's pregnant." . . . There'll be signs, too, in the family . . . And then usually, if the signs are there, the father will call all the girls and ask, "One of you is, uh, you know, you better say it before something really . . . something bad happens."

In other words, intimate knowledge of another's body can express itself in one's own bodily sensations—the bodily experience and information are, to a degree, intersubjective, and, at the very least, widely accessible.[34] Fijians believe that other bodily information can transcend one body and relocate in another in certain contexts. For example, if a person is too ill to go outdoors to urinate, another family member can be empowered by a healer to relieve this bodily need. Similarly, when a designated person drinks a bowl of *yaqona* directly after the chief, he or she can urinate in lieu of the chief so that, theoretically, he will not be inconvenienced by a need to empty his distended bladder during the important business of the ceremony.

Bodily information — particularly data concerning pregnancy — is accessible and knowable by its manifestations in others' bodies and in the environment. Disclosure, while presenting an apparent moral dilemma as a woman weighs her personal agenda against the obligation to neutralize the terrible potency of a covert pregnancy, is in some ways inescapable, whether or not it is voluntary. Communal access to the knowledge of the pregnancy is a foregone conclusion: the body will ultimately betray its secrets and become transparent to the community's gaze.[35]

Some Conclusions and Questions

In Fiji, the body cannot exclusively possess its secrets, nor can it escape from the pervasive and penetrating collective gaze. Attempts to hide one's bodily secrets turn the social world upside down. A concealed pregnancy threatens the community with its terrible power to capsize boats, poison food, cause children to lose weight, and undermine collective projects to sing or catch fish. Given the wide array of environmental mishaps it can cause, an undisclosed pregnancy represents the height of moral irresponsibility.

In a community in which the primary and explicit goal is to build its *kawa*, or descendants, denying a pregnancy's social existence threatens the very basis of the community. Just as a body does not own its secrets, it does not have exclusive claim to its reproductive powers, which also belong to the *mataqwali*. To the extent that *mana* in Polynesia is linked to control of generativity through the containment of women's reproductive powers, this resource must be regulated. It is understandable that it should be under social watch (see Shore 1982:185). Hence, the sequestration of this information fundamentally undermines the *mataqwali's* primary interest in its regeneration and indicates the new bride's failure to embrace the goals of her new community. Villagers in Fiji continually monitor individuals and their bodies for information regarding not only social enmeshment but also their potential dissonance from community interests. This surveillance is effective by virtue of the fact that bodies are extraordinarily compliant in relinquishing their secrets in their transparency to the community's gaze.

But if bodily secrets are ultimately uncontainable, and if, indeed, the individual recognizes the community's interest as paramount, what underlies these cases of resistance to voluntary disclosure? Why are there countless gripping personal testimonials arguing the danger of nondisclosure while simultaneously recounting rebellion against community interests?

In some instances, the impulse to conceal an unwanted pregnancy may be easily explained. To the extent that a pregnancy may reveal a history of sexual indiscretion that disgraces the kinship group, a woman might understandably seek to avoid certain reproach. At other times, women are reticent in speaking forthrightly of their early pregnancies and wait to confirm the pregnancy when asked — perhaps by a woman who has noticed her weight loss, or by a neighbor who heard an owl cry at her house — rather than raising the topic themselves.

In part, the thematic popularity of concealment narratives lies in their ability to dramatize the integration of the marginalized bride into her new kinship group with the birth of each child. The new bride's position in her husband's *mataqwali* is liminal until she produces children. As she shares her secret and then her child, she is drawn again into her community and her participation in the social order is affirmed. More importantly, the multiple narratives reassure that even when the prodigal individual is foolish enough to alienate herself from her community, her body resists the secret and allows her reintegration. The danger of separation from the community has been only an illusion. Hence, the community gaze guarantees that moral delinquency will be discovered and rectified, and that the alienated transgressor will be restored to the community. The liberation of secrets, like the sharing of food, invites social intimacy and restores solidarity.

The modes of regulating moral activity in the village, although in a far different context, are not unlike Foucault's description of the "uninterrupted play of calculated gazes" that induce a "state of conscious and permanent visibility" (1979:177, 201). In the Fijian village, there is the gaze of the attentive villagers enhanced by the openness of households situated close together. This watchfulness is encompassed by the omniscient sensitivity of the cosmos, indicating disruption in the integrity of the community through a variety of signs.

The clear visibility of the body and its secrets while caught in the penetrating collective gaze reflects a broad social concern with regulating and managing community affairs and regeneration and a need to control the activities of the community's members through local conventions of cosmic awareness and punishment of socio-moral transgressions. In addition, these narratives about the threat of non-disclosure evince both the intricate relationships between body, self, other, and cosmos and the conflation of their identities. We have seen how the *yalo* leaves the body to disclose information, and how bodily experience transcends personal boundaries to be manifest as somatic experience in others' bodies or as environmental mishaps. In perhaps its most graphic representation, the *yalo ni cala* flew from its body to publicly announce the sins of its flesh while the alarmed transgressor sat, captive to and defenseless against the gaze of her *yalo*'s audience. Within the narratives of non-disclosure (and implicit involuntary disclosure), the exclusive identity between the self and the body is further disrupted. Self and body are located in a socio-cosmic matrix as much as they are bound to each other.

Chapter 5
The Body as a Community Forum: Spirit Possession and Social Repossession

The Fijian self is unshielded from the community's gaze, located in both community and body. The body is transparent and permeable, permitting the essence of the self, the *yalo*, to spill out into the community. The fluidity of bodily boundaries also allows spirits (*niju*) and spiritual manifestations to enter and occupy the body. We have seen that the Fijian community directs and claims the body's productive and reproductive labors. In this chapter, we will examine a similar appropriation of the body's space as a community forum. Analogous to the concretization of care in anatomic space is the manifestation of social conflict via spirit afflictions—as visions, nightmares, or illnesses—within the body.[1]

Spirits enter or afflict the body in three major contexts: dreams, waking visitations that are publicly witnessed, and illness.[2] In all three of these instances, the body is transiently incapacitated to various degrees as the spirit makes its agenda known to the community of witnesses. In many cases, the spirit articulates moral transgression or disorder in the community; alternatively, the community is pressed to fathom the social etiology of the illness by searching for conflict or disruption within the village or *mataqwali*. Thus spirit illness or possession is a social rather than a personal event. The body's space is exploited as a forum to critique moral behavior in the community. What is often conceived of as private and personal in Western experience—whether secrets, reproductive choices, dreams, or illnesses—is appropriated for community purposes in Fiji. Once again, the self surrenders the body's space to the community.

Since these spirits are said generally to be stirred to afflict humans by a disruption in social relations, the body thus possessed—or inhabited—serves the community by presenting an opportunity for interpretation and discussion of social norms and conflicts. Personal conflicts, normally excluded from other channels of public expression, are simultaneously represented in the same forum. In the former instance, the personal body is manipulated by spirits in the service of the community; in the latter, the community members witness the personal interests of the individual. Since personal needs are traditionally subordinated to those of the community, powerful sanctions prevent giving them voice. While a personal agenda must ideally be suppressed, a spirit may articulate it.

Spirit visitations are occasions both for constructive interpretations of issues vexing a community and for mobilization of supportive measures for the afflicted individual.[3, 4] For an individual who is socially marginalized as a result of conflict with members of the *mataqwali* or village or through transient disability, these events provide a mechanism to relocate the experience of suffering and isolation into the community arena. The symbolic liberation or evacuation of the self from the body makes it clear that the self is integral to the community, not necessarily always to the body.

Niju Dream Visitations: Phenomenologic Dimensions

Fijian spirits and villagers generally manage to coexist without problems;[5] on occasion, however, *niju* interfere with village life. Although they exercise considerable caution in avoiding contact with *niju*, villagers commonly report the sensation of the presence or entry of a *niju* during sleep.[6] Nighttime *niju* visitations are unpredictable, although they may be precipitated by a person's misconduct or inopportune trespass into a *niju's* habitat.[7]

Although these visits occur erratically, their phenomenology is relatively consistent. Typically, the *niju* attempts to enter the body just at the onset of sleep and is most commonly experienced as a heaviness (*bibita ni lala*) or an inability to move the limbs. The force it exerts is often likened to a magnetic field. At this time, there is conscious awareness both of the *niju* presence and of being trapped in sleep or powerless to move the body. One woman described the sensations as follows:

When I'm sleeping, I often notice my body becomes heavy . . . [and then] I see the *niju's* face . . . If I see that *niju's* face, I'll be frightened . . . That heaviness . . . we are lying down, we are sleeping, and then, you'll want to turn . . . you'll want to turn and it isn't possible! . . . It is like something is forcing you to lie still; . . . that's what this heaviness is like. The strength of the *niju* is [like] a magnet that catches people.

Many also describe an urge to speak, but gibberish (*qoqoru*) flows out in lieu of intelligible speech. This same woman continued:

You are going to notice, at the time when your body is heavy . . . we attempt to talk, eh? It's like this: if I am lying here, and you, you are lying there, and the *niju* comes to me and not to you . . . me, I'm going to want to grab you . . . to make you come close to me, but it won't be possible for me to grab you, or [makes a sound as though she cannot speak] . . . or [I] am going to want to speak, but it won't be possible. That's the strength of it, the magnet the *niju* holds is strong indeed.

Another young woman explained, "You have trouble screaming; . . . you can't find your voice; . . . it's sort of, uh, locked somewhere." She elaborated further on the experience:

I mean, your hair sort of, uh, grows or something . . . I mean, eh, you just feel different when, um, some person from another world comes to you . . . I mean, your hair sort of grows or something, it sort of lengthens . . . And that time you'll be dreaming about something, eh? . . . One night I was sleeping, and um, I felt this thing, eh? And I felt that someone was touching my hair, and was touching my body, and I just woke up and screamed.

On some occasions, a person may apprehend the presence of a *niju* while awake. This is often manifested in a precipitous overwhelming need to sleep: "their body just feels heavy; they just want to sleep all of a sudden."

The *niju* presence may be only felt mildly, as in a certain uneasiness during sleep, or its force may be more proximal, as in the descriptions above. If the *niju* actually enters the body, it physically alters it. One woman explained:

If the *niju* enters you, if it enters you and occupies your body . . . your face is a different one, your voice is different . . . We'll know, your eyes will be all red . . . That's if the *niju* really enters you.

The episodes are brief and not experienced as painful; nonetheless, they are considered unpleasant. Persons who are awakened several times in one night by a *niju's* presence may seek the company of another human who can protect them (see also Herr 1981:345).

The sensations of heaviness and paralysis associated with *niju* visitations bear remarkable resemblance to supernatural visitation reported in other areas of the Pacific (Levy 1973:151–53; Baddeley 1985) and described as "the old hag" or otherwise in Newfoundland and North American folk narratives (Hufford 1982).[8] As David Hufford and others have suggested, these visitations share phenomenological features with hypnagogic hallucinations and sleep paralysis, which are associated with narcolepsy.[9]

What distinguishes Fijian *niju* visitations from the experiences described in the oral tradition reported by Hufford is that the community uses them as a medium of existential inquiry or a forum for conflict identification and resolution. On many occasions, the *niju* remains in the body it has entered in order to converse with the witnesses on hand. Afterward, the episode is reviewed with peers or within the *mataqwali*, where there is a shared reworking of the disruptive experience of the visitation and a collective negotiation of meaning.

In the following discussion, I avoid conjecture about the Fijian *niju* visitation's resemblance to other oral traditions of supernatural phenomena or psychopathologic symptomatology.[10] Instead of inquiring into the role of psychodynamic conflict, if any, in precipitating spirit visitations of nightmarish quality, I ground the interpretation of these events in "socio-dynamic" conflict. That is, we will explore how the experience connects the individual to the community through shared interpretations.

Spirit Visitation as a Text for Interpretation

The neurophysiologic epiphenomena of the *niju* visitation are of little interest to the community except as confirmation of the spirit's presence. Attention focuses rather on a careful exposition and analysis of the possible reasons for the visit. A select group of confidants is mobilized to assist in the interpretation or to corroborate the experience of the *niju* presence. In many cases, the visitation is exploited to critique behavior of the afflicted individual, as in the following account by a young woman who had gone to visit relatives:

All of us went bathing outdoors [at night and we were told], "Don't bathe with your clothes off" [because of the many *niju* in that area]. [Later when they were all asleep] a man came nearer and nearer to me,[11] I knew it was the *niju*, and when I was yelling, it didn't come out . . . I was yelling and yelling, but there was no sound coming out . . . All of a sudden, the yell just came out . . . Auntie got so mad at me, "Hey!" [she said,] "What did I tell you people, not to go and bathe out in the night!" For women it is tabu that we bathe outdoors at night.

In this case, visitation was seized as an occasion for an older woman to remind the younger generation about proper decorum in the village. In the following case, *Dauhina*, a *niju* that frequently preys on young women who bathe outdoors or wander alone at night, began to plague a young woman who was frequently criticized by a female relative for her wanderings in the evening. His persistent appearances culminated in the following scenario when, embodied as a man, he attempted to assault her.

This young woman had been made uneasy by a recurrent vision of a light near her house and once in her living room.[12] One evening she closed the door to her bedroom and lay prone to sleep. With no warning, a hand grasped her wrist, and when she turned she saw it was a man. During her struggle she reached over to turn on a new electric light; as she pressed the switch, the bulb burned out (and the light has not worked since). Unable to free herself from his grip, she screamed, "Mother, there's a man here!" When her mother entered her room, the man vanished.

At this juncture the frightened woman sought the advice of her grand-father, who summoned a group of men to offer *yaqona* to the *niju* disturbing her, along with a plea to discontinue his attentions. "You must stop trying to ruin my granddaughter!" he shouted. Her visions ended at once.

In this sequence of events, a conflict had escalated between this young woman and other members of her household regarding proper behavior. Occurring just when all parties had reached the limits of exasperation with one another, *Dauhina's* appearance created a crisis that simultaneously vindicated the opinions of the household members, while also mobilizing their assistance in expelling the menacing spirit on her behalf.

The *niju's* presence is exploited as an opportunity for members of a household to validate their common experience of the world. The following excerpt from my field notes relates the household's concern with what I reported as a disturbing dream and which they reconstructed as a *niju* visitation:

I awoke in terror one evening after a frightening dream in which I was confronted by a giant Fijian warrior with a painted face and wearing horns and a traditional grass skirt. I related the dream to members of the household, who carefully noted the details. Tai Vani quizzed me about its size and wondered aloud if it were one of the *juwawa*, or giant *nijus* that inhabited the tree near our compound. Her husband commented that while it sounded like an evil *niju*, he had never seen one with horns. Then he and his wife joked that perhaps I had seen a cow. On a more serious note, he suspected that the *niju* had followed me from another place. When I subsequently informed him that I had gone to Natadola the previous evening — a region said to be populated with many evil *niju* — he was confirmed in his opinion that it had indeed been a *niju bura* (bad niju) and chastised me for going out too often. When I told Liku of my dream, she said a frightening dream had disturbed her sleep. Mere, too, added that something had caused her to sleep uneasily the previous night. Tai Pita (who is considered to be *riva*, or crazy) listened carefully to my description and insisted he had seen the same figure outside the latrine the previous evening. His testimony, however, was discounted by the others as another one of his confabulations.

In this instance, the two women and the man who had felt something the previous evening affirmed my experience as frightening and real. The elderly couple evinced their concern by their empathic elicitation of the details of the apparition. Finally, Tai Vani's husband could not resist an opportunity to scold me for leaving the safety of the village unattended.

This episode underscores a cardinal feature of the *niju's* arrival: it frequently invites broad participation in the process of fathoming its meaning. The individual becomes an instrument of the community's collective interpretation—his or her experience is borrowed as an opportunity either for expressing consensus or difference. The dispossession of personal bodily experience becomes more apparent in waking, public spirit visitations, when the sentient self literally is silenced or absented from the body as the body becomes a substrate for collective participation.

The following account illustrates the embodiment and display of conflict through waking spirit visitations. Although I did not witness the episode myself, I later heard many versions that corroborated the phenomenological events yet differed in their interpretation.

A young woman from a remote outer island had recently given birth to a son while staying with distant relatives in a Nadroga village. The unfortunate woman had suffered great humiliation when the man with whom she lived[13] brought home a new wife to replace her. Her family had decided it best to send her to the village of her uncle's wife for the remainder of her pregnancy and the birth of the child. Brokenhearted, she acquiesced in her family's wishes and remained in a household where, although she was well cared for, she felt unhappy. The language and customs in Nadroga were markedly different from those of her island, and her hosts often criticized her nonconformity. Nonetheless, she was in no position to challenge their hospitality and charity.

Even after the birth of her son, she continued to face conflict with her hosts in her obstinacy in breaking with Nadroga postpartum dicta of behavior. One afternoon, when her baby was several weeks old, she fell into some sort of fit. One of the women who witnessed her lapse in consciousness described her eyes as rolling back in her head. This woman ran to fetch a Bible and held it up to her face, demanding to know whether she recognized it.[14] The woman shook her head to indicate no and the frightened hostess, suspecting that a *niju* had possessed her, asked who she was. The spirit within the woman spoke to indicate that it had come to take the mother and her baby back to her island. Shortly afterward the young woman regained her normal state of consciousness.

This episode was the subject of intensive household scrutiny and debate as alternative interpretations were advanced and evaluated. Some held that the woman had indeed been possessed of a *niju*; others were suspicious that, given the victim's apparent secondary gains, the event had been staged. However, this observation was not voiced in an unsympathetic way; the plight of the woman was unenviable and not subject to any other recourse. Any expression of dissatisfaction in her current situation could only be received as ungrateful and hence outside the realm of acceptable behavior. Only others could champion her cause, and, in the absence of a protector, a spirit gave voice to this end. In this case, the expression of personal interest in conflict with community norms and wishes was legitimated in its only permissible way. Like secrets, conflicts are likely to be manifest in public space through the medium of the body. Whether this episode was factitious, hysterical, or spirit-induced is moot. Relevant here is the mutual license granted and extended between the self and the community, lending voice to intolerable conflict between personal and community interests. Fijians themselves are not averse to psychodynamic or "socio-dynamic" interpretations of *niju* appearances. Indeed, *niju* appearances are nearly always exploited as an opportunity to identify social conflict, whether in the realm of interpersonal or intergroup relations. Finally, while the enactment of *niju* visitation may potentially be perceived as manipulative, it defuses social tensions by identifying and mending differences, and by invoking the *niju* as a mediator between an individual and his or her community. Furthermore, what materializes during the possession episode is not an actor or actress playing a role, as Bourguignon has suggested (1976b:52), but rather a self undisguised. What has been secret is revealed to the *mataqwali* or the village. Personal anguish or misconduct is relocated from the private inner experience of the self to a community forum.

On other occasions, an individual's body is occupied for the purpose of exposing the clandestine behavior of some other person in the group. That is, the community appropriates the body as a public forum for exposure of behavior dangerous to it, such as in the *yalo ni cala*'s incarnation described in Chapter 4.

The entrance of a *niju* into a person—whether while waking or asleep—is signaled by incoherent mumbling (*qoqoru*). One woman explained that

If someone goes like that [begins to *qoqoru*] . . . [we] have to wake them up . . . [The spirit] comes into you, and it can make you talk . . . Some people, when they, they get the spirit in them, they can say: "This one doing the *drau ni kai* [traditional medicine], this one make that one dead" . . . the Fijian *niju* is very strong . . . and it's not you who's talking, its the *niju*!

Often, witnesses encourage the *niju* to speak in lieu of waking up the person who is mumbling, either by demanding that the spirit reveal its identity or by crying "*kania, kania*" (literally, "eat it, eat it," which in this case may be interpreted as an injunction to "incorporate" the spirit) to the person in order to fix the spirit's presence and make the *qoqoru* intelligible. A woman described the curiosity surrounding a *niju* visitation as follows:

We want to know what it is they [the *niju*] want to say, why it was they came here, what it is they came here [for] . . . When the people are eating the *niju*, [we will say,] "*Kania, kania,* what is your name?" Eh? It is going to say, "My name is whatever" . . . For instance, it might say it is someone who has died, died a long while ago . . . [or it might say], "My name is . . . mmmmm" and it isn't possible to understand it . . . After that, there are some who say, "Hey, let's catch it, let's catch it!" And they twist the clothing. The *niju* can't leave that person he is in then . . . You, you are sleeping, you don't know that you are eating a *niju*. It is frightened too, it hates to be trapped in the body, it is going to say, "Please, I beg you to let me go, don't capture me."

Sometimes the *niju* is set free. On other occasions, however, the visitation is a valuable opportunity to elicit information useful to the community. This woman continued:

There are some *niju* that lie, there are some *niju* that tell the truth . . . There are some *niju* that come here to alert us about something we should know . . . that we should be frightened about . . . Some *niju*, the things they say are true, really true . . . They are wise, they are always watching. These days if it is apparent that someone is eating a *niju* . . . [We'll say], "*Kania, kania,* What is your name?" . . . Maybe it is a *niju* who has come to murder . . . because of the *dukaduka* [filth, breach of tabu] of not [being where one should] because the women of Nahigatoka have gone to stay at Yavulo, they are not [properly] in Nahigatoka, the homes are empty of people to care for them.

Sometimes a *niju* spirit specifies the reason for the punishment or visitation. In other instances the immediate social causes remain obscure, and their ambiguity is eventually exploited through various interpretations.

Since *niju* possession is by consensus a frightening experience, it is difficult to invoke a psychodynamic explanatory model for what appears to be an altruistic absenting from one's body in the service of the community. Yet, what may be initially experienced as personal terror is quickly relocated from personal to community awareness. The very substance of the *niju* arises from social conflict rather than spiritual essence. Sociodynamic forces materialize in *niju*, which, in entering human bodies become concretized in anatomic space. In other words, the disorder of the community is temporarily "possessed" by an individual, who embodies the social processes requiring resolution.

Niju visitations, then, though experienced as threatening to the integrity of the individual, ultimately reintegrate him or her into, rather than alienate him or her from, his or her community. This occurs either in flushing out an undisclosed transgression or literally enfleshing a morally objectionable relationship. Moreover, the episode — the personal space and experience — is repossessed and exploited as a public forum for the purposes of negotiation and resolution of conflict.

The Relocation of Illness to the Community

Niju presence also manifests itself in bodily space as illness, disability, bad behavior, and sometimes in personal failure. Suffering and misfortune are often attributed to supernatural forces conjured from a disgruntled human seeking personal vengeance or arising from a disruption of social order, which becomes a force seeking restitution. In these cases, punishment is not necessarily directed exclusively toward the offender, but is frequently visited upon innocent members of the group. It may be perpetuated for generations as afflicted *mataqwali* members struggle to identify an original transgression and deflect the missiles of misfortune that plague them. For example, the descendants of the *mataqwali* that killed, cooked, and feasted on a famous missionary, the Reverend Thomas Baker, over a century ago have suffered a certain failure to thrive, which they attribute to the un-Christian act of their forebears. The grass in that river valley village is said to be stained red with the dead clergyman's blood as an indelible souvenir of their misdeed.

Like *niju* visitation and possession, somatic symptoms are subject to multiple interpretations that are not necessarily mutually exclusive. Indeed, the fathoming of etiology of illness is central to Fijian healing. While personally catastrophic or painful, illness episodes are exploited by the community to expose conflict or to validate a particular group decision. Therapy is directed toward the dual purposes of making the individual comfortable and rendering the community peaceable. Long after moral breaches have been identified and rectified, they are resurrected to justify accusations, to vindicate moral opprobrium, or to serve as injunctions against future transgressions.

Mase Vavisi: Spirit Illnesses

Spirit or *niju* etiologies are always included in the differential diagnoses of illnesses. A spirit etiology is not mutually exclusive with other proposed causative agents of the illness. Similarly, the existence of an identifiable proximal cause of misfortune or accident, such as a shark attack, does not rule out the possibility of supernatural influence acting through natural agents. The explanatory models (see Kleinman 1978) for a spirit illness encompass a range of nonexclusive etiologic possibilities and emerge from the active engagement of the social network in plumbing the meanings of the illness. The local theories of causation continue to be reworked even after resolution of an illness in apparently inexhaustible ways, resembling the prolific exegeses of a particular text long after it has been authored.

This multi-therapeutic approach to illness has been documented widely in the South Pacific (see Parsons 1985). Clearly, spirit causation theories continue to flourish alongside biomedical education and technology and the traditional health practices. In Tahiti, for example, the failure of the usual medical therapies is taken as indication of spiritual causality (Hooper 1985:174). In Fiji, *dranu* or biomedical pharmaceuticals are frequently utilized as the first line treatment in illnesses of unclear etiology. Illnesses that prove refractory to these therapies may be ascribed to spirit causation and inspire an inquiry into the history of behavior that prompted supernatural intervention. The diagnosis of spirit illness is at times reluctantly made by default, as suggested by the words of this Nahigatoka villager:

See, if someone is sick, and then he or she has been taken to the hospital, and then nothing happens, he's not well, then we go to Fijian doctors, eh? And then if he's cured like that, then we say, "Oh, [it was a] *mase vavisi* [Fijian illness]." . . . If he's still not in good condition, and then somebody says, "Do some *yaqona* . . . it's somebody's fault, your family or your father is wrong somewhere . . . you have to present *yaqona* so that the kid could be well again."

Certain illnesses (such as seizures or a skin rash called *mula*) are closely associated with spirit involvement; other illnesses, by virtue of their cataclysmic nature or their temporal proximity to unscrupulous behavior or offense, may also invite these interpretations. At times, spirit causality is invoked in sheer desperation during a tragic event.

Traditionally in Fiji, "the guilt of a person is shared by his close relatives who are also likely to suffer from its ill-inflicting consequences" (Ravuvu 1987:296). Illness crystallizes and locates a collective transgression in the individual bodies of the collectivity (see also Das n.d.:4). Thus, an illness episode is recontextualized as a social and a personal experience. Once again, the personal space of the body is exploited as a substrate within which to identify social disorder and as a forum to censure immoral behavior. The relocation of experience to social space also integrates the afflicted individual into the community by allowing articulation and sharing of personal suffering. The inexpressible pain and isolation that often accompany debilitating illness in our own society find voice and support in the Fijian social milieu.

Human suffering provides unending opportunities for existential deliberation and introspection (see Sontag 1979; Tsongas 1986; Kleinman 1988a). In this context illness and misfortune are exploited toward restoration of social order and negotiation of meaning in Fiji. Historically and transculturally, medical theories have treated the diseased human body as a microcosm of a disordered environment; thus the anatomic space becomes a microcosmic representation of its social milieu. Our insistence in the West on making illness an exclusive property of the body it afflicts is actually the exception. According to Michel Foucault, "the exact superposition of the 'body' of the disease and the body of the sick man is no more than a historical, temporary datum" (Foucault 1975:3).

This notion of cosmic representation in the human body is well documented in the ethnographic literature from the South Pacific and elsewhere. For example, Samoan medical ideology conceptualizes physical malfunction as disruption in social equilibrium (Macpherson 1985:13). Similarly, Tikopians express ideas about social order in "metaphorical statements about the body and its well-being" (Macdonald 1985:69). Malfunction or deviance of the individual have unavoidable consequences for one's social group; "social disorder brings misfortune in the shape of sickness, sterility of land and people, or other disasters" (69–70). Furthermore, social well-being depends on harmonious relationships within the community (85). In the Cook Islands, as well, social discord is invoked as a causative element in illness. Consultation with healers provides an opportunity to probe one's misconduct and offenses (Baddeley 1985:139). The illness category *mate Maori* is associated with " 'wrong living,' especially the breaking of *tapu*" in New Zealand (Parsons 1985a:217). Finally, Richard Katz and Linda Kilner observe that in Fiji, "Sickness and health reflect the degree to which individuals and communities are living within the cultural ideals" (1987:212) and often specifically correlate with "some violation of cultural norms" (Katz 1981:66).

The homology between body and society in Fiji is suggested in the following description of division and distribution of a totem gift:

In Lebaleba Village, their totem-food [*cavu*] is a snake . . . If for example, me, if I happen to find a snake from the bush, I'll take it to them . . . [In] the villages in Nadroga we have three sections in the village: one, the top of the village, the middle, and the bottom one, eh? And that snake, those people at the top, the top of the village, they'll have the head, the people in the middle, they'll have . . . the middle part, and the people at the [bottom], they'll have the tail . . . They'll cook it, they'll divide it. Those people at the bottom, they can't eat the top part. Those people at the top, they'll eat the top part . . . Those people at the top, they can't eat the bottom, they have to eat their own share, their own portion.

Hence, the order of the social universe is represented in village cartography and *cavu* anatomy. This ordering of relations is continually reaffirmed, in this case in the distribution of community-owned food.

The relocalization of social pathology to the individual body is conceptually relevant to certain disease entities, such as anorexia nervosa or substance abuse, in Western experience as well (see, for example, Mackenzie 1985; Bordo 1993). Many social problems themselves, arising from political, racial, or gender oppression are medicalized so as to be managed as individual rather than societal disorders (Kleinman 1988a:21).

Even when pathology is attributed to the malfunction of the human body, it is inevitably stamped with cultural salience and social relevance; symptom becomes polysemic symbol, elaborated into multiple meanings on physiologic, personal, social, and cultural levels (see Kleinman 1988a). The individual may tumble into an existential abyss occasioned by the inexplicable pain or isolation of the illness experience, yet "local cultural systems provide both the theoretical framework of myth and the established script for ritual behavior that transform an individual's affliction into a sanctioned symbolic form for the group" (26).

In many cases, an illness is appropriated at the expense of an individual to censure morally objectionable behavior much in the same way as is done in the South Pacific. Susan Sontag traces the evolution through Western thought of the association of disease with divine punishment from the classical Greeks, for whom either an individual failing or a collective transgression could incite supernatural punishment in the form of illness. With the advent of Christianity, and consequently "more moralized notions of disease," she argues that "a closer fit between disease and 'victim' gradually evolved" (Sontag 1979:42). Collective sentiments "about evil are projected onto a disease," allowing an illness to develop metaphorical significance linked to corruption or unjustness in society (58, 71). Disease imagery, then, becomes a vehicle for expression of "concern for social order" (71). This capacity is not exercised without ambivalence, however, since, as Arthur Kleinman has observed,

The imagery of infirmity and disorder provokes moral questions that most social systems prefer not to encourage. In the current age, where image making is the essence of politics, no regime wants to expose these realities lest they threaten the naive optimism they seek to maintain in the population. (Kleinman 1988a:47)

Sontag sees this metaphorical working of illness as at odds with the individual and the society. While historically plagues have been interpreted as divine retribution for the ills of society, the contemporary AIDS crisis, which especially threatens individuals engaging in certain high-risk behaviors, identifies "a community of pariahs" morally blamed for contracting their illness (Sontag 1989:25). Vulnerability to disease is understood to be enhanced by particular indiscretions such as smoking cigarettes, using excessive alcohol, consuming high cholesterol foods, or avoiding screening mammograms, and, to a degree, individuals are held personally responsible for their health. The personal agency projected onto health maintenance recontextualizes it as matter of personal choice and control with particular consequences that must be individually weighed. Thus the fiction of personal responsibility for poor health sets up illness as a potentially socially alienating experience.

When the diseased body is regarded as symptomatic of the disordered community, healing practices are directed toward identifying and resolving the conflict and restoring the order. For example, Victor Turner found that among the Ndembu the tendency to locate etiology in social disorder has a "redressive function in interpersonal or factional disputes" (V. Turner 1964:360). The diviner/healer's difficult and dangerous task is to "publicly expose the hates that simmer beneath the outward semblance of social peace" (V. Turner 1967:146). In effect, therapy is directed toward both social and personal ends in being a "matter of sealing up the breaches in social relationships simultaneously with ridding the patient (*muyeji*) of his pathological symptoms" (V. Turner 1964:360). Similarly, Katz depicts healing in Kung culture as a "fundamental integrating and enhancing force" (1982:34). He distinguishes it from "curing" in its operation on the multiple dimensions — including the "physical, psychological, social, and spiritual" — of human experience. Healing, he argues, "involves work on the individual, the group, and the surrounding environment and cosmos." In the same way the Fijian healer, too, is the "community's emissary to unchartered realms of experience — areas of psychological, social, and spiritual ambiguity for the community" (Katz and Kilner 1987:215–16), whose role is fundamentally one of interpretation.

In western Fiji, certain persons are recognized as gifted in ascertaining the supernatural elements of illness episodes. These *daurairai* are consulted as specialists in cases in which a baffled community, family, or individual seeks guidance in making sense of illness or misfortune. However, the process of interpretation is often relegated to the *mataqwali* or community, becoming a joint venture. Such an occurrence provides an opportunity and a forum for the articulation and deliberation of moral and existential issues. As the community assumes "ownership" of the personal experience, the symptoms and the personal suffering are subordinated to community interests in resolving conflicts and reestablishing order. Needless to say, this process can culminate in crisis as latent tensions erupt into public debate during a community member's acute illness. Such a charged moment, however, may afford one of the very few appropriate occasions to mediate interpersonal conflicts within the community.

Ethnographic research in Tahiti reveals that there, too, illness episodes are exploited as opportunities for moral inquiry. Anthony Hooper observes that constant moral commentary on *ma'i* [sickness] of all kinds taps a whole hidden vein of local conflicts, tensions, and rivalries, and . . . can serve to crystallize and provide a focus for public opinion about the sick person and his or her associates. (1985:182)

Hooper questions why illness should be such a comfortable and satisfying means of airing and resolving disputes. Certainly, there are other far more straightforward sanctioned means of settling differences. He offers the explanation that Tahitians prefer to avoid confrontation; in sublimating debate about social discord to discussion about personalized illness, they sidestep the indelicacies of direct criticism (1985:182–83). While Fijians do share with the Tahitians a distaste for open confrontation, emotional debates about responsibility for illness often result in very direct accusations of culpability. Moreover, the active participation of the group in addressing the moral issues as opposed to exclusive reliance on a specialist suggests that the community stands to gain from the process.

The inherent uncertainty of diagnosis and the negotiation of competing etiological explanations allow the community to engage in the painful and difficult process of sifting, sorting, and reworking perennial existential issues. Although the ostensible goals are resolution of social disorder and personal illness, these conflicts are inherent in the competing interests of individuals and groups and the inescapable tensions created at the interface of traditional lifeways and encroaching alien values.

Admittedly, however, there are instances that afford a more rote interpretation of socio-moral delinquency. These cases by consensus closely associate particular transgressions with specific physical stigmata. Clearly, interpretation is more closely tied to moral policing than to sorting existential issues in a public forum. The majority of these situations appear to visit harm or illness on the guilty individual.

For instance, shortly before my arrival in Nahigatoka in 1982, there had been a fatal shark attack at the mouth of the Sigatoka River. The shark, a representative of the ancestral *vu* in this region, is often the vehicle of supernatural punishment. Tradition holds that an agreement has been reached with the shark: so long as the villagers protect it and respect certain requests, it will spill no blood in the river basin. Since the villagers had contracted with the shark for mutual protection, it was a virtual certainty that the victim had incurred the *vu*'s wrath in some way. One informant interpreted the mishap as punishment of this individual's unbridled greed in netting *cigana*. The victim of the shark attack was accused of violating tabu with his plans to sell the *cigana* for personal profit.

A plethora of tabus associate consumption of particular foods with subsequent illness or mishap. For example, breach of certain prenatal food tabus results in direct physical stigmata on the unborn fetus. By the same token, persons related to one another as kin in the *veibatiki* relationship (warriors and their chiefs) must refrain from consuming the food designated as belonging to the opposite group as discussed in chapter 3. One woman recalled her reluctance to eat fish, the food of her *bati*, in the presence of any members of that group, lest she choke on its bones. Similarly, one abstains from eating the *cavu* of another's *mataqwali* in that person's presence lest it cause an unspecified illness. If a person eats a chief's leftover food or an animal representing his *vu*, white spots (*vula*) will cover his body. Thus the social cicatrices incurred by such infractions are transferred to anatomic space, just as other transgressions are recapitulated as illness.

Other visitations of punishment are manifest as a variety of unusually sudden and lethal afflictions. Their temporal association rather than their specific symptomatology identifies them as punishment. These are often linked to a particular interpersonal conflict and the deliberate invocation of supernatural assistance by an individual for vengeful purpose. The following cases illustrate a variety of these situations:

A man in a neighboring village was observed deep in the bush after midnight by two young boys. He had removed all his clothes and mixed a bowl of *yaqona* over which he chanted something the boys could not hear. Three weeks later the man's daughter-in-law, whom he reputedly disliked, died unexpectedly. Her death was attributed to his curse.

A woman who had offended a high chief was in labor for the third time after experiencing two miscarriages. As she lay in bed, a large black dog walked into her room, paused for a moment, and departed. Another woman who shared the hospital room advised that the dog was the "owner of the place" as representative of the *vu* of the chief and that it heralded an imminent death in that *mataqwali*. Shortly thereafter the woman delivered a stillborn baby. Taking heed of the warning of her roommate, she offered *yaqona* to the high chief in apology for her offense against him. Shortly thereafter, she became pregnant, carried the pregnancy to term, and delivered a healthy infant.

Illness is often a direct result of sorcery practiced to avenge a social wrong. Not all spirit illnesses require human instigation, however. Misfortune can befall the perpetrator of an offense against a chief without his or her intention. A woman recalled a family's concern that a family member's stroke was a manifestation of their insubordination to their chief:

When Tai Merelita was sick . . . Tai Seru's wife . . . all Tai Seru's sons and daughters and granddaughters, they came to *bulubulu* [bury the wrongs] to [the village chief] . . . [They said they were] sorry, "We will not be disrespectful to you again . . . we will not be bad again to you, all our children will not be [bad again to you]" . . . And after that, Tai Merelita was out from hospital, she was home . . . The chiefs don't show their anger, but there'll be a time when somebody who has been . . . bad to him . . . will suffer.

When transgressions are flagrant or disputes and antipathies publicly known, there is less ambiguity in diagnosis. On the other hand, since would-be sorcerers conceal their activities, ample opportunity exists for speculation about human agency in illness etiology. Similarly, the success of the sorcery may be a means of vindicating or delegitimating the cause of the perpetrator. One elderly man confessed on his deathbed that for many years he had attempted to kill a chief with sorcery. Only an unrelenting history of failure had convinced him of the *mana*, or power, invested in this chief.

Not all spirit illness manifests itself as the direct consequence of personal transgressions of the moral code. On the contrary, an individual's illness is commonly regarded as reflecting the misconduct of other members of the *mataqwali*. The afflicted individual — often a child — is often perceived as an innocent, unwitting victim of punishment for the *mataqwali's* offense. In this case, disease must be localized in an individual who embodies the collective wrongdoing. That is, while the responsibility for misbehavior is distributed among the *mataqwali*, its manifestation is concentrated within a particular body; yet the *mataqwali* retains its connection to the punishment by assuming the collective task of rectifying the wrong. In sum, the body is first a designee of the *mataqwali* as a locus of pathology; in turn, the personally experienced illness is reclaimed from the individual as a community forum for moral inquiry. What has originally been displaced from the social to the individual is ultimately relocated in social space. This is similar to the role of the compliant participant in spirit possession: the individual bears the community's punishment, but also defers to community management of the experience. In both instances, the body's space is lent to the collective as a vehicle for social divination.

Seini's nearly tragic case of meningitis, discussed in Chapter 3, provides another illustration of the layers of interpretation that develop in response to critical illness. Despite initial diagnoses of an appetite disturbance and then bacterial meningitis, followed by a dramatic cure with biomedical treatment, her illness inspired discussion of the behavior of a relative of hers in the preceding generation. Another child had characterological flaws that amounted to antisocial behavior in the Fijian-village community. He was caught stealing on a number of occasions to the extreme exasperation of his household. Although he was chastised for this behavior, he was not held wholly accountable. Rather, a relative explained, a *niju drivadriva* (stealing spirit) must have inhabited him. This possession was again attributed to the multiple transgressions of a relative.

In another set of cases, the dramatic presentation of seizures in children that were refractory to traditional treatment with *dranu* prompted an immediate evaluation of the family's relations with the community. One mother recalled her concern when her eleven-month-old baby lapsed into a seizure that lasted for hours and failed to respond to the *dranu* she poured in the child's mouth. "Because of the length of time it affected her, [I thought] perhaps this is a *niju* . . . because with [ordinary] seizures, it is possible to end them just by giving medicine, eh?" Another mother recounted her baby's first seizure episode, summarized below.

Her baby had had fever and vomiting for several days when he started to seize at three in the afternoon. She sought her grandmother's advice and gathered several *dranu* to give the infant. These were to no avail; the seizures continued. At this juncture the family recalled a recent altercation with a villager who "always uses the *niju*." "Once a while ago, my father and one old man in the village argued with each other," she explained. Their dispute was on a Monday, and the child fell ill with seizures on that same Friday: "right after the fight, then came the illness." Her family determined the urgency of a *yaqona ni horo* (offering of apology) for the dispute. She recalled that the men had been explicit in relating the fight to the seizure illness: "If Waisake's illness . . . is due to our argument over the marriage you must drink [the *yaqona*] so that Waisake's sickness will end." As soon as the *yaqona* was accepted and drunk, Waisake's body relaxed. He was taken down the valley road to the hospital, where he was given an injection bringing the seizures to an end around nine in the evening.

Though accepting that her child's epileptic seizures (*kida*) will recur chronically, with each new seizure episode the mother pauses to reflect on her family's relational standing with other villagers. The second time the child had a seizure, she was certain there had been no infractions, but she feels the family is now especially cautious in its public conduct.

A more striking example of the individual's affliction as the nexus of multiple social and interpersonal conflicts is that of a young woman who was studying for a degree at the University of the South Pacific. Her story follows.

Ateca said that in the recent months she had been plagued by a series of persecutory nightmares filled with snakes, knives, stabbings, and the intuitive chill of somebody trying to inflict harm on her. After registering at the university, she returned home to her mother's home and fell ill. Ateca described the onset of her illness as an "uneasiness." At that time she asked her aunt to massage her stomach. She recalled, "When she stopped, I felt uneasy, you know? And then you know something . . . you know, something was like coming inside me, eh?

And I couldn't breathe properly, and I said, then I asked them again to massage me, eh? I asked about three people to massage me, two to massage . . . the [soles] of my feet, and uh, one on the palms of my hands; but when they left it, I felt something stopping my breath, eh? . . . I thought I was going to die that night."

Ateca continued that the sensations were like none she had experienced before. She felt a coldness creep through her body, starting in her legs and moving up. She asked her mother to pray for her. Ateca related, "When my mother came near me, and when she was massaging me, like, umm, *harivo elala* [she got goosebumps] you know?" Her mother placed a Bible on her and fetched hot water for her to stand in; she recalled standing in the pan four times before she noticed the heat at all. The following day she was seen in the outpatient department by a Fijian medical assistant who diagnosed trouble with her "womb" and gave her some tablets.

After the crisis passed, a Fijian woman seated next to her at the outpatient waiting area asked her mother whether Ateca was pregnant. Her mother had seen Ateca from a distance somewhat earlier and, not yet recognizing her, had remarked to herself that surely that was a pregnant woman. Ateca herself was confused about this. One of the staff at the university had thought she looked pregnant and advised her to go to the clinic for a test. The medical checkup was negative. Two weeks later, after her mother asked whether she might be pregnant, a second test was negative. Despite this result, she commented that she remained unconvinced since people continued to tell her that she looked pregnant. She also felt that her wanting to "spit" after eating suggested a pregnancy and wondered if the snakes in her dreams confirmed it. Although her last menstrual period was just days before I interviewed her, she was scheduled for an ultrasound the following day to rule out pregnancy definitively.

Her thoughts returned to her frightening illness episode. Just before it befell her, a strange woman had watched her on a bus. Ateca's hair had stood out when recalling this incident later, and she began to suspect that someone wished to curse her. At some point, she had a dream that she was crossing a river and spied a man who tried in vain to get hold of her. She shouted at him "*lavelave na yaqona vakaikai*" [make the *yaqona's* curse very strong] and felt certain he was trying to harm her with black magic.

Ateca remembered that on the evening of her illness, her mother had a premonition about the event, which was confirmed on seeing her daughter. She recalled, "I was, you know, changed, you know, my look, eh? I was changed, like you know, I, like . . . she said that eh, something was with me, like the devil was with me or something like that."

Ateca remained unsure of the cause of her illness but retained a nagging fear that she was the victim of somebody's hostility toward her family. She mentioned that she was very close to an uncle from her mother's village. One of this man's sons was the first boy from his province to travel to Suva for cadet officer training. Despite the boy's promising future, something odd happened, and he ran away from the training camp. Ateca's uncle had accused another villager of cursing his family. He said everyone knew of his participation in the family's poor fortune. Ateca thought that perhaps, since she was studying at the university, she was a target of this jealousy as well.

As we spoke, a torrential downpour engulfed Suva and Ateca called my attention to a foul smell, which she explained was the odor of the *buraga*, the devil's insect. When one smells it, the *niju* presence is felt and causes one's hair to stand out. She found the insect and showed it to me, saying that she had not seen a like one since last year and that perhaps our conversation had elicited its presence. She reassured me, however, that our talking about the events was protective.

The history of Ateca's illness unfolds in a melange of images and inter-pretations. She reveals her anxieties — manifest in her dream content — that her academic success jeopardizes her safety by inculcating envy and hostility in persons who remain in the village. She shares the burden of unorthodox success with her cross-cousin, who is similarly thwarted on the apparent threshold of nontraditional advancement. It is her uncle and her mother, however, who are sensitive to the latent malevolence and how it will be manifested in actions directed toward the *mataqwali*.

At the onset of the illness narrative, Ateca's body threatens to be consumed by the presence of these untoward forces. Her mother can actually sense bodily (*harivo elala*) the spirit within her. Ateca, on the other hand, experiences her body as distanced, her senses as deceiving her when she is unable to feel the hot water at her feet. Similarly, her intimate knowledge of her own body is brought into question by others' certainty that she must be pregnant. When her mother sees her on the road, she sees a pregnant Ateca, not Ateca as Ateca experiences herself; similarly, others — the women at the hospital and the university — see a pregnant woman in Ateca. Although she continues to menstruate she seeks alternative verification that she is pregnant as others say she is. Her body has been claimed by the spirit and those who interpret her symptoms.

Multiple and complex elements of interpersonal rivalry and assis-tance, existential anxieties accompanying one's departure from tradi-tion, embodiment of malice, and a mysterious appearance of the spirit eavesdropping on her tale (the *buraga*) are entangled in Ateca's narra-tive. The episode engages her family in questioning the meaning of their misfortunes at the brink of many successes. Members of the kin and com-munity networks are mobilized in their participation in the diagnosis and therapy of the disorder.

Most significantly, these other persons — her mother, aunt, uncle, and the women at the hospital and the university — experience the distur-bance firsthand through their own bodies and perception. They are able to experience that which Ateca cannot — and she trusts their knowledge of her body despite conventional somatic cues that contradict their in-terpretation. Hence, at the time when Ateca is most distanced from her own bodily experience — when her perception seems disconnected from sensory stimuli — her mother begins to share the sensation of the *niju* by attending to her own bodily sensation.

Thus, not only does the family engage in shared interpretation of the personal illness; they also somatically experience its sensory dimensions. In this way, while Ateca embodies social discord in her very unusual illness, her somatic experience is embodied in her mother. Fijians believe that to share private experience of *niju* presence disempowers it from accomplishing harm. Like the *buraga* conjured from the retelling of the events, the potentially frightening and alienating experience vanishes from the personal and rematerializes in the collective realm.

The Self in the Community: More Thoughts on Alienation and Integration

In Chapter 2 we explored the propensity of body/self alienation in a context in which the self is alternately conceived as both the body's master and its captive. In the former scenario, the exclusive authorship of the body is claimed by its occupant, allowing for extreme forms of cultivation of its surfaces and space. In the latter instance, the body's pain or discomfort traps the self in an unsharable experience. As Byron Good writes, "The world of pain becomes a special world, a world largely unshared and unsharable" (1992:47). The individual is isolated by virtue of an experience that defies articulation. In the West, illness more than alienates the self from the body, it alienates the self from its community by its capacity to stigmatize and isolate the self.

The profound alienation between self and community precipitated in illness has been abetted by the development of medical science that narrows the focus to disease at the expense of experience and meaning (see Kleinman 1988a) and endeavors to "subtract the individual" for the purpose of treatment (Foucault 1975:14). Far from facilitating transfer of somatic pain and discomfort by absorption and reclamation into the group, the clinical gaze reconstructs the illness experience as objectified pathology, a process in which the identified patient is draped, probed, and otherwise dehumanized. Emily Martin details the profound alienation of body from self and patient from physician in gynecological settings. She relates one woman's words describing her Caesarean section: "'They talked over me and to each other, but not to me. I felt like an object and not a human.'" Martin observes that, for a particular woman, there is a division between body and self in which "people are doing things to her body but paying no attention to her self" (Martin 1987:83). In this case, the surgeons attend to the body while the woman herself disappears.

Illness outside the context of the clinic can be equally alienating. Kleinman argues that diseases stigmatize by attaching

powerfully disconfirming cultural meanings onto the sick person . . . Thus, the stigmatized person is defined as an alien other, upon whose persona are projected the attributes the group regards as opposite to the ones it values. In this sense, stigma helps to define the social identity of the group. (Kleinman 1988a:159)

Thus, the location of personal illness in social space may benefit the collective, but at tragic cost to the individual. In fact, Sontag has argued that contemporary illness metaphors have created a "profound disequilibrium between individual and society," casting them as adversaries (Sontag 1979:72).

Himself a sufferer of a chronic, progressive, debilitating spinal tumor, Robert Murphy observes that illness alienates the self from the body and the community simultaneously in causing "diminution of the self, which is further magnified by debasement of others" (Murphy 1987:93). He writes:

The individual has also been alienated from his old, carefully nurtured, and closely guarded sense of self by a new, foreign, and unwelcome identity. And he becomes alienated from others by a double-barreled mechanism: Due to his depreciated self-image, he has a tendency to withdraw from his old associations into social isolation. And, as if in covert cooperation with this retreat, society— or at least American society—helps to wall him off. (108–9)

He sums up the tragic condition of the afflicted: "They have experienced transformation of the essential condition of their being in the world. They have become aliens, even exiles, in their own lands" (111).

The social isolation of the chronically ill and disabled is entrenched by the inability to communicate one's suffering to one's community that locks one into mute suffering. Pain becomes a "force that so shapes the world that sufferers often describe themselves as inhabiting a world that others can never know" (Good 1992:30). Murphy attests from his personal tragedy:

Nothing is quite so isolating as the knowledge that when one hurts, nobody else feels the pain; that when one sickens, the malaise is a private affair; and that when one dies, the world continues with barely a ripple. (Murphy 1987:63)

Compare this sentiment to the case of a Jiuta, a middle-aged Fijian man with a history of a seizure disorder:

Jiuta had initially experienced seizures in elementary school, when he said that *niju* impersonating human forms began to appear to him. His somewhat inconsistent account of his affliction was filled with allusions to a persecutory *niju* whom he felt would one day return to harm him again. He suspected that the original visitation of this illness was effected by the jealousy of another villager about rights for land use he was to inherit. The *niju*, who generally impersonated a woman with red hair, had warned him of the consequences when she returned to him. Finding this unendurable, he had begged his brothers and sisters not to leave him alone. "Every time I'm staying by myself," he explained, "that's the time she came here." Finally, he took his plight to a Protestant minister who called a gathering of the church members one evening to pray collectively to chase the evil spirit away. The minister advised him that they would pray and "the time you go to sleep, [it will be] like you are seeing someone who is praying for you." Jiuta was later able to report to the congregation the remission of symptoms and his peace of mind.

In this case, too, the suffering of chronic illness is compounded by its isolating effects; this is illuminated in Jiuta's desperate plea to his family not to run away from him. Although the community does not assume responsibility for the etiology of this illness, it removes the afflicted individual from his or her social isolation by communal participation in prayer to prevent further visitation.

The integration of the afflicted person into the community in Fiji contrasts with the Western tendency to encapsulate and remove from view the stigmatized. For example, the proliferation of "support groups" in our own society that address the practical and emotional needs of afflicted individuals has its inception in the experience of profound alienation by virtue of unique or isolating experience. This institutionalized support engenders a community of co-sufferers that can legitimate a discourse of complaint and alienation within the group. This sort of group, comprised of members for whom social marginalization is a central experience, is itself on the fringe of social space; while providing a community for its members, it cannot promise reintegration into the non-affiliated community.

Conclusion

Within the context of *niju* or *yalo* possession, the sense of personal agency over the body is disconfirmed. Indeed, in certain extreme situations somatic experience is distanced and the body is potentially alienated from the self—through either the bodily immobilization of a *niju*, the silencing of voice by a *yalo ni cala*, or others' acquisition of intimate bodily information and its incorporation into their own bodily experiences. However, the lapse in personal agency is not unprecedented as part of the landscape of common experience of the body; therefore, Fijians do not expect exclusive personal control of their bodies. Moreover, when a person feels displaced from his or her body, there is a concomitant pull into the community by virtue of its appropriation and integration of the experience.

The inherent ambiguity that veils *niju* possession and illness is exploited by the *mataqwali* or village for moral and existential inquiry.

Bodily disorder, whether via possession or illness, is conceived of as a manifestation of social disharmony that has been concretized and identified in anatomical space. This conflict is restored to its original place in its recontextualization as a community concern. Although the sufferer superficially appears as a hapless victim whose body has been kidnapped for social ends, he or she is not condemned to the isolation that illness so often confers in Western society. The potentially alienating bodily and emotional discomforts initially experienced by an individual are absorbed by the community as it negotiates the meaning of the illness.

It is not that Fijians do not suffer through their bodies; rather, this experience cannot be privatized. Not contained within a body, illness is claimed by the collective. It is both the right and the obligation of the family, *mataqwali,* and village to read illness like a text, to absorb it into collective experience, and ultimately to give it meaning. Hence what is often "unshared and unsharable" in Western experience is exactly what establishes connection to the social world in Fijian experience.

Chapter 6
Cultural Metaphors: Body and Self

> Where is the Melanesian's "me"? [. . .] The psychological "me" and the physical body do not always correspond to each other. His "me" is not fixed.
>
> —Leenhardt (1979:84)

We have explored the ways in which the Fijian body is situated within the socio-cosmic matrix, as well as how it embodies the collective. Although core identity begins with a relationship to a body, it includes the community. Bodily experience transcends the individual body, is diffused to other bodies, and is even manifest in the environment. Self-essence (concretely identified in the *yalo*) likewise transcends the body to affiliate with the collective. The two, body and self, do not share a mutually fixed or exclusive identity; their common substrate is the collective.

These elements of Fijian embodiment differ from Western folk models that posit the discreteness of embodied experience, the firm anchoring of identity to the body, and the sense of personal authorship of that body. As we have seen, in fact, embodied experience is quite contingent on how the self is situated in a relational matrix. We will review the evidence for this correlation below.

Authorship of the Body

The cultivation of the body has reached grand proportions in contemporary Western society. This ethic of work on the self, characterized by the exploitation of "visible signs" of prestige and their "careful and ostentatious staging" (Foucault 1988:85) flourishes in the rich culture medium of twentieth-century capitalism (see B. Turner 1984). Pursuing the assumption that "The body, a social product which is the only tangible manifestation of the 'person,' is commonly perceived as the most natural expression of innermost nature," Pierre Bourdieu argues that individuals rationally calculate the type of manipulation of their appearance from which they stand to profit (1984:192, 202). In other words, we see the cultivation of self-presentation through manipulation and exploitation of bodily symbols, a concept in accord with capitalist-derived values encouraging competitive work on the self to promote it above other selves. To the extent that we can identify core societal values and their analogues in body morphology in the West, we can predict what sort of work on the body represents an avenue to prestige. For example, not only have we identified a trend toward an idealized female shape that was thin and progressively tubular a decade ago, but we have since witnessed its evolution into a toned, no-longer-emaciated form. Since these particular attributes have been aesthetically pleasing by virtue of their association with health, vigor, youth, and, to an extent, an advertisement of one's participation in cultivating the body, individuals could shape their bodies to create and project an image. (In the mid-1990s there has been a resurgence of the overly thin body represented in the "waif look.") Our fickleness with respect to preferred attributes may reflect our tendency to equate prestige with limited accessibility — hence the need for a moving target.

Given our experience in contemporary Western culture, we might suppose that within other cultures people would be similarly motivated to represent themselves through their bodies and that they would associate aesthetically pleasing forms with what is relatively valued in their cultural milieu. So, for example, we might speculate that in the Fiji Islands, where abundance of food is prized, the cornerstone of prestige would lie in displaying one's wealth in food through one's obviously well-fed body. We might be further tempted to conjecture that Fijians would be highly motivated to attain such corpulence. This hypothesis is misguided, however. It is the ability to be generous with food rather than to possess it that confers prestige in Fiji. Food is used to potentiate social relations. In this setting, it no longer behooves individuals socially to invest themselves in cultivating their own bodies, but instead, in cultivating those of others — for therein lies their ability to provide for and nurture others, not so much to access channels of prestige as to fortify their embeddedness in a plexus of social relations.

The Fijian body is not a primary vehicle for expression of personal identity or excellence. Rather, it provides a means of integrating the self into the community. The task of the individual is to establish his or her social presence by engaging in the complex protocols of informal and formal care. Inasmuch as care is elaborated through the availability and distribution of food and through attention to appetite, it is indexed in changes in body morphology. Therefore, a body encodes social meanings as concretized care, and as such exhibits the collective handiwork of its community's laboring on its form.

The cultivation of bodies, then, represents the cumulative efforts of the collective; their care, or *vikawaitaki,* is embodied in the members of the community. For this reason, there is complacency with respect to the self-reflexive cultivation of the personal body, with a complementary motivated interest in nurturing and otherwise caring for others' bodies, which will manifest this *vikawaitaki* in their robust forms.

As a result of this ethic, Fijians are not at all inattentive to body shapes. In fact, they are particularly vigilant with respect to changes in weight that reveal nurturing or negligence on the part of the care-giving collective. This exceptional vigilance directed toward body shape and weight changes is evident in the proliferation of insults and compliments critiquing body shapes, in the rhetoric emphasizing a desire to nurture others, and in the elaborate etiquette that encompasses guests in a network of care within each household. The Fijian, on the other hand, devotes himself or herself to cultivating social relationships, not to intensifying his or her relationship to the body, which in any case is seen as within the province of the community. Hence, regulation and cultivation of, and responsibility for the body shifts from the personal to the collective domain. The self, therefore, while certainly connected to its body, is not its exclusive agent.

This ethos stands apart from the penchant for personal cultivation of the body in the West, where personal identity and agency are expressed through the discipline and cultivation of the body rendering it, in Ivan Illich's words, "a progressive embodiment of self" (1980:1326). The Western self guards the body as its exclusive domain and seeks to legitimate the cultivation of this personal space. The cultural constitution of the body as an appropriate arena for the projection of qualities of the self and the legitimation of the intensive cultivation of the body's space for this purpose reflect the agenda of a society that indulges and supports autonomy and independence as paramount values.

Whereas, in the West individual selves are embodied, in Fiji the collective is embodied in its members. This fundamental difference accounts for differences in the authority to cultivate bodies, designating it as a personal or collective privilege respectively. In both instances, bodies are cultivated by manipulation of symbols referring to core cultural values. It is, however, the nature of the representation of the body — whether as a personal or collective showplace — that ultimately localizes the self as a part of, or apart from, the collective.

Alienation and Integration: A Reprise

As demonstrated in the data on the Fijian self, and as Leenhardt made clear about the nature of the Canaque self (1979), the locus of personal identity resides in relationships; bodies are, to a degree, undifferentiated, belonging to a collective. Fijians do, of course, also experience themselves as embodied agents but their core identity is inclusive of their community. By contrast with Western experience (see Giddens 1991:218), Fijian identity is not only anchored in the self or in the body. The conceptualization of the body/self relationship in the West lends itself to our own particular myths about the discreteness of the personal body. The differentiated nature of personal experience in the West, along with the firm conviction that the individual is the personal author and agent of bodily experience, not only permits the personal cultivation of bodies in this (Western) cultural milieu, but also allows extreme objectification of bodies and fosters the body/self alienation when the myth of personal control is disrupted by an illness.

The formulation of the self as the independent operator of a body engaged in the attainment of an ideal form pits the self in a perpetual struggle against its body. As a result of the body's exploitation as a forum for projection of the self rather than of the collective, embodied experience is often formulated as an entrapment of the self. The body is objectified and alienated as something against which to struggle.

This sense of alienation is amplified in the context of illness experience. Inherently destabilizing to the integrity of the individual, illness disconfirms the illusion of personal control over the body, generating anxiety as one is confronted with the strangeness of dyscontrol. Within the differentiated concept of self and body, illness experience is also potentially isolating, as it catapults the individual into an unsharable experience. In essence, the notion of the discreteness of bodies and the personal responsibility and authority over them generate conditions allowing simultaneous personal alienation from one's body and community.

Illness also disrupts the smooth day-to-day experience of the collective in Fiji. But in contrast to the isolating nature of illness in the West, illness in Fiji — whether manifest in physical symptoms or *niju* visitation — though personally uncomfortable, is characteristically shared and claimed by the community. The collective appropriates the individual body as a forum to negotiate and articulate the meaning of the social conflict identified by the illness. The etiology of the illness is traced from a socio-moral transgression within the *mataqwali*, rather than of the individual, underscoring the inseparability of selves within the collective.

Far from isolating the individual, illness integrates him or her into the collective by diffusing the experience among its many members. This is accomplished either concretely—as in the case of the mother who experienced the *niju* presence in her daughter's body or in the accommodation of a sick person's need to urinate by transferring the urge to another person—or more abstractly, in a collective interpretation of the meaning of an affliction to the community. The attempts to repair the social rupture reintegrate the afflicted individual into the collective, since his or her body represents its substrate. Already familiar in the popular narratives about the *niju's* disempowering force over the body, the absence of agency over the body in illness is not strange to the Fijian.

Similarly, the responsibility for the welfare of individuals as explicitly manifest in their bodily form lies with the social unit that feeds them. Negligence suggested by a weight loss or failure to thrive is identified in an individual body, but is attributed to the community. This returns us to the clinical question which puzzled me when I arrived in Fiji. How are we to understand the virtual absence of anorexia nervosa in this cultural context? The answer, it now seems clear, is that anorexia nervosa, characterized by the suppression of appetite and refusal to eat, is a logical impossibility within the traditional Fijian concept of self and body.[1]

In part, the alienation from the body experienced by the anorectic relates to the profound disruption of personal authorship of bodily experience: disconfirmation of her insistence that hunger can be suppressed or that the body can continue to exist without being fed. It is the anorectic's refusal to relinquish this myth of control that is pathologizing. Consider the contrast between anorexia nervosa and *macake*, the Fijian appetite disorder. *Macake* is characterized by a *loss* of appetite—not a *suppression* of it. This lack of appetite is immediately noticed by the community of caregivers and (almost always successful) efforts are instituted to restore appetite by administering the appropriate treatment. Hence the experience of *macake* confirms and solidifies the grounding of self in the familial and collective matrix, whereas that of anorexia nervosa rejects it.

The Body in the Socio-Cosmic Matrix

We have illustrated the embodiment of the collective within individual bodies via the concretization of care in bodily dimensions and of social conflict in anatomic space. Self-identity, rather than being fixed to the body, is firmly entrenched in the collective. This primary identificatio with the community is manifest in the disembodied self, the *yalo*, as it wanders from the body during sleep to tattle on its body and affiliate with its community. Precisely when bodily information threatens to sever connection with the collective (through an undisclosed pregnancy or breach of the adultery tabu), the *yalo* (*yalo ni bukese* and *yalo ni cala*, respectively) disengages from the body and seeks to affirm its allegiance to and integration within the collective. The manifestation of the disembodied *yalo* vividly portrays the self as more closely affiliated with the collective than the body.

Hence, we have come to see the collective embodied (manifest in bodily dimensions and symptom), and the self disembodied (manifest in the wandering *yalo*). We have also explored the body as it is reconstituted in the socio-cosmic corpus — that is, through manifestations in others' bodies and in the environment. Bodily presence erupts into the environment through a variety of signs in the case of a secretly pregnant woman: the owl crying at her home, the boat that makes no headway in rough seas, the choir that cannot sustain a high note, the child who "goes thin."[2]

Consider the following two scenarios:

A young boy approached his grandmother while she was bathing in the sea. Pointing at her right breast, he asked her, "Grandmother, whose breast is that to drink?" (*O cei na mea cucu?*).[3] She answered, "That one was your father's to drink." Indicating her left breast, he then continued, "Whose breast is that *to drink*?" She told him it had been his auntie's to drink.

A pregnant woman recounted that, at the end of a previous pregnancy, she and a friend, also then pregnant, had delivered their babies at the same time. At the time of her friend's delivery, her friend's younger sister was herself in the early stages of a pregnancy, but neglected to disclose this information despite the fact that she was caring for her postpartum sister. This friend had been breast-feeding her baby, but being in the vicinity of her sister's hidden pregnancy, she stopped lactating. The friend's family then approached the narrator to ask if she could supply the breast milk for this infant, which she agreed to do. She concluded by saying that she made sure to be responsible about disclosing each of her own pregnancies lest anything untoward befall those with whom she was in contact.

These anecdotes illuminate the body's intimate grounding within the collective. In the first scenario, the child highlights the interpersonal belongingness of his grandmother's breasts. He appropriates them as someone's to drink, in the service of nursing and nurturing that person, ignoring that it is his grandmother to whom they are physically attached. In the second story, a woman harboring a secret pregnancy causes her sister's inability to nurse her infant. The narrator lends her breast milk to her friend's baby, while emphasizing her awareness of the potential effects she may have on others' bodies (like her friend's secretly pregnant sister) in the context of her own current pregnancy. Challenging the personal exclusivity of the body, these narratives underscore the ways in which the body is situated in the collective.

The translocation of bodily experience is not part of the mundane world. *Yalo* are not said to wander from bodies unless stirred by an extreme threat to community integrity; *niju* are reported to enter bodies more frequently, but it is still not an unremarkable phenomenon. The havoc of an undisclosed pregnancy is far more commonly observed (or experienced firsthand), however. As one woman explained to me in describing the potent ramifications of an undisclosed pregnancy, "We [Fijians] have a lot of beliefs, but this one is true." Despite the fact that these occurrences represent a departure from routine events, they remain firmly fixed on the horizon of possibility and, therefore, elemental to the local understanding and experience of selfhood and embodiment in Fiji.

Cultural Metaphors: The Embodied Self, the Embodied Collective

In conclusion, we have examined how, in Fiji, the collective participation in nurturing is indexed in the body. Moreover, the collective appropriates, shares, and diffuses personal bodily experience within the context of the individual's embeddedness in the social corpus. By contrast, we have reviewed the ethic of bodily cultivation as a personal endeavor in Western society. Embodied experience is framed very differently within these two contexts; in Fiji, the body, self, and collective are intimately connected, but identity between body and self are not fixed.

Fijian embodied experience is inclusive of community processes and transcendent of the body's physical boundaries. Conflation of body identity with that of the collective reveals our Western notions about the discreteness of the body, the circumscription of bodily experience, and finally, the fixed identity between body and self, as our own particular cultural metaphor. Like the Fijian woman defending her cultural conviction that secret pregnancies are dangerously potent, we too may protest that our belief is "true," but if we do, we lose the opportunity to appreciate how our notion of selves established in discrete bodies mediates the experiences of alienation and isolation from a community.

By contrast, the Fijian self is located in a community as much as in a body. Accordingly, bodily surfaces and dimensions are not objectified as entities to manipulate self-reflexively, nor is embodied experience potentially isolating or alienating. The body is the very substrate that indexes and records the history and complexity of social relations within the collective. The body, then, mediates and substantiates the relationship between the self and the collective, while social processes are constitutive of both bodies and selves. Whereas we, in the West, privilege the notion that self and identity are lodged in the personal body, in Fiji, self, identity, and body are embedded in the socio-cosmic matrix.

Hence, we have unraveled the paradoxical disinterest in personal cultivation of the body in Fiji, despite the pervasive rhetoric about bodily dimensions. Fijians may admire a particular bodily form, but they rarely feel motivated to sculpt their bodies to match it since they do not constitute the body as an object to struggle with or against. On the other hand, the personalization and the objectification of the body in Western discourse frames the experience of the self in the body differently. The identification of self with a cultivated, bounded, and individuated body engenders a potentially antagonistic relationship between the body and its governing self. The ensuing alienation—both that of body from self and self from community—flourishes in cultural milieux that cast the body as a reflexively, personally managed resource.

Epilogue: On Being *Gwalili* in the West

> There, in front of us, where a broken row of houses stood be-
> tween us and the harbor, and where the eye encountered all sorts
> of stratagems, such as pale-blue and pink underwear cakewalking
> on a clothesline, or a lady's bicycle and a striped cat oddly sharing
> a rudimentary balcony of cast iron, it was most satisfying to make
> out among the jumbled angles of roofs and walls, a splendid ship's
> funnel, showing from behind the clothesline as something in a
> scrambled picture—Find What the Sailor Has Hidden—that the
> finder cannot unsee once it has been seen.
>   —Vladimir Nabokov, *Speak, Memory*

In my absence from Nahigatoka, I have noticed that my thoughts have
gradually turned less and less toward speculating what feast might be
being discussed over *yaqona* in Tai Vani's cookhouse, wondering whether
mangoes were still in season, or imagining a circle of women who were
no doubt coaxing a new baby to take his first step. However, at very
unpredictable times, vivid scenes still replay themselves in my thoughts,
and even more unpredictably, letters arrive from overseas—both events
for which I am thankful.

One of my dearest friends from Nahigatoka sent a letter to me soon
after my departure, describing the gossip and goings-on of our village.
She noted my absence, still relatively fresh, and confessed that she was
gwalili (lonely) without me. She distinguished this word by translating
it into English, since she supposed it was one I had never had occasion
to hear or to use while I was in Fiji. Indeed I had been unfamiliar with
the word, but its appearance in her letter presented an opportunity to
reflect on the *gwalili*-ness that has crept into my positioning in my native
social universe.

I suspect that my friend's loneliness has long passed, while the existential conditions for my own are quite inseparable from my lived experience as a Westerner. It is simultaneously the prize and the price of ethnographic work to step out of one's taken-for-granted universe, only to emerge from the field with a sense of forfeiture attending the richness and wonder of the experience.

My most difficult lesson in Nahigatoka — that of relinquishing what I could of my privacy and autonomy to become a self in the collective — is being unlearned as I recultivate the independence and autonomy that serve the American so well. And consequently, as a member of a community that makes a virtue of operating alone, I must bear the cost of being *gwalili*.

Just as my entry into Nahigatoka and understanding of the Fijian ethos were accompanied by the frustration, confusion, and elation I felt as I tried to fathom what gave meaning and substance to the Fijian world, my re-entry into the West has occasioned a similar disruption in taken-for-granted experience. I am now very aware that much of my focus on the ethnographic material has been conditioned not only by my intrinsic Westernness but also by my not-uncomplicated return home. Thus I realize that, to a large extent, I have exploited in my analysis the once-hidden elements of alienation accompanying the trappings of Western experience that I have not been able to "unsee." While I consider myself fortunate beyond my greatest expectations to have become embedded in the Fijian community, my experience there cannot help but deepen my subsequent experience of *gwalili*.

Appendix A:
Glossary and Language Notes

Standard Fijian and the Nadroga Dialect

While there is a Standard Fijian language (*Viti Raraba*), the number and diversity of the indigenous regional dialects is staggering, as even neighboring villages may have distinctive vocabularies (see Geraghty 1983). As a result, Standard Fijian is used as a lingua franca among Fijians of different provinces, as well as for communication between native Fijians and Fiji Indians. The Nadroga dialect, used in areas of western Fiji, is not mutually intelligible with Standard Fijian, which is substantially derived from the Bauan dialect (Geraghty 1988).

Evidence indicates that the eastern Fijian languages share a common development with a proto-Polynesian language, whereas the western Fijian languages "share more features exclusively with Melanesian than with Polynesian languages" (Geraghty 1983:348, 389). Moreover, western and eastern Fijian languages continued to evolve independently on either side of the central plateau of Viti Levu (348–49). While, given the overlap in vocabulary and grammar, the indigenous languages translate easily from one to another, their remaining dissimilarities point to important differences in custom between eastern and western Fiji, which have been glossed over in the depiction of Fijians as a culturally unified group.

GLOSSARY OF KEY NADROGA DIALECT TERMS

The glossary below includes key terms in the Nadroga dialect. Singular and plural forms of the noun are the same in most cases. Pronunciation of certain consonants varies from the English pronunciation approximately as follows:

Written as: Pronounced:
     b   mb
     c   th
     d   nj
     g   ng
     j   ch
     q   ngg

baca—ill, illness

bati—(Standard Fijian) warrior, or warrior class

beci—disgraceful

bito—a structural kinship division encompassing several *vuwere*, or family/households

bori/bori vina—full, well-sated after a meal

bori ho—an expression signifying that one is full after a meal

bosi la—calf of the leg

bulagi—leftover food

cavucavu—to confess; an illness which afflicts sexually experienced brides for which the only cure is to name all the men she has had sexual relations with before marriage

cavuka—postpartum illness (akin to psychosis)

cawa dina—literally "true food," refers to starchy staple crops and includes taro, cassava, yams, sweet potatoes, plantains, and breadfruit

cigana—a minnow-like fish, also referred to as "whitebait," that makes infrequent seasonal appearances in the Sigatoka River; considered a great delicacy, its arrival is greeted enthusiastically

colacola vina—healthy; also used as a greeting; connotes robust appearance with respect to weight

dalahika—a traditional remedy for *macake*

dagia na ogaoga ni vanua—idiomatic expression meaning to fulfill traditional responsibilities; literally, "carrying the responsibilities of the land on [one's] shoulders"

Dauhina—a *niju* that preys on young women; his name, literally, "always shining," refers to his visibility as a light

daurairai—a seer or diviner of spirit illnesses

dokadokaya—deserving of respect

dranu—traditional Fijian herbal therapy

drau ni kai—traditional Fijian herbal therapy

dukaduka—transgression or breach of tabu; literally, "filth"

gwalili—lonely

hevuhevu—ceremony offering *yaqona* and sometimes a gift on entering a village

holi—fundraiser

holi ti—event during which one group makes a food gift of tea items to another group

horo—ritual atonement

icavu or *cavu*—usually an edible plant or animal which represents either the collective village or *mataqwali* and refers to the genitals (male and female) of its members; often translated as "totem"

ihevu—first fruits ceremony

ilava/kea ilava—the accompaniment to the *cawa dina*, usually meat or vegetable dishes

itovo vavisi/na itovo—Fijian custom; etiquette befitting a Fijian

itovo vina—correct behavior

iyau—traditional goods often used in prestations and exchange, including mats, barkcloth, and fabric

jubu vina—well-formed shape (connoting robust)

julou—excuse me

kabekabe—food prepared by one household to take to another household as a contribution to some special event or to help feed a guest staying there

kaikai—strong

Kalou—the Christian God

kana valevu—"eat a lot"; a rhetorical invitation at meals to guests, encouraging them to eat their fill

kanakana lo—one who eats secretly (a grave offense); often meant as an insult

kana vaosi na tavioka—literally, "eating and finishing [wasting] the cassava"; idiomatically refers to married women who have not borne children

kawa—descendants

kawaitakinia—caring; concerning oneself with

kea ilava—see *ilava*

kerekere—formal request for help or for something material; please

kese levu—"big belly"; generally regarded as an insult

kua ni leqwa—don't worry

kune bura—a condition during the first trimester of pregnancy characterized by vomiting and poor appetite

kwekwe—gossip

layahewa—"skinny legs"; generally regarded as an insult

lewa vina—a good woman

lila—skinny; a pejorative description referring to body shape

Loju ni Hevu—Wesleyan church service dedicated to the presentation of the first harvest to the church for a blessing

[e] *luju elala*—"going thin"; idiomatically alludes to a person's weight loss

macake—an appetite disturbance

magisi—a feast, usually given for a special or ritual occasion; can also be a gift of food accompanying a social exchange

malaya—a variety of fish caught in the Sigatoka River

mana—the inherent power in a chief, Fijian spirits, or traditional Fijian practices, such as a *yaqona* ceremony

mase—illness

mase vavisi—Fijian (spirit-caused) illnesses

matakarawa—ceremony or offering reciprocating a *hevuhevu*

mataqwali—a division of the segmentary patrilineage which characterizes and organizes Fijian kinship structure; it is frequently translated by ethnographers and now even ethnic Fijians as "clan"; most villages are comprised of anywhere from two to five or more *mataqwali*

Matavitokani—youth group with the Methodist Church

mea—third person possessive pronoun used for drinkable items

ogaoga—a community or *mataqwali* function (event)

na tadoka ni vasucu—somatic illness afflicting postpartum women

niju—spirit or parahuman being; it can either appear in human form or enter a human and manifest itself as a voice, an illness, or as a bodily heaviness

qoqoru—gibberish or mumbling

riva—crazy or mentally ill

roqoroqo—formal visit to a family with a new baby

seigwane vina—a good man

tabua—whale's tooth; the most prestigious item in ceremonial exchange

Tai—grandmother or grandfather

talanoa—stories, or telling stories

tauvu—a relationship between two people whose ancestral *vu* were friends

tavale—cross-cousin with whom a joking relationship is established

turaga ni koro—village spokesman

urouro—fat

vabausia—a belief

vakaturaga—Standard Fijian for *vaturaga*; in a chiefly way; denoting exemplary behavior

vanua—land, or structural kinship division encompassing *yavuha*

varokorokotaki—respect, knowing one's place in relation to others

vavinavina—a ceremonial offering of *yaqona* to thank a person or a collective, usually for help or hospitality

veibatiki—(Standard Fijian) a relationship of a warrior *mataqwali* to a chiefly *mataqwali*; there are stringent food tabus associated with their relationship *vikawaitaki*—care in the sense of concern, bothering about others, paying attention to others' needs

vilomani—loving, empathizing with, caring about the general welfare of others

vinaka—thank you; also, no thank you

viqwaravi—to take care of others, e.g., a child, or guests, at a meal

viwekani—kin

visiko—formally organized visit from one community or group to another on the occasion of the new construction of a building or sometimes in the event of an illness

viwaletaki—joking discourse

vu—an ancestral deity, often represented in the form of an animal such as a dog or a shark

vudi—plantain; the *cavu* of Nahigatoka Village

vulagi—guest

vuwere—household unit; conceptualized as a kinship or spatial term

waci—a leafy green vegetable

waiwai—Fijian body oil; made from coconut oil with a variety of scented additives such as sandalwood and flowers

were levu—a traditional dwelling made entirely with natural materials; the chief of each village ought to occupy one even if other villagers live in the more permanent cement and corrugated tin structures

yaca—name; namesake

yalo—the essence of the self that can wander from the body under certain circumstances; sometimes translated as spirit or soul (see Capell 1941a)

yalo ni bukese—a *yalo* that wanders from a secretly pregnant woman

yalo ni cala—a *yalo* that is formed of the essence of wrong-doing (usually adultery)

yaqona—kava root (*piper methysticum*), a non-fermented beverage used recreationally and ceremonially; the beverage, which is mixed from the pounded or chewed root with cold water, is mildly psychoactive

yato—to walk; to walk like

yavuha—kinship structural division, encompassing several *mataqwali*

Appendix B: Research Methods

Elements of the research presented in this text include data collection through observation, ethnographic interviewing, and the administration of a survey questionnaire on attitudes toward diet and body shape (Figure B-1). Analyses and conclusions are drawn primarily from the observations and interviews; data generated by the survey are used to supplement conclusions by documenting the prevalence of weight problems and certain body-shape preferences, and by correlating dietary attitudes and behaviors with other social factors.

Field data were mainly collected during my residence in the chiefly household of Nahigatoka from January 1988 through April 1989. Some additional data were gathered in the spring of 1994 during a three-month stay. Throughout the period of data collection observations were recorded daily in a journal. During the first several months of 1988 I worked primarily in the local outpatient and maternal and child health clinics as a medical student and participated in household or village activities. I spent the remaining months administering the survey questionnaire, conducting ethnographic interviews in Suva and Nahigatoka, and continuing to observe and participate in village life. My hosts included me in daily household activities and invited me to attend or participate in ceremonial or *mataqwali* functions. They seemed genuinely delighted that I took an interest in these events.

Methodological difficulties are inherent in conducting in-depth ethnographic interviews with persons of the opposite sex in Fiji. First, my access to observation was somewhat limited by being a woman in settings in which men and women are traditionally segregated; my status as a "special guest," however, occasionally took precedence over my gender, enabling me to observe various ceremonial events from a choice spectator's vantage point. More important, male/female relationships in Fiji are characterized by either rigid avoidance or extreme familiarity (for example, in the exchange of ribald jokes). Since it was difficult to stray from the rather stereotyped modes of relating to men, my in-depth interviews are almost exclusively with women.

Survey of Attitudes Toward Diet and Body Shape

Beginning in April 1988, I attended several workshops on nutrition sponsored by the Fiji National Food and Nutrition Committee (NFNC) and
traveled with members of this committee to survey several villages in the
Sigatoka Valley region for an NFNC project. I later returned to four of
these villages (Bemana, Keiyasi, Nadroumai, and Wauosi), as well as to
Nahigatoka and Lomanikaya, and administered a formal questionnaire
to a total of 301 men and women in order to collect further data on
dietary behaviors and attitudes toward body shape.

The goal of this survey was to document and quantify the Fijian attitudes about diet and body shape that had emerged from my initial
informal interviews and observations. There were several advantages to
collecting survey data rather than only conducting interviews. First, the
information from survey data corroborated the data collected from a
more limited sample of persons interviewed in-depth. Second, it allowed
some access to men's attitudes toward diet and body shape.[1] Finally, this
questionnaire allowed cross-cultural comparisons of attitudes toward
body shape, insofar as it employed a technique of eliciting responses
to a series of cartoon drawings of gradated shapes similar to those used
in studies that have sought to document perceptions of female body
shapes in Western societies (see Furnham and Alibhai 1983; Powers and
Erickson 1986).

The questionnaire was developed after extensive interviewing to determine culturally appropriate categories and phrasing of questions.
After an initial format was developed, it was piloted and revised twice in
two different villages (Bemana and Wauosi), then subsequently administered to 172 women and 129 men ranging in age from 15 to 84 in four
additional villages—Keiyasi, Lomanikaya, Nadroumai, and Nahigatoka.
A variant of the Nadroga dialect is spoken in all the villages selected for
the survey, and all but Lomanikaya (which is located 30 km offshore on
the island of Vatulele) are located in the Sigatoka Valley region. Keiyasi
is remote, approximately one hour's drive from Sigatoka Town by way of
an unpaved road; Nahigatoka is within walking distance from the town;
and Nadroumai is approximately 12 km from the town by way of a paved
and unpaved road.

In each village, the *turaga ni koro* (assistant to the chief in organizing
village affairs) was contacted either personally or via the public health
team, and arrangements were made for my research assistant (a Fijian
woman from a Sigatoka Valley village) and myself to stay in the village
for several days while administering the questionnaire. On all occasions,
formal *yaqona* presentations were made to request permission to do the
survey and to obtain the village's cooperation; permission and help were

graciously offered in a complementary presentation. Several educated women were recruited in each area to help in administering the survey, and the *turaga ni koro* determined which *mataqwali* should be surveyed on which day. All available men and women over age 15 were encouraged to participate. The host village either asked a designated *mataqwali* to provide a household at which members might gather or offered the use of the community hall for administration of the survey.

On the appointed day, *mataqwali* members arrived at their convenience[2] and either my research assistant or I explained in the Nadroga dialect directions for completing the survey. Because we had anticipated problems with the numbered responses, portions of the questionnaire were displayed on large posters to demonstrate how to complete these sections. Participants were offered the choice of filling out the eight-page survey on their own or with the assistance of one of the young men or women recruited to help, my research assistant, or myself. Since many of the subjects had only a primary school education and since the dialect was presented in an unfamiliar written form,[3] most of the subjects gave verbal responses, which were recorded on their questionnaire forms by one of the assistants. Administration of the survey required approximately one hour per respondent.

After the survey forms were completed, participants were weighed and measured and their blood pressures checked. The substantial proportion of the sample group identified as hypertensive were advised of this and referred to an appropriate facility. Body-mass indices were calculated at a later date and supplied to the villages, district nurses, the Fiji NFNC, and the Fiji School of Medicine for their information and data bases. Villagers were not required to fill out a survey to have their blood pressure checked, but this service seemed to add incentive to come to the gathering and participate. In general, participants were very concerned about learning whether they were affected by hypertension (*jubu ni dra*), but relatively uninterested in knowing their weight or height.

The rate of participation in each village is unknown, since accurate information about the resident adult population was not available. Daytime absence from the village for school or employment may have selectively excluded a higher percentage of the younger sample population than others. In addition, a desire to have blood pressure checked may have selectively encouraged participation from individuals concerned about their health or with a history of hypertension. However, since Fijians are generally curious about hypertension and relatively unaware of risk factors (such as age, obesity, smoking, and heredity), and since many had never had their blood pressure checked, it is doubtful that any particular risk group was overrepresented in the sample.

Vanua:———————— Naba:————

Siki ni higa:————

VATATARO NI TOLA
BALESIA NA CAWA QEINIA NA IBULIBULI NI LALA

MATAI NI WAHEWAHE — IJUKUJUKU NI ECOLA YAHILA QEINIA NA VUWERE
[Mo toqaia na ihau dodonu i na kea yaloganiba he volaia e na laini.]

Muyaca ruarua:———————————— I yabaki vica? ————————

I hi bere ni vamau ☐   E vica na luvemu? ————————

I vamau ho ☐   Eri yabaki vica na luvemu?————————

I videi ho ☐

I dawai ho ☐   I loju ca?————————

Rara o huhu mai ke? ————————

I no koto mai vei nikua? ————————   E yabaki vica na lemu no koto oke? ————

O bau vainono i na tauni: io ☐   sikai ☐

I vei? ————————

Yabaki ca coko o na koto mai tauni?————————

I vei coko na vanua i vavalagi o bau no mai ke? ————————

Vatagedegede ni vuli? ———————— kalasi:——— form: ——— torocake: ————

Lemu cakacaka: ————————

I bau dau wilikia na Fiji Times: sikai ☐   vagauna ☐   vihiga ☐

I bau dau wilikia na niusiveva he na mekesini ca coko tale? ————————

LEMUJU VUWERE

NA ECOLA eri yabaki 15 la cake, eri no koto i na lemuju were

Yaca	Vikucasi qea na i taukei i were	Yabaki vica	Cakacaka	Balavu	Bibita	BMI	N/S

KWAYAHEWA eri no koto i na lemuju were:

Yaca	Vikucasi qea na i taukei i were	Higa ni sucu		Balavu	Bibita	N/S

E vica coko na ecola eri no koto i na lemuju vuwere? ————————

NA CALEVU NI REWASIA NA ILAVO

Rausia e vica na ilavo miji kou ma i na lemuju juku cakacaka i na tahila na macawa rua:

Cakacaka ———————— $ —————

Cakacaka ———————— $ —————

Rausia e vica na ilavo muju kou ma i ————————————————— **i na yabaki a osi:**

Na basa: $ —————

Na Lihi: $ —————

Hila tale na calevu: $ —————

E vica na ilavo muju holia i na yabaki a osi:

I na loju $———————— I na ogaoga varara $————————

WERE:

Were vaca:			E no koto na lemuju:		
	Were block	☐		Rejio	☐
	Were kava	☐		Livaliva	☐
	Were kai	☐		Bola ni wai kakaholi	☐
	Were biju	☐		Kasi	☐
	Were vavisi	☐		Video	☐
	Were vakenani	☐			
	Flat	☐			

Were ni vo vaca:	dre	☐	E vica na rumu ni moce? —————————
	hovawai	☐	
	qwara	☐	

Were ni kuro:
Miji vayagatakinia vata qeinia e hila tale na vuwere: io ☐ sikai ☐

E no koto i yaloga ni were: io ☐ sikai ☐

Vahala: quto ☐ varamasi ☐ kasi ☐

OGAOGA NI RARA:

Na gauna vaca a tara ke na i osiosi ni homase i na lemuju rara? ————————— O vahala: io ☐ sikai ☐

O la muni i na homase. io ☐ sikai ☐

O kou mai ke a yavalu na cawa· io ☐ sikai ☐

Na cawa ca? ————————

Na gauna vaca a tara ke na i osiosi ni holi i na lemuju rara? ————— O bau holi ke: io ☐ sikai ☐

A vica? ——————— $ —————

O holia e hila na cawa i na loju ni hevu i na yabaki a osi?

I na loju: ☐ Na cawa ca? ————————————

Na tale vunau: ☐ Na cawa ca? ————————————

I were levu· ☐ Na cawa ca? ————————————

KARUA NA WAHEWAHE — NA KANA

	Na ca muju kania a ni yavi:
Qe na qwata:	
Qe na higalevu:	
Ji i na va:	
Qe na yavi:	

Na ca muju kania na higa
tabu osi qe na higalevu? ———————————————————————————

Kodaki e hila na lemu vunilagi me
vahigalevu, na cawa ca i na vahala ke? ——————————————————

Na ca miji seia koto:

waci	☐	vijua	☐	vuji	☐	kuvukuvu	☐
qovi	☐	doko	☐	jaina	☐	tovu	☐
maoli	☐	kumala	☐	baigani	☐	niu	☐
		tavioka	☐	kulu	☐	vinaji	☐

Miji dau kou valevu tahila mai vei kemuju cawa: seisei ☐ makete ☐

Na cawa ca miji dau volia mai na sitoa? ———————————————————

Bara rausia e vica na ilavo muju
vayagatakinia i na voli cawa i na macawa a osi? ———————————————— $ _____

Bara rausia e vica na i lavo muju vayagatakinia i na voli vaqona i na macawa a osi? ____ $ _____

E bau yavala na gauna e bau leqwa na cawa i lemuju were: io ☐ sikai ☐

Na gauna vaca honi? —————————————————————————————————

Na ca miji dau tara ni dau yaco me kodaki honi?———————————————————

Na ca lemu numia balesia na lemu kana? ————————————————————

[Oria wavoki na naba me la vata na lemu numia:]

I bau vinasia mo vihautakinia lemu kana:
   Valevu   1   2   3   4   5   6   7   Sikai hara ga

Kodaki mo vihautakinia lemu kana,
na cawa ca i na kania valevu?———————————————————————————

Kodaki mo vihautakinia lemu kana,
na cawa ca i na muhukia: ————————————————————————————

O bau tovolia ho mo tosonia cake na lemu kana:
   Valevu   1   2   3   4   5   6   7   Sikai hara ga

Balesia na ca? ——————————————————————————————————————

O rewasia vina he sikai:
   Rewasia vina   1   2   3   4   5   6   7   Tasi rewasia vina

O bau tovolia ho mo muhukia na lemu kana:
   Valevu   1   2   3   4   5   6   7   Sikai vahila

Balesia na ca?——

O rewasia vina he sikai:
   Rewasia vina   1   2   3   4   5   6   7   Tasi rewasia vina

Na ca lemu numia balesia na kemu bibita:
   Donu   1   2   3   4   5   6   7   Tasi donu vuako

I bau vinasia mo levulevu he mama (he kua ni vihautakinia na kemu bibita):
   Levulevu   1   2   3   4   5   6   7   Mama

I bau dau kawaitakinia na kemu bibita:
   Valevu   1   2   3   4   5   6   7   Sikai vahila

I bau dau tasi bori:
   Vigauna   1   2   3   4   5   6   7   Sikai vahila

Na ca lemu numia balesiko ni o tasi bori? _____

Na ca i dau tara ke? _____

I bau dau kana vahivisia:
   Vigauna   1   2   3   4   5   6   7   Sikai vahila

Na ca lemu numia balesiko ni o kana hivisia? _____

Na ca i dau tara ke? _____

O bau dau majua ni hivisia na lemu kana:
   Vigauna   1   2   3   4   5   6   7   Sikai vahila

I bau dau majua ni hewahewa na lemu kana:
   Vigauna   1   2   3   4   5   6   7   Sikai vahila

I bau dau majua ni bura na lemu kana:
   Vigauna   1   2   3   4   5   6   7   Sikai vahila

I bau dau marautaki ni vina na lemu kana:
   Vigauna   1   2   3   4   5   6   7   Sikai vahila

I bau dau majua ni o vakanira vabura na lemu vuwere:
   Vigauna   1   2   3   4   5   6   7   Sikai vahila

I bau dau marautaki ni o vakanira vina na lemu vuwere:
   Vigauna   1   2   3   4   5   6   7   Sikai vahila

I bau dau majua ni o vakanira bura na lemu vunilagi:
   Vigauna   1   2   3   4   5   6   7   Sikai vahila

I bau dau marautaki ni o vakanira vina na lemu vunilagi:
   Vigauna   1   2   3   4   5   6   7   Sikai vahila

I bau dau kawaitakinia na cawa i dau kania:
   Valevu   1   2   3   4   5   6   7   Sikai hara ga

I bau dau kawaitakinia na cawa eri dau kania na lemuju vuwere:
   Valevu   1   2   3   4   5   6   7   Sikai hara ga

I hau dau kawaitakinia na cawa eri dau kania na lemuju vunilagi:
   Valevu   1   2   3   4   5   6   7   Sikai hara ga

E manasiko koto e hila na baca?   mase ni huka: ☐
                                          jubu ni dra: ☐
                                          caisisi (tibi): ☐
                     e hila tale na mataqwali na baca: ☐ _____

Na cawa ca coko i dau kania mo cola vina ke? _____

Na cawa ca coko i dau muhukia
he vatabuniko mo cola vina ke? _____

Na vuanikai he na wainimase he na dranu
ca coko i homia koto mo cola vina ke? _____

Na cawa ca coko eri vamakali i vuako? _____

KATOLU NI WAHEWAHE — NA IBULIBULI NI LALA

Na kwa mo tara: E na varaitaki vuako e yavalu na iyaloyalo ni ibulibuli ni ecola. Vatakea na lemu numia balesia na ibulibuli yahila i na lemu toqaia wavoki na naba e volekasia na voha i na imawi he na kea i ha i na imatau. E sikai na i hau ni taro dodonu he cala okwe, na lemu numia ga. Mo volaia na i hau i na veva e holi wa.

Rairai vina	1	2	3	4	5	6	7	Rairai bura
Qwaravi vina	1	2	3	4	5	6	7	Tasi qwaravi vina
Dau kana vina	1	2	3	4	5	6	7	Tasi dau kana vina
Colacola vina	1	2	3	4	5	6	7	Gogo
Kawa vina	1	2	3	4	5	6	7	Kawa bura
Vinumi	1	2	3	4	5	6	7	Kocokoco
Ciqaciqa	1	2	3	4	5	6	7	Yalo bura
Dokai	1	2	3	4	5	6	7	Beci
Lima tawa	1	2	3	4	5	6	7	Lima gwalala
E dodonu me levulevu	1	2	3	4	5	6	7	E dodonu me mama

Na ca i numia balesia na kemu ibulibuli? ————————————————————

Balesia na ca e kodaki ke na lemu numia okwe? ——————————————————

[Mo jigitakinia na ibulibuli mai na iyaloyalo ni seigwane he na iyaloyalo ni lewa:]

1) O kua e vina tahila (mai na iyaloyalo ni seigwane):————————————————

    O kua e vina tahila (mai na iyaloyalo ni lewa): ——————————————————

2) O kua miri vimouci: ————————————————————————————

3) O kua i vinasia mo moucia: ——————————————————————————

4) O kua eri vinasia lemu i jubujubu mo moucia: ————————————————————

5) O kua e vinasia lemu wetai mo moucia: ————————————————————

6) O kua e moucia lemu wetai: ——————————————————————————

7) O kua i vinasia me moucia lemu wetai: ————————————————————

8) O kua e moucia o luvemu yalewa e vulau ju ho: ————————————————————

9) O kua i vinasia me moucia o luvemu yalewa e vulau ju ho:————————————————

10) O kua e moucia o luvemu seigwane e huravou ju ho: ————————————————

11) O kua i vinasia me moucia o luvemu seigwane e huravou ju ho: ——————————————

12) O kua i vuara na iyaloyalo ni seigwane e leidani valevu i na lemuju rara: ——————————

13) O kua i vuara na iyaloyalo ni lewa e leidani valevu i na lemuju rara: ——————————

14) O kua i vuara na ibulibuli ni seigwane e rairai bura tahila: ——————————

   Bara tara vaca me kodaki honi na kea ibulibuli? ——————————————

15) O kua i vuara na ibulibuli ni lewa e rairai bura tahila: ——————————

   Bara tara vaca me kodaki honi na kea ibulibuli? ——————————————

[Oria wavoki na naba me la vata na lemu numia:]

I vei kodaki lemu taletakinia mulala:

| Valevu | 1 | 2 | 3 | 4 | 5 | 6 | 7 | Burasia |

O bau vinasia me hilanihila mulala:

| Valevu | 1 | 2 | 3 | 4 | 5 | 6 | 7 | Sikai hara ga |

I bau marautakinia he majuatakinia mulala:

| Marautakinia | 1 | 2 | 3 | 4 | 5 | 6 | 7 | Majuatakinia |

O bau vinasia mo vihautakinia kemu ibulibuli:

| Valevu | 1 | 2 | 3 | 4 | 5 | 6 | 7 | Jua hara ga |

I na tara vaca me vihau? ——————————

E rewa mo bau vihautakinia kemu ibulibuli:

| Valevu | 1 | 2 | 3 | 4 | 5 | 6 | 7 | Tasi rewa |

O bau tovolia ho mo vihautakinia:

| Valevu | 1 | 2 | 3 | 4 | 5 | 6 | 7 | Tasi vahila |

Na ca o tara ke? ——————————

I bau dau kawaitakinia na kemu ibulibuli:

| Valevu | 1 | 2 | 3 | 4 | 5 | 6 | 7 | Sikai vahila |

I bau dau vakawaia na kemu ibulibuli:

| Valevu | 1 | 2 | 3 | 4 | 5 | 6 | 7 | Sikai vahila |

I bau dau vakawaia na ibulibuli e yavalu tale na ecola:

| Valevu | 1 | 2 | 3 | 4 | 5 | 6 | 7 | Sikai vahila |

I bau marautakinia he majuatakinia elala o lemu wetai:

| Marautakinia | 1 | 2 | 3 | 4 | 5 | 6 | 7 | Majuatakinia |

I bau vinasia mo vihautakinia na kea ibulibuli:

| Valevu | 1 | 2 | 3 | 4 | 5 | 6 | 7 | Sikai hara ga |

I na tara vaca me vihau? ——————————

E rewa mo vihautakinia na kea ibulibuli:

| E rewa | 1 | 2 | 3 | 4 | 5 | 6 | 7 | Tasi rewa |

O bau tovolia ho:

| Valevu | 1 | 2 | 3 | 4 | 5 | 6 | 7 | Sikai vahila |

A bau hila na gauna a luju ke mulala: io ☐   sikai ☐

Na gauna vaca honi? ——————————

Na ca a manasiko? ——————————

I bukese ho okwe?   io ☐   sikai ☐

Kodaki o bau bukese ho, na ca lemu numia balesia mulala, na gauna o bukese ju ke:

| Donu | 1 | 2 | 3 | 4 | 5 | 6 | 7 | Tasi donu |
| Matau | 1 | 2 | 3 | 4 | 5 | 6 | 7 | Tasi matau |

[Vatakea na kedru bibita na vikwa okwe i na leju rairai vina he taletaki na ecola:]

Havahava:	Bibita	1	2	3	4	5	6	7		Tasi bibita
Ihuluhulu:	Bibita	1	2	3	4	5	6	7		Tasi bibita
Rauniulu:	Bibita	1	2	3	4	5	6	7		Tasi bibita
Na roka ni lala	Bibita	1	2	3	4	5	6	7		Tasi Bibita
Sasauni:	Bibita	1	2	3	4	5	6	7		Tasi bibita
Ukuuku:	Bibita	1	2	3	4	5	6	7		Tasi Bibita
Na ibulibuli ni lala	Bibita	1	2	3	4	5	6	7		Tasi bibita
Vidokai	Bibita	1	2	3	4	5	6	7		Tasi bibita
Colacola vina:	Bibita	1	2	3	4	5	6	7		Tasi bibita

I bau dau vayagatakinia na kirimu ni
mata me vabucobuco ke (kodaki na Ambi Cream): —————————————— io ☐   sikai ☐

I bau dau bena: ——————————————————————————— io ☐   sikai ☐

I bau dau tereni he vakaikai lala: —————————————————— io ☐   sikai ☐

Na vakaikai lala ca i dau tara? ——————————————

Bara e rausia vica na ilavo o
vayagatakinia i na voli lemu ihulu i na yabaki a osi? ——————————

O dau kawaitakinia valevu na kemu irairai: i mata ☐   okwe ☐

Kodaki i mata, nigica honi? ——————————————

KAVA NA WAHEWAHE-NA VIKWA BIBITA I NA LEJU COLA
[Vatakea na kedru bibita na vikwa okwe i na leju cola:]

Cola vina:	Bibita	1	2	3	4	5	6	7		Tasi bibita
Vinumi:	Bibita	1	2	3	4	5	6	7		Tasi bibita
Mamakuju:	Bibita	1	2	3	4	5	6	7		Tasi bibita
Leiqwaravi vina:	Bibita	1	2	3	4	5	6	7		Tasi bibita
Viqwaravi	Bibita	1	2	3	4	5	6	7		Tasi bibita
Lima tawa	Bibita	1	2	3	4	5	6	7		Tasi bibita
Vidokai:	Bibita	1	2	3	4	5	6	7		Tasi bibita
Varokoroko:	Bibita	1	2	3	4	5	6	7		Tasi bibita
Kawa vina	Bibita	1	2	3	4	5	6	7		Tasi bibita
Rairai vina:	Bibita	1	2	3	4	5	6	7		Tasi bibita
Kana vina:	Bibita	1	2	3	4	5	6	7		Tasi bibita
Dagia na oga ni vanua:	Bibita	1	2	3	4	5	6	7		Tasi bibita
Yalo havu:	Bibita	1	2	3	4	5	6	7		Tasi bibita
Vuli:	Bibita	1	2	3	4	5	6	7		Tasi bibita

Qi vavinavinatakinia na lemu vivuke i na haumi taro. Kodaki i vinasia mo kwaya e hila na kwa, qi kerekere mo volaia i ra. Vina valevu.

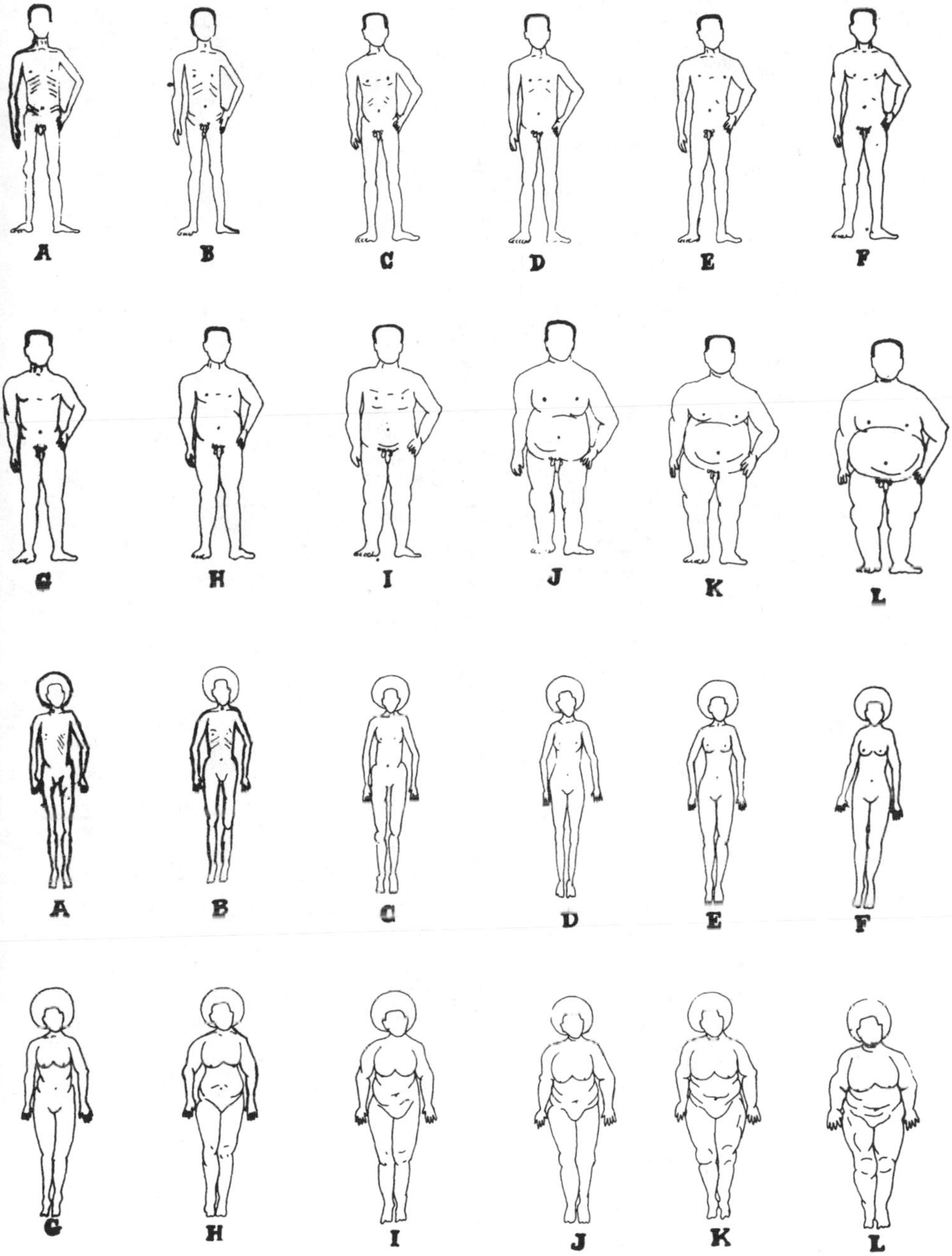

Figure B-2. Gradated male and female body shapes. Female drawings adapted by permission from Furnham and Alibhai 1983.

Appendix C: Graphic Representations of the Data

The gradated body shapes accompanying the charts in Figures C-1 through C-12 below are adapted by permission from Furnham and Alibhai 1983. The format for the graphs in Figures C-14 through C-19 is also adapted by permission from that paper.

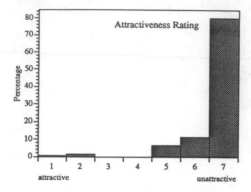

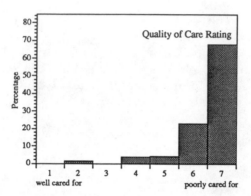

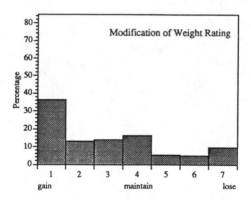

Figure C-1. Selected summary of ratings by women for female shape A.

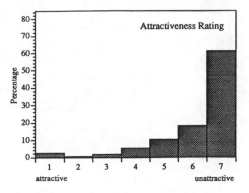

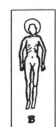

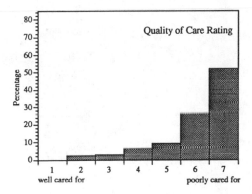

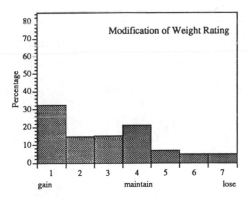

Figure C-2. Selected summary of ratings by women for female shape B.

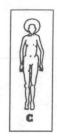

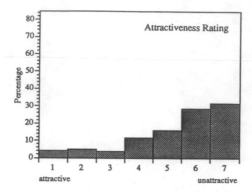

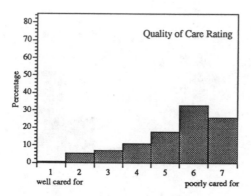

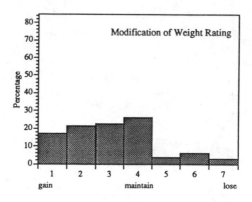

Figure C-3. Selected summary of ratings by
women for female shape C.

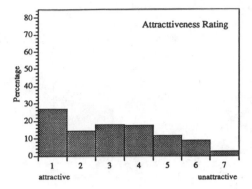

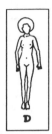

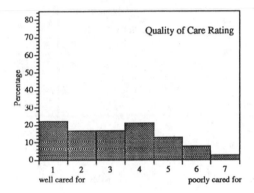

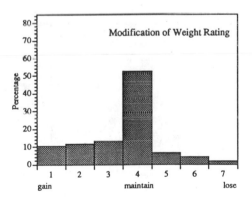

Figure C-4. Selected summary of ratings by women for female shape D.

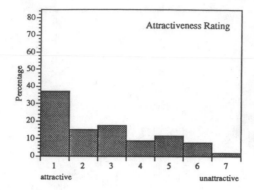

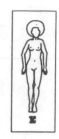

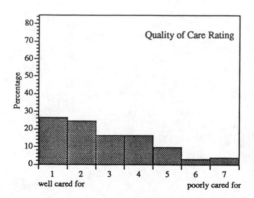

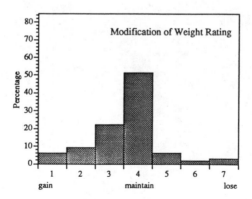

Figure C-5. Selected summary of ratings by women for female shape E.

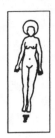

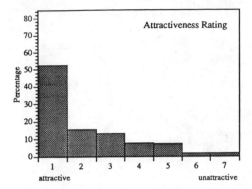

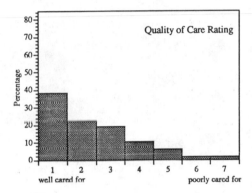

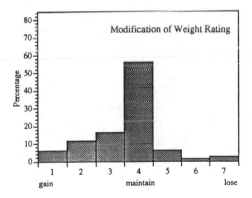

Figure C-6. Selected summary of ratings by women for female shape F.

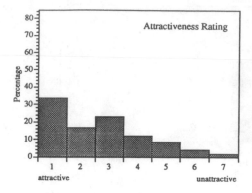

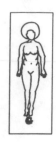

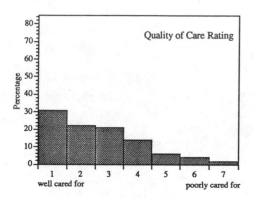

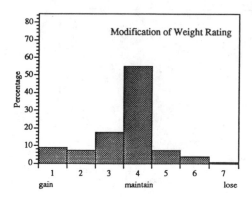

Figure C-7. Selected summary of ratings by women for female shape G.

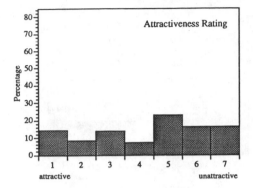

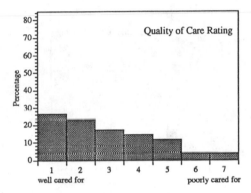

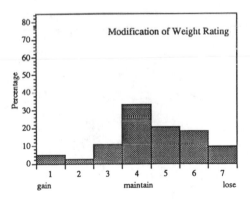

Figure C-8. Selected summary of ratings by women for female shape H.

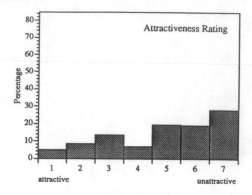

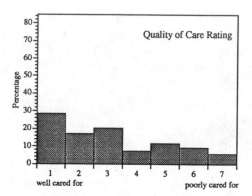

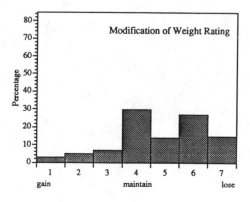

Figure C-9. Selected summary of ratings by women for female shape I.

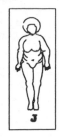

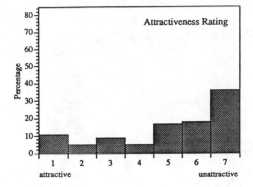

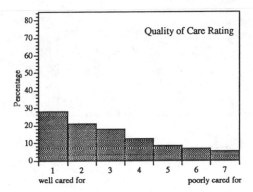

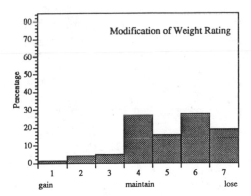

Figure C-10. Selected summary of ratings by
women for female shape J.

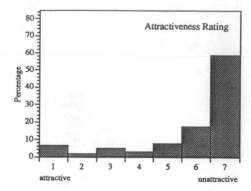

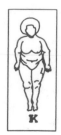

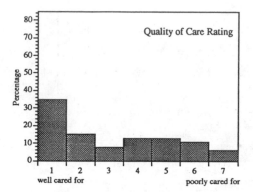

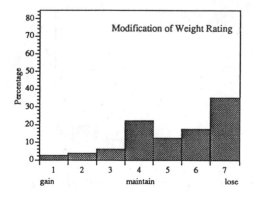

Figure C-11. Selected summary of ratings by women for female shape K.

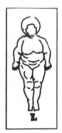

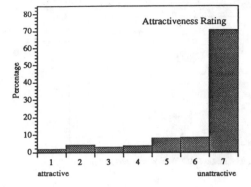

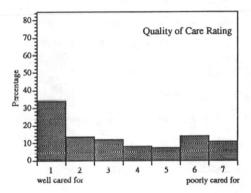

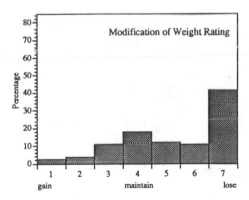

Figure C-12. Selected summary of ratings by women for female shape L.

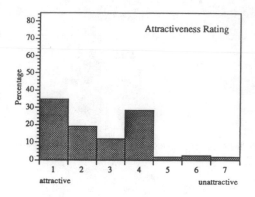

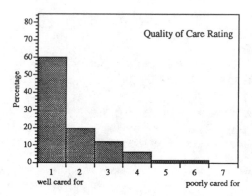

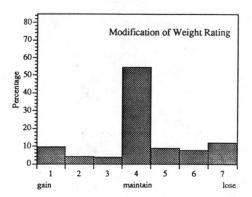

Figure C-13. Selected summary of ratings by women for perceptions of self.

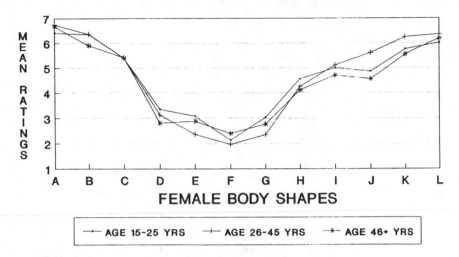

7 = Least Attractive
1 = Most Attractive

Raters are Women

Figure C-14. Age group comparisons of attractiveness ratings of female body shapes.

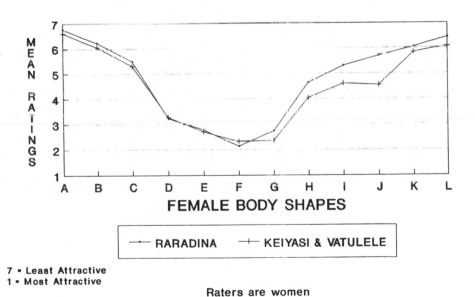

7 = Least Attractive
1 = Most Attractive

Raters are women

Figure C-15. Village comparisons of attractiveness ratings of female body shapes.

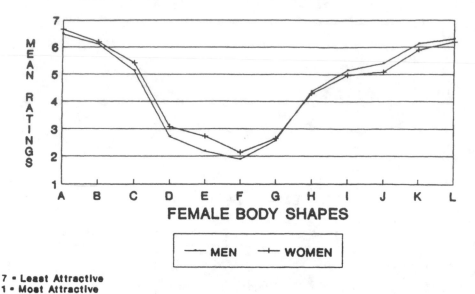

7 • Least Attractive
1 • Most Attractive

Figure C-16. Gender comparisons of attractiveness ratings of female body shapes.

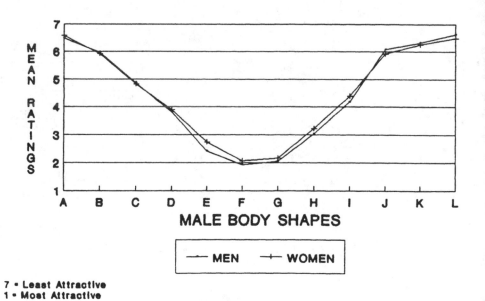

7 • Least Attractive
1 • Most Attractive

Figure C-17. Gender comparisons of attractiveness ratings of male body shapes.

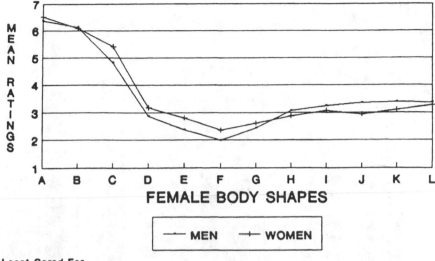

7 • Least Cared For
1 • Most Cared For

Figure C-18. Gender comparisons of quality of care ratings of female body shapes.

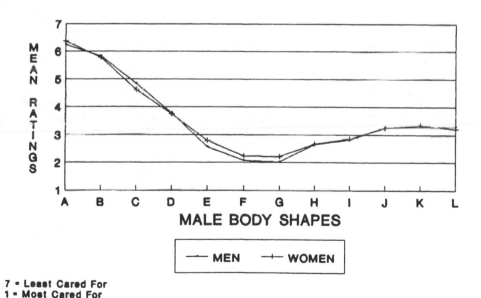

7 • Least Cared For
1 • Most Cared For

Figure C-19. Gender comparisons of quality of care ratings of male body shapes.

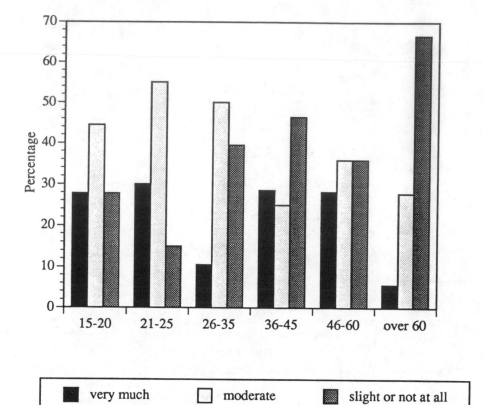

Figure C-20. Modification of diet to decrease food intake in women by age (in years). With the exception of women over 60 years of age (among whom a greater proportion show a desire to diet than among younger women) there is no clear association between desire to diet and age of women surveyed.

Notes

Introduction

1. Actually, there is a reported case of an ethnic Fijian woman who died secondary to complications of anorexia nervosa (Brock 1994). The prevalence of eating disorders is believed to be quite low relative to other populations (Abusah 1992, 1994) although it has not been formally documented. (But see addendum to this chapter, p. 6.)

2. The category "Western" is an admittedly problematic, but necessary, simplification for the purpose of comparison with very different cultural contexts. Here Western subsumes mainstream cultural practices in contemporary North America and Western Europe.

3. There is good evidence within the developmental psychology literature that while an infant's capacity for emergent relatedness is part of an innate developmental sequence, there is sufficient flexibility to allow cultural imprinting on the forms and experience of relatedness (Stern 1979.100, 200, 200, 244).

4. K. E. Read is a notable dissenter from this view in his paper on morality among the Gahuku-Gama in the Eastern New Guinea Highlands (1955:275).

Chapter 1

1. For a comprehensive ethnographic account of the Fiji Islands, see Deane (1921), Thompson (1940), Quain (1948), Sahlins (1962), Roth (1973), and especially the works of Fijian sociologist Asesela Ravuvu (1983, 1987, 1988). Fijian society, with its rich linguistic and cultural diversity, is far from monolithic. Most ethnographic data in this book are drawn from traditions local to the Nadroga/Navosa Provinces, and specifically, the Jubuniwai District.

2. I was in residence in the chiefly household in Nahigatoka for fifteen months between January 1988 and April 1989. My data reflect demographics and conditions in Nahigatoka at that time although supplemental data were collected during an additional three month trip to this site in 1994.

3. Fijians cultivate various starchy root crops such as taro, cassava, yams, and sweet potatoes. Bananas, plantains, breadfruit, eggplants, peppers, and leafy green vegetables are also tended on the plantations for family consumption or sale. In some areas cash cropping (mostly sugar cane and coconut) generates income.

The complement to the traditional starchy staple foods (*cawa dina*) is termed *na ilava* and varies considerably according to local fauna in the microecological environments. Villagers in the river valley enjoy freshwater fish, eels, prawns, and shellfish, whereas those in coastal and outer island villages dine on reef and ocean fishes. While mutton, beef, chicken, and fish are also sometimes purchased in town or at the market, the cattle, pigs, and chickens kept in the village as livestock are reserved almost exclusively for feast occasions.

4. Even the most remote villages commonly have shops that stock dried, processed, and canned goods. Sugar, flour, butter, rice, and soap are among the most popular commodities. In towns such as Sigatoka, supermarkets stock frozen and other Western-style foods to supplement the traditional diet. These foods, however, are regarded as inferior by the older generations and are said to make older persons ill.

5. It is projected that Fiji's tourist industry will soon become the nation's largest source of income; by 1990, it already employed about 6.6 percent of the country's workforce (Gibson 1990:34). The Coral Coast is Fiji's most developed and prosperous tourist area.

6. Video-cassette recordings of movies introducing media images of Western and other lifestyles became available in the Sigatoka area in the mid-1980s. Broadcast television subsequently became available in some parts of Fiji in 1992, after most of the data for this study had been collected.

7. *Yaqona* is an unfermented beverage made from kava root. Its presence is ubiquitous at formal and informal gatherings in Fiji.

8. All personal names of informants are pseudonyms and in some cases identifying features have been changed to protect confidentiality while preserving context as much as possible. My decision to use pseudonyms reflects my own (Western) orientation toward privacy and disclosure rather than any interest in anonymity expressed by my informants.

9. Throughout this book, the term "Fijians" refers to ethnic (indigenous Melanesian) Fijians only. Although this label fails to distinguish intraethnic differences within this population, I believe there is a sufficiently consensual Fijian identity to warrant this usage.

10. Abel Tasman, in 1646, was the first European to sight the Fiji Islands, although the treacherous coral reefs surrounding Fiji prevented him from landing. The next Europeans to come to Fiji were Captains Cook and Bligh in the late 1700s. Traders arrived in the early 1800s (Williams 1982) to exploit natural resources, including sandalwood, beche-de-mer, copra, and, eventually, sugar.

11. See Belshaw (1964), Nayacakalou (1973), and Ali (1980) for analyses of Fijian political structure as it relates to elements of prior traditional Fijian political organization and to the influx of the Indian population over the last century.

12. I draw heavily on Ravuvu's (1987) characterization of the Fijian ethos as tied to the practices of "sharing and caring" in following sections and chapters.

13. Recent physiometric evidence in the archaeological record suggests that the Fijians' proto-Oceanic forbears were indeed much larger than present day Fijians. Captain Cook noted the "fine physiques and freedom from disease" of the pre-contact Fijians, as well (Keith-Reid 1988:5). Moreover, the Fijian's perception of the demise of their traditional diet is well substantiated. Nutritional studies have demonstrated that "the dietary patterns and foods consumed in the island region have come to resemble those of the poor cities of North America and Europe" (1988:5). Unfortunately, this Westernization of the Fijian diet has been implicated in the rapidly increasing incidence of nutrition-related dis-

eases, most notably diabetes, cardiovascular disease, and hypertension (Thaman 1993:25; Johnson 1983).

14. Richard Katz and Linda Kilner maintain that in the pursuit of their art, Fijian healers aspire to a set of behaviors called *na gaunisala dodonu* or the "straight path." Respect, togetherness, kindheartedness, and "love for all" are elements of this ideal type (Katz and Kilner 1987:210).

15. For example, a young woman had been crippled since birth, reportedly because her mother, a commoner, had named her for an extremely chiefly woman. This sort of pretension was said to be met with disapproval from spirits. Levy describes a similar phenomenon in Tahiti (1973:181–82).

16. *Holi* (derived from *holia*, to give) are commonplace in Fijian villages. Usually a person of some status is selected to be the chief guest or to lead the *holi* with a sizable opening donation.

17. It is not at all unusual for a Fijian villager to have no savings. In fact, reserve cash is the exception rather than the rule. When emergency funds are needed they can be readily borrowed or one of a variety of fundraising activities can be held.

18. Throughout this book, interviews are translated from the Nadroga dialect to reflect informants' words and meaning as accurately as possible. The interviews conducted in English reflect some pidginization, which I have preserved in the transcription.

19. At the time of her story, one Fiji dollar was worth approximately seventy U.S. cents.

20. Legitimate authority in Fiji is determined by "seniority of descent in the male line," although seniority with respect to age and knowledge of protocol are also factors in designating leadership status (Nayacakalou 1975:32–33). Lineages are ranked according to the relative seniority of their founding ancestors (32). Chiefs and the members of a chiefly family have the authority to make decisions on behalf of their kinship group or village as a whole and are accorded obedience and privilege (35, 81). Chiefly men and women are repositories of ancestral spiritual powers, or *mana*. They control access not only to land resources, but also to clan deities. Disrespect for their authority is thought to invoke the displeasure and consequent retribution of ancestral deities.

21. Fijians traditionally eat, drink *yaqona*, conduct meetings, and relax while sitting on woven mats on the floor.

22. The head is the most sacred portion of the body, thought to be the repository of the spirits of one's ancestral kin. Fijians are ever-conscious of avoiding the physical space around another's head and consider indiscriminately touching another person's hair or head to be *tabu*. For example, a person who searches another's scalp for lice or nits, or cuts another's hair must first ask permission and then communicate respect afterward by a *hobo* while crouching or sitting on the ground. A Fijian who must reach or walk over another accompanies this action with an apologetic "*julou*," the rough equivalent of saying, "excuse me [for trespassing through the space near your head]."

23. Whereas Fijians use relatively few terms to map the terrain of the individual body, terms designating social relationships are highly elaborated and differentiated as detailed in the text. For example, anatomical areas such as finger, hand, and arm are referred to by their general category, *lima*. Moreover, although there are names for internal organs, they do not often find their way into general use and a Fijian might have difficulty naming a particular organ.

In short, the anatomy of the social corpus is well-explored in contrast to the internal organs of the individual body.

24. Individual names are chosen by a family to establish a namesake (*yaca*) connection to other members of the *mataqwali*. The two namesakes address each other as *Yaca*, and have a relationship in which each is especially indulgent and respectful of the other's requests. Commonly, a person has many *yaca* and the name identifies him or her as part of a family as well as an individual. In a similar vein, Bradd Shore has described how names in Samoa "establish relationships more clearly than they suggest personal identity" (1982:145).

25. This is especially apparent in western Viti Levu, where legend has it that a Tongan prince came ashore long ago and fathered the Fijian race at Vuda. For a discussion of this paradoxical coexistence of exogamic and cross-cousin marriage prescriptions, see Lévi-Strauss (1985: chapters 5, 11).

26. *Qalu* (in Standard Fijian, *vakalolo*) is a Fijian delicacy prepared from caramelized sugar, coconut cream, and pounded taro or cassava. Since desserts are seldom served in Nadroga, this dish is reserved for special occasions, such as grand-scale feasts or the arrival of esteemed guests. It is proper to set aside the first portions for the chief of the village (regardless of whether or not he or she will attend the feast or is in residence in that household) and for any guests present in the village before serving it to the party for which it is intended.

27. A person may not enter or reenter a village — even one's own — after an extended absence without a formal presentation of *yaqona* to the chief or the head of the particular household with whom one will be staying (*hevuhevu*). The individual seeks permission to stay and pardon in advance for any inconvenience or offenses he or she may cause. The virtually axiomatic granting of the request is effected in the counter-presentation of *yaqona*, the *matakarawa*. In some villages in Nadroga, the acceptance is sometimes offered before the actual request.

28. Bradd Shore describes how "social resources are revitalized" within the context of material exchange in Samoa (1982:169–70).

29. The polite form of request in standard Fijian is *yalo vinaka*, which roughly corresponds to "please." Although the slightly modified *yalo vina* is used occasionally in Nadroga, it is normally replaced by *kerekere*, a word derived from the verb *kerea* (to give) that has been reported to refer to a season in which refusals were forbidden (Mauss 1967:29).

30. Possessive pronouns designate objects as belonging to categories based on their edibility, drinkability, and inalienability. Inalienable "possessions" include kin relations and anatomic parts, which in theory cannot be wrested from the individual. They denote a unique category of relationship of the personal and social body to the self.

31. Most notable is the avoidance tabu for a woman and her husband's brother or *daku* (literally, "back"), who must demonstrate their mutual respect by not addressing each other. For example, in some cases a woman might refrain from entering a room if she knows her *daku* is present. These tabus are observed to varying degrees depending on the context.

Chapter 2

1. Garner et al. (1980) demonstrate the changing weight and circumferential measurements of *Playboy* centerfolds and Miss America Pageant winners during the 1960s and 1970s. Although this shift in female body shape standards

is convincingly documented, it must be remembered that to make their point the authors have used two of the most notably sexist institutions in the United States. This selectivity calls into question the degree to which these ideals do in fact reflect a popular consensus and, moreover, how females who have not been co-opted by the values reflected in these institutions might view these so-called ideals.

2. Diagnostic criteria for anorexia nervosa and bulimia nervosa specifying "undue influence of body shape or weight on self-evaluation" among symptoms indicating diagnosis (American Psychiatric Association 1994:545, 550) are problematic in their relativity to changing cultural norms that legitimate and reinforce certain kinds of bodily preoccupation.

3. Obesity condenses two of three types of stigmata described by Goffman by simultaneously being an "abomination of the body" and indicative of "blemishes of individual character" (Goffman 1963:4).

4. Historically, bodily urges that conflict with cultural norms have precipitated a sense of alienation from the body, if not psychopathology. For example, at the turn of the century, hysteria became associated with sexual impulses at a time when Victorian morals delegitimized female sexuality (see Showalter 1985). Cultural and religious mores prescribing ascetic behavior are attempts to reign the body in by curbing and reformulating its desires. In the same vein, bodily urges that are deemed undesirable are objectified or reified in appropriate cultural or religious contexts as demons, which then become alienated from the self. See Csordas (1990:14–15) and Bilu and Beit-Hallahmi (1989) for cases in which bodily urges are reified as spirits.

5. A vast literature documents and describes the virtually infinite means of decorating and adorning the body. These processes range from ritual scarification to application of cosmetics to enhance attractiveness, to the veiling and covering of the body to privatize it.

6. This assessment was based on these subjects' responses to cartoon drawings of female bodies that varied from emaciated to morbidly obese.

7. These data provide an introductory insight into preferences for certain shapes and their associations with particular values or attributes. Ethnographic interview data, presented later in this chapter, make the survey data more meaningful by relating them to more complex processes informing the cultivation of bodies in Fiji.

8. Weight status was assessed by measuring height and weight and then calculating the Body Mass Index (BMI). This simple formula (weight [kilograms]/ height [meters] squared) is a standard clinical method for determining a person's weight status relative to the norm. BMIs of 20 to 25 constitute a healthy body-weight range; those between 25 and 30 fall into the overweight range; and BMIs above 30 fall in the obese category.

9. There is, for example, an impressive congruence between men's and women's responses concerning attractiveness and quality of care ratings for the randomly presented male and female gradated body shapes (Figures C-16–C-19).

10. The data suggest a markedly higher prevalence than projected from the preliminary results of a Fiji National Food and Nutrition Committee survey in Suva and Nausori in 1985 (Fiji NFNC Newsletter 1986:1) and results reported earlier in a study conducted by the Fiji School of Medicine (Hawley and Jansen 1971).

11. Although overweight and obesity are relative categories with respect to cultural experience of normative and ideal and the construction of aesthetic

standards, there is biomedical evidence that obesity and overweight (as measured to some extent by the BMI) are risk factors for morbidity and mortality from a variety of diseases (Gray 1989). Other data suggest, however, that obesity may also confer certain health benefits (Ernsberger and Haskew 1987). Nonetheless, given the high prevalence of diabetes and cardiovascular disease — both associated with overweight — among ethnic Fijians, it is likely that the culturally perceived "normative" weight does contribute to morbidity.

12. This hypothesis, developed in the first few months of my fieldwork, reveals my Western ethnocentric assumption that persons formulate an approximation of the ideal as a goal in cultivation of the body/self. I had so taken this for granted that when I began administering the survey I was startled by respondents' complacency regarding manipulating the weight of these shapes. I initially surmised the question had been mistranslated or misinterpreted, but in retrospect I find the response entirely consistent with the relative lack of interest in attaining an ideal shape.

13. The word *tupu* in the Maori language (likely an etymon of the Nadrogan *jubu* [in Fijian *tubu*], or vice versa) also refers to "a power to thrive and grow" and is related to a person's *mana* (Mackenzie 1989:53). Shore (1989:140–41) also reviews the link between *tupu* and *mana* in Polynesia.

14. Propriety dictates that a woman's leg be covered at least to her knees. In a formal situation she is required to wear a *sulu ira*, a garment reaching below her ankles, but while working in the household or on the plantation her calves may be exposed.

15. Several Tongan women at the University of the South Pacific described large calves as a salient feature in Tonga in judging the relative attractiveness of a woman. They noted that while their legs should be covered, traditional dances do allow women to display their calves.

16. There is actually a great deal of balanced structure to the Fijian diet, although it does not follow Western biomedically based nutritional categories. For example, all meals must include *cawa dina* (starchy root and other staple crops) with *kea ilava* (its relish, or meat); many meals include broth made from meat or greens, with sugared tea afterward. Fruits are not traditionally eaten with meals, and green vegetables infrequently appear on the meal table in Nahigatoka.

Chapter 3

1. Totemic foods (*icavu* or *cavu*) are not always reserved for their "owners" if, for example, they are not particularly rare. Even in these cases, however, persons generally claim to relish their totemic food. I am not aware of any present-day prohibitions on the consumption of one's *icavu*, although there is evidence that historically these may have been forbidden foods (Capell 1941:60). The *icavu* must be distinguished from foods derived from the *vu* (such as the shark in Nahigatoka), which are strictly tabu.

2. As a general rule, the head of any animal is considered to be the choice portion; the tail is the correspondingly least desirable part. Etiquette demands that when an animal is divided for serving the head should be given to the chief or to a distinguished guest if either is present; otherwise it is served to the senior member of the household.

3. The designation of prohibited and prescribed foods may be the most visible

and frequent marker of the relation between different *mataqwali*, especially today, when, for example, the warrior class is no longer mobilized for its traditionally designated communal duties.

4. The expression "*qalu kania*" literally means to eat the *qalu* one has prepared oneself, and figuratively indicates a situation in which a man marries a woman from his own village, comparing not sharing food with failing to participate in social exchange. Just as it is (theoretically) unthinkable to marry in one's own village within the exogamic tradition, it is unimaginable to prepare an elaborate dish like *qalu* and not distribute it to other households. Both are axioms of social interchange.

5. Ritual marking of transitional life events and exchanges are both characteristically accompanied by a *magisi, yaqona, iyau* (traditional wealth including mats and barkcloth), and the prestigious *tabua* (whales' teeth). For a comprehensive discussion of ceremonial exchange see Sahlins (1962).

6. A cash gift generally accompanies ceremonies officially opening new structures. Practically it is meant to defray the debts accumulated during the course of construction. Symbolically it demonstrates concretely the *mana* of the giver; therefore motivating a chief to make a large donation.

7. On each of my subsequent trips to Nahigatoka, the large yam of the 1989 harvest has been fondly recalled by my hosts.

8. The requirement of inviting passersby to join a group extends also to gatherings for drinking *yaqona*. These omnipresent sessions complement the community solidarity fostered through sharing meals.

9. The frequency of *kabekabe* contributions became most apparent to me when I had occasion to visit distant villages while administering my survey. For the main noonday meal, cooking responsibilities were divided and assigned to the village's separate *mataqwali*; in the evenings, women brought their additional *kabekabe* to our host's household to help feed us. When I accompanied a household member to her husband's village on the distant island of Nayau, in the Lau Group, a succession of villagers arrived at mealtime and placed their *kabekabe* of boiled root crops and seafood at the threshold of the house, bidding us to eat heartily and enjoy our meal.

10. *Kua ni kana vanasi* is a common expression used to indicate that someone is only picking at his or her food. It probably reflects the stereotype of the (supposed) affectations of young ladies educated at the Fiji School of Nursing and a presumption that women who have experienced urban life and earned wages in hospitals are less traditional in their behavior and more concerned with their appearance than are traditional Fijians.

11. My weight status was the focus of constant attention throughout my fifteen months in Nahigatoka. My hosts frequently compared my more filled-out habitus at that time with my much thinner body during my short visits in 1982 and 1986. Several months after my arrival in 1988, when my initial weight gain was obvious, villagers commented that I was looking healthier. Although my own Western-based issues around body shape made me reluctant to allow my household to make a hobby of fattening me, their behavior did underscore the imperative to demonstrate *viqwaravi* and *vikawaitaki* toward an important guest. After fifteen months and nearly fifteen extra pounds attesting to their superb skills in *viqwaravi*, the owner of the house where I stayed returned from her year-long absence in Australia to see me off. On greeting me, she exclaimed to her relatives that I was still so thin and wondered how they could possibly send me home to my parents.

12. Supernaturally caused illnesses are discussed at length in Chapter 5.

13. The untoward effects on food and on the world in general of pregnant women who are hiding their pregnancies are discussed in Chapter 4.

14. Although I hesitate to use a Western diagnostic nosology in a case where the illness category may substantially differ from the local understanding of this man's behavior, for descriptive purposes Tai Pita appeared to suffer from a chronic, psychotic illness. The local understanding of his eccentricities was that he was *riva* (crazy).

15. I deliberately use Heidegger's language since his ideas on care (*sorge*) address a vacuum in modern, Western society — and further illustrate the cultural gap in relative notions about how the individual is interwoven into the fabric of the social world (see Heidegger 1962). The Fijians have traditionally understood care as a central feature of their interdependent lives, without the benefit of the philosopher.

16. The frequency of mealtime guests in a Fijian household is much higher than in Western households. This is partially due to the obligation to open the household to passersby, and the unavailability of restaurants or lodges in village areas to accommodate travelers. Moreover, the recurrent mobilization of kin groups to attend *holi*, meetings, or mortuary events necessitates frequent travel to distant areas and the concomitant provision of hospitality to travelers.

17. As I discuss in the next chapter, there is explicit hope that feeding a new bride will be rewarded in her regenerating their *mataqwali*. In addition to the careful attention to the diet during pregnancy to avoid teratogenic harm to the fetus, to effect an easy delivery, and to reflect ethnonutritional theories about prenatal care, the desire to feed pregnant women seems to reflect symbolic connections between production and reproduction. Pregnant women present problems with respect to their care, not only because of their eccentric cravings (e.g., for unripe, salted mangoes) but also because of a common and very troubling loss of appetite ascribed to a condition known as *kune bura*, which superficially resembles hyperemesis gravidarum (extreme morning sickness). Women in the first trimester of pregnancy are also thought to show a drastic weight loss in both their faces and bodies, and are therefore encouraged to eat well. Toward the end of the final trimester, however, women are discouraged from eating heartily in an effort to avoid a difficult delivery due to a large infant.

18. *Isa* is an interjection that expresses a multitude of emotions depending on the context. Generally it implies an empathic concern with another's problems.

19. There are sound practical reasons for monitoring a Fijian child's growth and appetite. A 1988 cross-sectional study of children twelve and under in a rural village found 66.7 percent of the sample deficient in their calorie intake and 23 percent deficient in their protein intake (Robertson et al. 1988:30). Moreover, whereas malnutrition was virtually unknown fifty years ago (Johnson 1983:19), pediatric cases are now reaching alarming prevalence in both rural and urban areas, having increased from a total of 68 seen at the Colonial War Memorial Hospital in Suva in 1975, to 178 in 1980 (Lambert 1981:12). More recent reports suggest a slight decrease, with only 47 admissions for malnutrition in the same hospital in the first five months of 1988 (Robertson et al. 1988:3); in the Nadroga health catchment area, the number of recorded pediatric malnutrition cases dropped from 53 in 1983 to 15 in 1987 (Gerona 1988). This illness is probably underreported, however, despite the diligent efforts of the maternal and child health staff nurses in village clinics to identify and treat cases.

The increase in malnutrition is blamed in part on the introduction of Western foods and the concomitant decline in the percentage of breast-fed babies (see Lambert 1981:11). These data illustrate that despite a household's best efforts at *vikawaitaki*, the goal is not always achieved.

20. *Vadabe* refers to a folk illness relating a child's weakened condition to its mother's getting pregnant at an inappropriately short interval between her previous and her current pregnancies. Strict postpartum tabus prohibit sexual intercourse for up to one year; in this sense, a child who is *vadabe* reflects its parents' moral failings.

21. Vasenaca is criticizing this family's ability to provide for their household's needs. Although cassava is a staple crop, it is considered a poor man's food. While perfectly adequate for meals, cassava has the lowest protein content of all the Fijian starchy foods (Aalbersberg 1994). It is not an appealing offering for afternoon tea, when baked goods are often preferred, in particular by children.

22. Vasenaca is making an oblique reference to sacrifices she made in her generosity. Eggs are considered somewhat of a luxury, as is store-bought milk. The way she fed the child is a reflection of her *vikawaitaki*.

23. This Fijian "appetite disorder" must be distinguished from the Western psychiatric category of eating disorders. The appetite disturbance, *macake*, is conceived of culturally as a physiologic, not a psychiatric, illness.

24. Fijians use appetite disturbance as a marker of concern in illness to the exclusion of conventional biomedical symptoms, such as fever. This was made painfully clear to me during one of my own illness episodes. I had complained of high fever and swollen lymph nodes for several days before I was forced to decline meals because of my inflamed tonsils. As soon as my hosts realized I was no longer eating, I was rushed to a local healer, who administered *dranu* and fed me a sweet potato to ascertain its effects on curing my inability to eat. Happily, my symptoms quickly responded to this treatment.

25. The tenor of these comments reflects the level of crisis the child's illness and refusal to eat had precipitated.

26. It is important to note that the acceptance of the *drala* was the ostensible issue to be negotiated. After the child took the medicine, the return of her willingness to eat was a foregone conclusion. The negotiation of appetite in Fiji is not commonly called for — with the exception of very small children. This is forestalled by prophylactic administration of medicines to prevent appetite disturbance. There is no indigenous notion that appetite itself is a negotiable issue; people conceive of eating as both life-sustaining and pleasurable, in contradistinction to the Western notion that appetite is an impulse subject to autonomous control. Indeed, in the Western context the control of appetite is often targeted for negotiation in interchange between anorectic patients and their families. See Minuchin et al. (1978) for a fascinating discussion of the negotiation of this symptom in "anorectic families," and Kahn (1986) and Mageo (1989) for discussions of the control of appetite elsewhere in Melanesia and Polynesia.

27. At this time I had become convinced the child had meningitis, and so intervened in her care. It is not clear when or even whether the family would have modified the diagnosis of appetite disturbance to allow for the possibility of seeking care at the local hospital. Since they relied on my medical assistance from time to time, it is also possible that my presence made them more complacent about Seini's medical care. Even months after Seini's discharge from the hospital, Tai Vani, who understood the diagnosis to have been *mase ni mona*

(brain sickness), maintained that her illness had been rooted in her poor appetite. Members of her *mataqwali* later considered the possibility of spirit etiology; this aspect of her case is discussed in Chapter 5.

28. There are syndromes nearly identical to *macake* in other areas of the South Pacific, including *fefie* in Tonga and *popome* in the Solomon Islands. Although some biomedically oriented researchers have suggested that the whitish covering on the tongue and oral lesions associated with high consumption of sweets reflect oral thrush (candidiasis), this hypothesis has not been clinically proven. I argue that although the symptoms of these two illnesses may overlap, *macake* comprises a far broader category of complaints that focus on appetite disturbance as the cardinal symptom rather than on the physical signs described in the text.

29. The cravings for and consumption of sweet foods sometimes experienced with *macake* only superficially resemble the carbohydrate cravings associated with bulimia. The cultural and personal understanding of *macake* motivates the afflicted individual to seek treatment to augment the appetite for appropriate foods.

30. There are several *dranu* given for *macake*, including *dalahika, drala*, and *sisinitodro*, which are gathered locally and produced as they are needed for treatment. They are all bitter, unpleasant-tasting concoctions, yet children are generally compliant in taking them on a regular basis.

31. I never observed a case in which a treat or a meal was withheld from a child as a punishment. Parents and caretakers do take steps to curb children's consumption of sweets, but they tend to be quite indulgent by comparison with American practices.

32. There is a Tongan appetite disturbance, *puke he faka'avanga*, of which successful cure depends on members of the social network's noticing a lapse in appetite and weight loss. According to Tongan informants, this fairly common illness is initiated when a spirit regularly visits and feeds one in a dream, causing the afflicted person to be sated during the day and to accept only the dream food as primary sustenance. Neither the afflicted individual nor members of the social network may explicitly acknowledge the dreams or the suspicion that a spirit is feeding the individual. A cure is effected when the condition is tacitly observed and treated through appropriate channels. After the fact, the dreamer can acknowledge the spirit's visits. Although one woman developed a signal to circumvent this by saying "We are going on a picnic," this illness generally demands the social network's vigilance in monitoring its members for changes in appetite and body shape. Despite similar requirements to monitor appetite and body shape, I am not aware of a similar illness category in Fiji.

Chapter 4

1. The proverb that serves as an epigraph to this chapter hints at the inescapability of the public gaze, which is the topic for discussion in this chapter. More loosely rendered, it means, "You cannot cover up an act which would normally leave a visible and distinct mark," thus refering to the stigmata that reveal secrets (Pulea 1986:66).

2. The concepts of public and private have arguably evolved as an outgrowth of the modern state dividing these two domains according to surveillance capa-

bilities (Giddens 1991:151). In some ways, because the surveillance in the village is so all-encompassing, privacy is not a meaningful notion. These concepts are used here to indicate the subjective relative exposure of personal experience.

3. Depending on their scope, communal functions (*ogaoga*) often demand village-wide participation. Men are expected to help construct shelters of posts and corrugated tin roofing, to dig earth ovens for cooking, and to pound the ceremonial *yaqona*. Women are charged with butchering meat and preparing the various dishes. Sometimes foods are prepared in the respective households and later brought to the public area, but on most occasions the cooking is done communally. Given the elaborate preparations required for *magisi* in supplying the varieties and sheer quantities of foods, communal cooking is a laborious process. For moral and practical reasons, everyone is expected to participate. Women who are frequently found absent are openly criticized.

4. See also Ravuvu (1987:267) for his comments regarding the importance of continuing the lineage.

5. Marriages were traditionally arranged by the respective *mataqwali* with a view toward building strategic alliances. For example, a family may have sought to create ties with a particular village or chiefly family to gain access to resources or enhance their prestige. Today some marriages are still arranged, although many may reflect the couple's choice. But even in the case of these "love-marriages," as they are dubbed, the family exercises its discretion in facilitating or discouraging the match.

6. Jack Goody observes that in allocating "the reproductive powers over women," the bridewealth, or transfer of property to the groom's kin, is a "kind of prospective childwealth" (1976:8). However, the characterization of the exchange accompanying Fijian marriage ceremonies as "bridewealth" greatly oversimplifies its meaning. As one informant pointed out to me, the exchange is a "way of respecting the kinship . . . that has been formed."

7. In some cases, a man might prefer to ensure his prospective bride's fertility by impregnating her before actually marrying her. For example, a woman who had run away from her home to her fiancé's village was repeatedly warned that he would send her home if she did not become pregnant. They eventually married when she was in her second trimester of a pregnancy.

8. See Chapter 5 for a detailed description of the community monitoring of Ateca's "suspected pregnancy." In this case, a young woman allowed her mother's and others' knowledge about her pregnancy to override her personal bodily experience. In other words, the community astutely perceived information that was not even available to the individual.

9. Although many Fijians enjoy unripe mangoes, this craving is particularly associated with pregnancy. Apparently it has similar associations in Tahiti (Levy 1973:143).

10. Coinciding with the careful monitoring of body shape for signs of pregnancy is an elaborately stipulated protocol regarding the nurturing of a pregnant and postpartum woman. She is fed according to what will not harm her fetus (the most common tabus are pork and prawns) and what will strengthen her (green vegetables, which are not usually favored in the Fijian diet, along with various broths, particularly of the tiny shrimp found in the river). In the final stages of her pregnancy, she is encouraged to eat only lightly and is given a series of *dranu* to lubricate the birth canal. For up to three months in the postpartum period she is relieved of all her usual household chores so that she may regain her strength. Indeed, her primary responsibilities are to nurse her infant and to

eat the food that is prepared and brought (*kabekabe*) to her. If these standards of care are not adhered to, women in the postpartum period are susceptible to *na tadoka ni vasucu* and *cavuka*, two illnesses precipitated by strain during this time. *Na tadoka ni vasucu*, which is characterized by weakness and severe headaches, is relatively benign and treated with a *dranu, totodro*. *Cavuka*, a much more serious consequence of postpartum stress, is locally characterized by "speaking nonsense" and "craziness" and corresponds to a "postpartum psychosis" in Western psychiatric nosology.

11. Illness and misfortune commonly reflect immoral behavior and social discord. This is discussed in detail in Chapter 5.

12. This woman was beaten by her fiancé when he discovered her oral contraceptives. This illustrates the widespread entitlement of husbands, and indeed entire *mataqwali*, to women's reproductive rights. While I do not intend to justify this violence by my argument that the body is "owned" less by the individual than by its social group, its context helps to illuminate its meaning.

13. This phrase is translated literally as "eating and finishing the cassava." It is used idiomatically to refer to women who fail to become pregnant. The saying implies that feeding a woman incurs a debt that she must repay in human resources to the *mataqwali*. One woman explained that it refers to a situation in which "the wife has been using up all the [sweat from his hard work] without . . . repaying . . . you know, the sweat that [the husband] has . . . done on the land . . . that has been feeding her." In her work in New Guinea, Kahn also finds that "sexual energy is conceptualized as food energy" (Kahn 1986:111). Ravuvu has also described the ostracism of barren women (1978:32).

14. The traditional remedy for infertility is a special bath (*hili*), which is usually administered by a woman recognized as having healing skills. Infertility is also traced to a *dukaduka*, or transgressions, in the past of the family a woman has married into. This association has been noted elsewhere in the South Pacific, as well (Kirkpatrick 1977:325).

15. The transfer of emotional or physical pain from personal to social experience through the articulation of symptoms or anxieties is thought to be therapeutic in Fiji.

16. The cultural sanctioning of disclosure of sexual transgressions has an interesting parallel in Foucault's description of the history of the "confession of the flesh" within the Catholic church as a means of transforming "desire into, discourse" (1980:19–21).

17. This syndrome, with its symptoms of burning on urination and urinary frequency, bears remarkable resemblance to "honeymoon cystitis" (a urinary tract infection in the setting of sexual intercourse).

18. There is similar concern with a man's sexual behavior, for example, with his pregnant and postpartum wife. He and his wife are expected to exercise abstinence in late pregnancy and for up to one year after the birth of their child. If he engages in sexual intercourse with his wife shortly before she delivers the infant, the couple fear that his semen will be splashed across the face of the child as tangible evidence of their transgression. Sometimes an infant's grandmother (usually on the maternal side) will sleep with her daughter for an extended period to forestall the husband's advances. Some say that a woman is supposed to avoid making herself attractive to her husband in the postpartum period; the husband is encouraged to drink *yaqona* late with other men rather than approach his wife. If the wife does become pregnant soon after the birth of a baby, the infant is thought to suffer; this casts a moral shadow on the couple.

See Quain (1948:351) and Thompson (1940:85) for additional comments on postpartum tabus on sexual behavior.

Although during his early twentieth-century tenure in Fiji Deane observed that "the amount of sexual immorality and promiscuous intercourse during the last forty years is appalling" (Deane 1921:148), Thomson observed that compared with the oft-cited moral licentiousness of the Polynesian women, "who were as lax as the Melanesians were strict in their social code," the Fijians' sexual mores were relatively conservative (Thomson 1908:234). Contemporary Fijian women are expected to be chaste before marriage and faithfully monogamous after marriage. Fijians do not live in an ideal world, however; in practice many women and men are sexually experienced before marriage, and there are many children born out of wedlock. As a rule, families attempt to supervise the social activities of their daughters and sisters strictly, and they discourage romantic liaisons outside of marriage or formal engagement.

This vested concern may be compared with Foucault's argument in *The History of Sexuality* that discourse on sexuality in the eighteenth century reflected an interest in building a "population." He wrote, "it was essential that the state know what was happening with its citizens' sex, and the use they made of it, but also that each individual be capable of controlling the use he made of it" (Foucault 1980:26). This is not the explicit reason for Fijians' concern with the sexual histories of their society's members, but arguably it may implicitly shape their mores.

19. The fact that Herr's data were collected in Fulaga, which is in many ways culturally distinct from Nadroga, may have some influence on this observation. In her work published in 1941, Dorothy Spencer documented the therapeutic role of confessing, and observed that an admission of sexual transgressions was elicited from both men and women (Spencer 1941:66–67). Although I do not have enough data to establish the frequency with which the confessional is invoked for therapeutic purposes, Fijians clearly consider it therapeutic to relocate problems from the private to the social realm.

20. *Yalo* has been translated as "spirit" or "soul" (Capell 1941a:286), but encompasses the notion of the essence of a person. It has the capacity to detach itself from the body on occasion (usually during sleep) and to visit or enter other persons. *Yalo* generally wander from bodies in the liminal states of illness, near-death, undisclosed pregnancy, or, as described here, wrongdoing.

21. This informant used the common expression *na niju a kana okwe*, literally, "the spirit was eaten here," to describe an instance in which a spirit actually enters the body of a human and speaks through him or her. The concept of possession includes the entry of both *yalo* and *niju* (another class of spirits) into the body. The interactions between humans, *yalo*, and *niju* are discussed in detail in Chapter 5.

22. To catch a spirit (*tobokia*) is to entrap it in a human's body. This is done by twisting a corner of the clothing of the person who begins to manifest signs of possession. Tradition holds that spirits do not much relish being caught, and often offer information in exchange for their release.

23. At this point, my informant was highly amused by her narrative. Apparently she considered it ironic that a *yalo* should appear in the presence of its embodied self. This seems to have been an unusual event.

24. The *mataqwali* executes this public punishment for a serious transgression. In this case, it is clear that the kinship group accepts responsibility for the moral discipline of its members.

25. This inadvertent participation in moral disclosure is a complex issue which is discussed at length in the next chapter.

26. I was unable to fathom the meaning of either this act or that of throwing a stone into the sea.

27. Fijians indicated that the association between undisclosed pregnancy and its manifestations is empirically and overwhelmingly validated in experience.

28. Residency in Fijian households is often quite fluid, allowing for guests to come and help with chores for an extended period of time, if desired.

29. This young woman had told me of her suspicions that she was pregnant very early on when ostensibly seeking medical advice. She also confided in another woman, who must have told a number of persons in the household, because several people had knowledge of it. Thus the pregnancy was no secret, although it had not been properly disclosed. She was ambivalent about her pregnancy because her resources were already strained in caring for one child as a single parent.

The requirement for formal disclosure in this case distinguishes it from the nonspecific disclosure allowable in the description of *cavucavu*. This difference may be due to the relative gravity of the secret; it may also be derived from the complex protocols in introducing a child to its new social world. See Ravuvu (1983:52–61) for a detailed account of these traditional practices.

30. Although theoretically a measles vaccine should prevent the illness, a number of immunized children were treated for measles at the Sigatoka District Hospital during this period.

31. Parallel cousins — the children of two brothers or two sisters — are classificatory siblings by Fijian kinship reckoning. The same-sex classificatory or biologic sibling of a parent is also in the relationship category of parent — a classificatory mother or father — to the offspring. In this case, a parallel cousin of the child's mother (that is, the child's mother's mother and the child's mother's cousin's mother are biological sisters), is referred to as mother by the child.

32. It is worth remembering that, in Fijian ethno-psychology, worrying caused by social disruption or loss is primarily manifested in a loss of appetite.

33. It is not entirely clear how Jioji's mother weighed the decision whether to disclose her pregnancy or to seek temporary childcare for her son. Some women are ashamed to speak directly of their pregnancies; they wait for the information to reveal itself through various signs so that someone will ask them whether they are pregnant. What can be inferred here is her experience of herself as toxic to her son and her concern about that.

34. This example somewhat resembles Csordas's description of "somatic modes of attention" as "culturally elaborated ways of attending to and with one's body" (1993:135–56).

35. The timing of the revelation is, of course, only a relative matter, since an obviously gravid belly and then an infant will be the ultimate natural manifestation of this "secret" in any case. What distinguishes this event in Fiji, however, is the premature release of the secret from the individual body, either to other bodies or into the environment at large.

Chapter 5

1. Fijian spirits are not homogeneous. They may be roughly divided into three categories: *yalo*, the essence of a human being (living or dead) or some action

or aspect of a human being (such as a *yalo* of wrongdoing [*yalo ni cala*] or of pregnancy [*yalo ni bukese*]); *niju*, or parahuman beings; and *vu*, or ancestral spirits.

The actions of *yalo* are discussed in Chapter 4. *Vu*, often manifest in living animal forms such as a dog or a shark, may entangle themselves with human lives either when they are personally offended by immoral acts or when their assistance is solicited by humans for purposes of revenge. *Niju* may also assist in avenging a personal wrong. Alternatively, they may prey upon humans who provoke them with their trespasses. Although some are conceived of as relatively innocuous and reside in villages while rarely disturbing their human neighbors, others have gained formidable reputations as agents plaguing humans. These *niju* frequently assume human forms for purposes of trickery or inflicting harm. However, a spirit presence is not necessarily always materialized in human or even visible form. Often it manifests itself simply as a force, a voice, or an illness.

Since Fijians themselves use these terms to refer to a rather ambiguous range of possibilities, I collapse the categories of supernatural powers and manifestations as *niju* or "spirit" related without designating the particular type in this chapter.

2. A detailed case of a waking visitation is offered in the *yalo ni cala* episode described in Chapter 4.

3. Despite the potential secondary gain attached to a spirit affliction through legitimating a personal agenda, a great deal of ambivalence attends these visitations, as indicated by the panoply of prophylactic measures to discourage them (e.g., lemon leaves and Bibles are left near the bed to ward off spirits, and toes and fingers are curled when a spirit approaches). To a degree, this ambivalence may derive from the inconvenience of being a public scapegoat for community ills; on the other hand, it may stem from discomfort in articulating personal needs.

4. Erika Bourguignon highlights several features of possession trance that are relevant to spirit possession in the Fiji context. She characterizes possession trances as "an impersonation of another being on an occasion when there are witnesses" (1976b:53) and likens them to "playing of roles before an audience" (52) whereby "the individual may be able to modify social constraints and the behavior of others and thus enlarge the scope of actions open to himself" (51–53). Similarly, Bilu and Beit-Hallahmi show that the *Dybbuk*—the traditional Jewish variant of spirit possession—effects a "working alliance between society and a selected group of deviants," allowing the expression of conventionally forbidden urges and desires (Bilu and Beit-Hallahmi 1989:138 and 143).

5. For example, there are several *niju* called *juwawa* (giants) that have lived near the chiefly compound in Nahigatoka Village as long as anyone can remember. They have been quiescent in the past several years, however, with no sightings reported. Another *niju*, *Dauhina* (known as *Daucina* in standard Fijian) seems ubiquitous in the island group and also quite active in Nahigatoka.

6. The specter of the *niju* is often invoked to frighten children ("Watch out, there are *niju* out there!"), shrug off the inexplicable (*Bara sa niju*, "Maybe it's the devil"), or portray a human with disagreeable qualities (e.g., *mata vaniju*, "devil face").

7. Wandering alone at night, particularly for young women, is discouraged, and is often enough provocation for a *niju* visitation. Some areas are known to be populated with contentious *niju* who prey on humans unlucky enough to

tread on their grounds. Near Natadola Beach, *niju* are said to live under the water and periodically drown unsuspecting swimmers.

8. Alternatively, these may be reconstructed as psychopathologic symptoms. A psychiatric case report formulates one such woman's phenomenologic experience, akin to what the Fijians describe, as "multi-modal hallucinations with delusions" (Douglass and Hays 1987:57).

9. According to Hufford, the crucial point, however, is that the clinical reconstruction — or "dis-interpretation," as he aptly puts it — is merely a description of physiological events that fails to account for their cross-culturally consistent interpretation as paranormal (Hufford 1982).

10. A reduction of the phenomena of *niju* visitation to its neurophysiologic basis fails to provide a satisfying account of the local meanings and contexts of these events.

11. In this particular case, the man appeared to be her father; when she screamed, he disappeared. A favorite ploy of the *niju* is to seduce or inspire confidence in a would-be victim by disguising itself as an attractive or trusted man or woman.

12. *Dauhina* is often manifested as a light, usually white or green. His name literally means "always shining."

13. A formal wedding ceremony is often delayed in Fiji, so it is not unusual for a couple to be functioning as a married pair before their marriage is legal.

14. Since *niju* are sometimes associated with a Christian concept of the devil, Fijians often invoke prayer or Christian symbols such as the Bible to protect themselves against harm or visitations from spirits.

Chapter 6

1. In fact, many features of the Fijian cultural milieu militate *against* the emergence of symptoms of anorexia nervosa. For example, as opposed to Western cultures in which anorexia is prevalent, in Fiji there is a disinclination to diet to look thin, a lack of explicit knowledge about the economy of calories in the body through food intake and energy expenditure, and a mealtime vigilance in tracking any appetite changes. Most important, however, is the different relationship of the Fijian with his or her body, which is not culturally made into an object for personal, self-reflexive control and cultivation.

2. An owl is said to cry at midnight at the home of a person whose death is imminent, another time at which the *yalo* can wander from the body, and at which there is the threat of social rupture by the impending death.

3. The exact translation is crucial to the point here. The possessive pronoun is *mea*, which literally translated means "[whose] to drink."

Appendix B

1. The almost-exclusively female research assistants were probably able to administer the questionnaire to both sexes because of its similarity to a standard government bureaucratic activity in which traditional gender restrictions are somewhat suspended.

2. In cases of participants too infirm or busy to leave home, an assistant administered the survey in their households.

3. Although the Nadroga dialect is not officially a written language, its sounds are virtually identical to those in Standard Fijian, and the questionnaire successfully used Standard Fijian orthography to represent the Nadroga dialect in written form (see Appendix A).

Bibliography

Aalbersberg, Bill. 1994. Personal communication. July.

Abusah, Prosper. 1992. Letter to the author. October 12.

——. 1994. Letter to the author. February 20.

Abraham, Susan et al. 1983. "Eating Behaviours among Young Women." *Medical Journal of Australia* 3:225–28.

Ali, Ahmed. 1980. *Plantation to Politics*. Suva, Fiji: University of the South Pacific.

American Psychiatric Association. 1994. *Diagnostic and Statistical Manual of Mental Disorders*. 4th ed., rev. Washington, D.C.: American Psychiatric Association.

Baddeley, Josephine. 1985. "Traditional Healing Practices." In *Healing Practices in the South Pacific*, ed. Claire D. F. Parsons. Honolulu: Institute for Polynesian Studies.

Battaglia, Debbora. 1995. "Problematizing and the Self: A Thematic Introduction." In *Rhetorics of Self-Making*, ed. Debbora Battaglia. Berkeley: University of California Press.

Becker, Anne. 1986. "Food for Thought." Manuscript.

——. 1988. "Diet and Body Image in a College Population: A Sample Survey." Manuscript.

Bell, Rudolph M. 1985. *Holy Anorexia*. Chicago: University of Chicago Press.

Belshaw, Cyril. 1964. *Under the Ivi Tree: Society and Economic Growth in Rural Fiji*. Berkeley: University of California Press.

Biggs, Bruce. 1985 "Contemporary Healing Practices in East Futuna." In *Healing Practices in the South Pacific*, ed. Claire D. F. Parsons. Honolulu: The Institute for Polynesian Studies.

Bilu, Yorum and Benjamin Beit-Hallahmi. 1989. "Dybbuk-Possession as a Hysterical Symptom: Psychodynamic and Sociocultural Factors." *Israeli Journal of Psychiatry and Related Sciences* 26:138–49.

Bok, Sissela. 1983. *Secrets*. New York: Vintage Books.

Bordo, Susan. 1993. *Unbearable Weight: Feminism, Western Culture, and the Body*. Berkeley: University of California Press.

Bourdieu, Pierre. 1984. *Distinction*. Cambridge, Mass.: Harvard University Press.

Bourguignon, Erika. 1976a. *Possession*. San Francisco: Chandler & Sharp.

——. 1976b. "Possession and Trance in Cross-Cultural Studies of Mental Health." In *Culture-Bound Syndromes, Ethnopsychiatry, and Alternate Therapies*, ed. William P. Lebra. Honolulu: University of Hawaii Press.

Boyarin, Jonathan and Daniel Boyarin. 1995. "Self-Exposure as Theory: The

Double Mark of the Male Jew." In *Rhetorics of Self-Making*, ed. Debbora Battaglia. Berkeley: University of California Press.

Brock, Philip. 1994. Personal communication. February.

Bruch, Hilde. 1973. *Eating Disorders*. New York: Basic Books.

Brumberg, Joan Jacobs. 1988. *Fasting Girls: The History of Anorexia Nervosa*. Cambridge, Mass.: Harvard University Press. Reprint. New York: Plume, 1989.

Bynum, Caroline Walker. 1985. "Fast, Feast, and Flesh: The Religious Significance of Food to Medieval Women." *Representations* 11 (Summer): 1–25.

Capell, A. 1941a. *A New Fijian Dictionary*. Suva, Fiji: Government of Fiji. Reprint, 1984.

———. 1941b. "The Nature of Fijian Totemism." *Fiji Society* 2:59–67.

Cash, Thomas F. 1990. "The Psychology of Physical Appearance: Aesthetics, Attributes, and Images." In *Body Images: Development, Deviance, and Change*, ed. Thomas F. Cash and Thomas Pruzinsky, New York: Guilford Press.

Chu, Godwin C. 1985. "The Changing Concept of Self in Contemporary China." In *Culture and Self*, ed. Anthony J. Marsella, et al. New York: Tavistock.

Clunie, Fergus. 1977. "Fijian Weapons & Warfare." *Bulletin of the Fiji Museum*, no. 2.

Cooper, Peter J. et al. 1984. "Women with Eating Problems: A Community Survey." *British Journal of Clinical Psychology* 23:45–52.

Csordas, Thomas. 1990. "Embodiment as a Paradigm for Anthropology." *Ethos* 18:5–47.

———. 1993. "Somatic Modes of Attention." *Cultural Anthropology* 8:135–56.

———, ed. 1994. *Embodiment and Experience: The Existential Ground of Culture and Self*. Cambridge: Cambridge University Press.

Das, Veena. n.d. "What Do We Mean by Health?" Manuscript.

Dean, Eddie with Stan Ritova. 1988. *Rabuka No Other Way*. Suva, Fiji: Marketing Team International.

Deane, Rev. W. 1921. *Fijian Society, or the Sociology and Psychology of the Fijians*. London: Macmillan.

Dimuri, Josefa. 1988. "Rabuka Warns on Constitution." *Fiji Times*. December 10, 1.

Douglas, Mary. 1971. "Deciphering a Meal." In *Myth, Symbol, and Culture*, ed. Clifford Geertz. New York: W. W. Norton.

———. 1982. *Natural Symbols: Explorations in Cosmology*. New York: Pantheon.

Douglass, Alan B. and Peter Hays. 1987. "Three Simultaneous Major Sleep Disorders." *Canadian Journal of Psychiatry* 32:57–60.

Durkheim, Emile. 1933. *The Division of Labor in Society*. New York: Macmillan. Reprint New York: Free Press, 1964.

Ernsberger, Paul and Paul Haskew. 1987. "Health Implications of Obesity: An Alternative View." *Journal of Obesity and Weight Regulation* 6:2–81.

Errington, Shelly. 1977. "Order and Power in Karavar." In *The Anthropology of Power: Ethnographic Studies from Asia, Oceania, and the New World*, ed. Raymond D. Fogelson and Richard N. Adams. New York: Academic Press.

Ewing, Katherine P. 1990. "The Illusion of Wholeness: Culture, Self, and the Experience of Inconsistency." *Ethos* 18:251–78.

Fajans, Jane. 1985. "The Person in Social Context: The Social Character of Baining 'Psychology.'" In *Person, Self, and Experience*, ed. by Geoffrey White and John Kirkpatrick. Berkeley: University of California Press.

Fallon, April. 1990. "Culture in the Mirror: Sociocultural Determinants of Body

Image." In *Body Images: Development, Deviance, and Change*, ed. Thomas F. Cash and Thomas Pruzinsky. New York: Guilford Press.

Feldman, W. et al. 1988. "Culture versus Biology: Children's Attitudes Towards Thinness and Fatness." *Pediatrics* 81:190–94.

Fiji Food & Nutrition Newsletter. 1986. "A Peep at the Scales." 7(1):1.

Firth, Raymond. 1963. *We, the Tikopia*. Boston: Beacon Press.

Fisher, Seymour. 1974. *Body Consciousness*. New York: Jason Aronson.

Foster, Robert J. 1990. "Nurture and Force-Feeding: Mortuary Feasting and the Construction of Collective Individuals in a New Ireland Society." *American Ethnologist* 17:431–48.

Foucault, Michel. 1975. *The Birth of the Clinic*. New York: Vintage Books.

——. 1979. *Discipline and Punish*. New York: Vintage Books.

——. 1980. *The History of Sexuality*. Vol. 1. New York: Vintage Books.

——. 1988. *The Care of the Self*. New York: Vintage Books.

Furnham, Adrian, and Naznin Alibhai. 1983. "Cross-Cultural Differences in the Perception of Female Body Shapes." *Psychological Medicine* 13:829–37.

Garfinkel, Paul E. and David M. Garner, 1983. "The Multidetermined Nature of Anorexia Nervosa." In *Anorexia Nervosa: Recent Developments in Research*, ed. Padraig L. Darby et al. New York: Alan R. Liss.

Garner, David et al. 1980. "Cultural Expectations of Thinness in Women." *Psychological Reports* 47:483–91.

——. 1983. "An Overview of Sociocultural Factors in the Development of Anorexia Nervosa." In *Anorexia Nervosa: Recent Developments in Research*, ed. Padraig L. Darby et al. New York: Alan R. Liss.

——. 1984. "Comparison Between Weight-Preoccupied Women and Anorexia Nervosa." *Psychosomatic Medicine* 46:255–66.

Gatty, Ronald. n.d. "Foods of the Fijian People, Book One of the Fijians: Life and Language of a South Sea Island People." Manuscript.

Geertz, Clifford. 1983. *Local Knowledge*. New York: Basic Books.

Geraghty, Paul. 1983. *The History of the Fijian Languages*. Honolulu: University of Hawaii Press.

——. 1988–89. Personal communication. Suva, Fiji.

Gerona, Rudy. 1988. Address at a Fiji National Food and Nutrition Committee Workshop, Keiyasi Village.

Gibson, Penny. 1990. "Cashing In on a Boom Industry." *Pacific Islands Monthly*, March, pp. 34–36.

Giddens, Anthony. 1991. *Modernity and Self-Identity: Self and Society in the Late Modern Age*. Stanford, Calif.: Stanford University Press.

Gilligan, Carol. 1982. *In a Different Voice*. Cambridge, Mass.: Harvard University Press.

Goffman, Erving. 1959. *The Presentation of Self in Everyday Life*. New York: Doubleday/Anchor.

——. 1963. *Stigma*. Englewoods Cliffs, N. J.: Prentice-Hall.

Good, Byron J. 1977. "The Heart of What's the Matter: The Semantics of Illness in Iran." *Culture, Medicine and Psychiatry* 1:25–58.

——. 1992. "A Body in Pain — The Making of a World of Chronic Pain." In *Pain as Human Experience: An Anthropological Perspective*, ed. Mary-Jo DelVecchio Good, et al. Berkeley: University of California Press.

Good, Byron J. et al. 1985. "Reflexivity, Countertransference and Clinical Ethnography: A Case from a Psychiatric Cultural Consultation Clinic." In

Physicians of Western Medicine, ed. R. A. Hahn and A. D. Gaines. Dordrecht: D. Reidel.

Good, Byron and Mary-Jo DelVecchio Good. 1982. "Toward a Meaning-Centered Analysis of Popular Illness Categories: 'Fright Illness' and 'Heart Distress' in Iran." In *Cultural Conceptions of Mental Health and Therapy*, ed. A. J. Marsella and G. M. White. Dordrecht: D. Reidel.

Goody, Jack. 1976. *Production and Reproduction.* Cambridge: Cambridge University Press.

————. 1982. *Cooking, Cuisine and Class.* Cambridge: Cambridge University Press.

Gordon, Deborah B. 1988. "Tenacious Assumptions in Western Medicine." In *Biomedicine Examined*, ed. M. Lock and D. R. Gordon. Dordrecht: Kluwer Academic Publishers.

Gray, David S. 1989. "Diagnosis and Prevalence of Obesity." *Medical Clinics of North America* 73(1): 1–11.

Hallowell, A. Irving. 1967. *Culture and Experience.* New York: Schocken Books.

Harris, Grace Gredys. 1989. "Concepts of Individual, Self, and Person in Description and Analysis." *American Anthropologist* 91:599–612.

Hawley, T. G. and A. A. J. Jansen. 1971. "Weight, Height, Bodysurface and Overweight of Fijian Adults from Coastal Areas." *New Zealand Medical Journal* 74:18–21.

Hecht, Julia A. 1985. "Physical and Social Boundaries in Pukapukan Theories of Disease." In *Healing Practices in the South Pacific*, ed. Claire D. F. Parsons. Honolulu: Institute for Polynesian Studies.

Heidegger, Martin. 1962. *Being and Time.* Translated by John Marquarie and Edward Robinson. New York: Harper & Row.

Herr, Barbara. 1981. "The Expressive Character of Fijian Dream and Nightmare Experiences." *Ethos* 9:331–52.

Holland, Dorothy and Andrew Kipnis. 1994. "Metaphors for Embarrassment and Stories of Exposure: The Not-So-Egocentric Self in American Culture." *Ethos* 22:316–42.

Hooper, Anthony. 1985. "Tahitian Healing." In *Healing Practices in the South Pacific*, ed. Claire D. F. Parsons. Honolulu: Institute for Polynesian Studies.

Howard, Alan. 1990. "Cultural Paradigms, History, and the Search for Identity in Oceania." In *Cultural Identity and Ethnicity in the Pacific*, ed. Jocelyn Linnekin and Lin Poyer. Honolulu: University of Hawaii Press.

Hufford, David J. 1982. *The Terror That Comes in the Night.* Philadelphia: University of Pennsylvania Press.

Illich, Ivan. 1986. "Body History." *Lancet* (December 6): 1325–27.

Islands Business. 1982. "The Diet of Death." November.

Ito, Karen L. 1985. "Affective Bonds: Hawaiian Interrelationships of Self." In *Person, Self, and Experience*, ed. Geoffrey White and John Kirkpatrick. Berkeley: University of California Press.

Johnson, J. S. 1983. "A National Food and Nutrition Policy for Fiji." *Food and Nutrition* 8:19–26.

Johnson, Patricia L. 1981. "When Dying is Better than Living: Female Suicide among the Gainj of Papua New Guinea." *Ethnology* 20:325–34.

Kahn, Miriam. 1986. *Always Hungry, Never Greedy.* Cambridge: Cambridge University Press.

Katz, Richard. 1981. "Education as Transformation: Becoming a Healer among the !Kung and the Fijians." *Harvard Educational Review* 51(1) (February):57–78.

——. 1982. *Boiling Energy.* Cambridge, Mass.: Harvard University Press.

Katz, Richard and Linda A. Kilner. 1987. "The Straight Path: A Fijian Perspective on a Transformational Model of Development." In *The Role of Culture in Developmental Disorder,* ed. Charles M. Super. San Diego, Calif.: Academic Press, Inc. 1987.

Keith-Reid, Robert. 1988. "Pacific Food." *Islands,* April/June, pp. 4–8.

Kikau, Eci. 1981. *The Wisdom of Fiji.* Suva, Fiji: Institute of Pacific Studies.

Kirkpatrick, John and Geoffrey M. White. 1985. "Exploring Ethnopsychologies." In *Person, Self, and Experience,* ed. Geoffrey White and John Kirkpatrick. Berkeley: University of California Press.

Kirkpatrick, John T. 1977. "Person, Hierarchy, and Autonomy in Traditional Yapese Theory." In *Symbolic Anthropology: A Reader in the Study of Symbols and Meanings,* ed. Janet L. Dolgin, David S. Kemnitzer, and David M. Schneider. New York: Columbia University Press.

Kleinman, Arthur. 1978. "Concepts and a Model for the Comparison of Medical Systems as Cultural Systems." *Social Science and Medicine* 12:85–93.

——. 1988a. *The Illness Narratives.* New York: Basic Books.

——. 1988b. *Rethinking Psychiatry.* New York: Free Press.

Koskinen, Aarne A. 1968. **kite: Polynesian Insights into Knowledge.* Helsinki: Finnish Society for Missiology and Ecumenics.

Kumar, Vijendra. 1988. "Radical New Charter For Fiji." *Pacific Islands Monthly* 59(11)(November):16–17.

Laing R. D. 1965. *The Divided Self.* Harmondsworth: Penguin.

——. 1971. *Self and Others.* Harmondsworth: Penguin.

Lambert, Julian. n.d. "The Effect of Urbanization and Western Foods on Infant and Maternal Nutrition in the South Pacific." *Food and Nutrition Bulletin* 4(3):11–13.

Langness, Lewis. 1976. "Hysterical Psychoses and Possessions." In *Culture-Bound Syndromes, Ethnopsychiatry, and Alternate Therapies,* ed. William P. Lebra. Honolulu: University of Hawaii Press.

Lasch, Christopher. 1979. *The Culture of Narcissism.* New York: Warner Books.

Leenhardt, Maurice. 1979. *Do Kamo.* Chicago: University of Chicago Press.

Lévi-Strauss, Claude. 1963. *Totemism.* Boston: Beacon Press.

——. 1985. *The View from Afar.* New York: Basic Books.

Levy, Robert I. 1973. *Tahitians: Mind and Experience in the Society Islands.* Chicago: University of Chicago Press.

Lieber, Michael D. 1990. "Lamarckian Definitions of Identity on Kapingamarangi and Pohnpei." In *Cultural Identity and Ethnicity in the Pacific,* ed. Jocelyn Linnekin and Lin Poyer. Honolulu: University of Hawaii Press.

Linnekin, Jocelyn and Lin Poyer. 1990. "Introduction." In *Cultural Identity and Ethnicity in the Pacific,* ed. Jocelyn Linnekin and Lin Poyer. Honolulu: University of Hawaii Press.

Loudon, Bruce. 1988. "One Year After the Coup." *Pacific Islands Monthly* 59(6)(June):17.

Ludvigson, Tomas. 1985. "Healing in Central Espiritu Santo, Vanuatu." In *Healing Practices in the South Pacific,* ed. Claire D. F. Parsons. Honolulu: Institute for Polynesian Studies.

Lutz, Catherine. 1985. "Ethnopsychology Compared to What? Explaining Behavior and Consciousness among the Ifaluk." In *Person, Self, and Experience,* ed. Geoffrey White and John Kirkpatrick. Berkeley: University of California Press.

Macdonald, Judith. 1985. "Contemporary Healing Practices in Tikopia, Solomon Islands." In *Healing Practices in the South Pacific*, ed. Claire D. F. Parsons. Honolulu: Institute for Polynesian Studies.

Mackenzie, Margaret. 1977. "*Mana* in Maori Medicine—Rarotonga, Oceania." In *The Anthropology of Power: Ethnographic Studies from Asia, Oceania, and the New World*, ed. Raymond D. Fogelson and Richard N. Adams. New York: Academic Press.

———. 1985. "The Pursuit of Slenderness and Addiction to Self-Control." In *Nutrition Update*, Vol. 2, ed. Jean Weininger and George M. Briggs. New York: John Wiley & Sons.

Macpherson, Cluny. 1985. "Samoan Medicine." In *Healing Practices in the South Pacific*, ed. Claire D. F. Parsons. Honolulu: Institute for Polynesian Studies.

Mageo, Jeannette Marie. 1989. "'Ferocious Is the Centipede': A Study of the Significance of Eating and Speaking in Samoa." *Ethos* 17:387–427.

Markus, Hazel R. and Shinobu Kitayama. 1991. "Culture and Self: Implications for Cognition, Emotion, and Motivation." *Psychological Review* 98:224–53.

Marsella, Anthony J. 1985. "Culture, Self, and Mental Disorder." In *Culture and Self*, ed. Anthony J. Marsella, et al. New York: Tavistock.

Martin, Emily. 1987. *The Woman in the Body*. Boston: Beacon Press.

Mauss, Marcel. 1967. *The Gift*. New York: W. W. Norton.

Meigs, Anna. 1984. *Food, Sex, and Pollution*. New Brunswick, N.J.: Rutgers University Press.

Millman, Marcia. 1981. *Such a Pretty Face: Being Fat in America*. New York: Berkeley Books.

Minuchin, Salvador et al. 1978. *Psychosomatic Families*. Cambridge, Mass.: Harvard University Press.

Moore, Dan C. 1988. "Body Image and Eating Behavior in Adolescent Girls." *American Journal of Diseases in Children* 142:1114–18.

Morris, Charles. 1962. *Mind, Self, and Society from the Standpoint of a Social Behaviorist*. Volume 1 of the Works of George Herbert Mead. Chicago: University of Chicago Press.

Murphy, Robert F. 1987. *The Body Silent*. New York: Henry Holt.

Murray, D. W. 1993. "What is the Western Concept of the Self? On Forgetting David Hume." *Ethos* 21:3–23.

Narokobi, Bernard. 1983. *The Melanesian Way*. Papua: Institute of Papua New Guinea Studies; Suva, Fiji: Institute of Pacific Studies of the University of the South Pacific.

Nayacakalou, R. R. 1975. *Leadership in Fiji*. Melbourne: Oxford University Press.

Parkinson, Susan. 1983. "Food and Health in the South Pacific." Manuscript. Suva, Fiji.

———. 1990. "The Feeding of Infants and Young Children." In *Food and Nutrition in Fiji: A Historical Review*, Vol. 1, ed. A. A. J. Jansen, S. Parkinson, and A. F. S. Robertson. Suva, Fiji: University of the South Pacific.

Parsons, Claire. 1985a. "Notes on Maori Sickness Knowledge and Healing Practices." In *Healing Practices in the South Pacific*, ed. Claire D. F. Parsons. Honolulu: Institute for Polynesian Studies.

———. 1985b. "Tongan Healing Practices." In *Healing Practices in the South Pacific*, ed. Claire D. F. Parsons. Honolulu: Institute for Polynesian Studies.

Pollock, Nancy. 1985. "The Concept of Food in a Pacific Society: A Fijian Example." *Ecology of Food and Nutrition* 17:195–203.

———. n.d. "The Relationship of Energy Intake and Expenditure to Body Fatness in Wallis." Manuscript.

Pope, Harrison G. et al. 1985. "Bulimia in the Late Nineteenth Century: The Observations of Pierre Janet." *Psychological Medicine* 15:739–43.

Pope, Harrison G. and James I. Hudson. 1984. *New Hope for Binge Eaters.* New York: Harper and Row.

Powers, Pamela D. and Marilyn T. Erickson. 1986. "Body-Image in Women and Its Relationship to Self-Image and Body Satisfaction." *Journal of Obesity and Weight Regulation* 5(1):37–50.

Premdas, Ralph R. 1986. "Ethnic Conflict Management: A Government of National Unity and Some Alterative Proposals." In *Politics in Fiji*, ed. Brij Lal. Sydney: Allen and Unwin.

Pulea, Mere. 1986. *The Family, Law and Population in the Pacific Islands.* Suva, Fiji: Institute of Pacific Studies of the University of the South Pacific.

Quain, Buell. 1948. *Fijian Village.* Chicago: University of Chicago Press.

Ravuvu, Asesela. 1978. "Sex Attitudes and Family Size in Fiji." *Pacific Perspective* 7:31–35.

———. 1983. *Vaka i Taukei: The Fijian Way of Life.* Suva, Fiji: Institute of Pacific Studies of the University of the South Pacific.

———. 1987. *The Fijian Ethos.* Suva, Fiji: Institute of Pacific Studies of the University of the South Pacific.

———. 1988. *Development or Dependence.* Suva, Fiji: Institute of Pacific Studies of the University of the South Pacific.

———. 1991. "A Fijian Cultural Perspective on Food." In *Food and Nutrition in Fiji: A Historical Review*, Vol. 2, ed. A. A. J. Jansen, S. Parkinson, and A. F. S. Robertson. Suva, Fiji: University of the South Pacific.

Read, K. E. 1955. "Morality and the Concept of the Person Among the Gahuku-Gama." *Oceania* 25:233–82.

Ritenbaugh, Cheryl. 1982. "Obesity as a Culture Bound Syndrome." *Culture, Medicine and Psychiatry* 6:287–94.

Robertson, Annette et al. 1988. "Prevalence Rate of Malnutrition Among 0–12 Year Olds in Nakavu Village, Namosi." Suva: Manuscript.

Rosaldo, Michelle Zimbalist. 1984. "Toward an Anthropology of Self and Feeling." In *Culture Theory: Essays on Mind, Self, and Emotion*, ed. Richard A. Shweder and Robert A. LeVine. Cambridge: Cambridge University Press.

Rosaldo, Renato. 1984. "Grief and a Headhunter's Rage: On the Cultural Force of Emotions." In *Text, Play, and Story: The Construction and Reconstruction of Self and Society*, ed. E. Bruner. Washington, D.C.: American Ethnological Society.

Roth, G. K. 1973. *Fijian Way of Life.* Melbourne: Oxford University Press.

Routledge, David. 1985. *Matanitu: The Struggle for Power in Early Fiji.* Suva, Fiji: Institute of Pacific Studies of the University of the South Pacific.

Sahlins, Marshall. 1962. *Moala: Culture and Nature on a Fijian Island.* Ann Arbor: University of Michigan Press.

———. 1985. *Islands of History.* Chicago: University of Chicago Press.

SAS Institute, Inc. 1990. *SAS Procedures Guide*, Version 6. Third edition. Cary, N.C.: SAS Institute, Inc.

Scheper-Hughes, Nancy and Margaret M. Lock. 1987. "The Mindful Body: A Prolegomenon to Future Work in Medical Anthropology. *Medical Anthropology Quarterly* 1 (March): 6–41.

Schwartz, Donald M. et al. 1983. "Eating Disorders and the Culture." In *Anorexia

Nervosa: Recent Developments in Research, ed. Padraig L. Darby et al. New York: Alan R. Liss.

Shilling, Chris. 1993. *The Body and Social Theory.* London: Sage Publications.

Shore, Bradd. 1982. *Sala'ilua: A Samoan Mystery.* New York: Columbia University Press.

———. 1989. "*Mana and Tapu.*" In *Developments in Polynesian Ethnology,* ed. Alan Howard and Robert Borofsky. Honolulu: University of Hawaii Press.

Showalter, Elaine. 1985. *The Female Malady.* New York: Penguin Books.

Shweder, Richard A. and Edmund J. Bourne. 1984. "Does the Concept of the Person Vary Cross-Culturally?" In *Culture Theory: Essays on Mind, Self, and Emotion,* ed. Richard A. Shweder and Robert A. LeVine. Cambridge: Cambridge University Press.

Silverstein, Brett, Barbara Peterson, and Lauren Perdue. 1986. "Some Correlates of the Thin Standard of Bodily Attractiveness for Women." *International Journal of Eating Disorders* 5:895–905.

Silverstein, Brett et al. 1986. "Possible Causes of Thin Standard of Bodily Attractiveness for Women." *International Journal of Eating Disorders* 5:907–16.

Sontag, Susan. 1979. *Illness as Metaphor.* New York: Vintage Books.

———. 1989. *AIDS and Its Metaphors.* New York: Farrar, Straus and Giroux.

Spencer, Dorothy M. 1937. "Fijian Dreams and Visions." In *Twenty-fifth Anniversary Studies,* ed. Daniel S. Davidson. Publications of the Philadelphia Anthropological Society 1. Philadelphia: University of Pennsylvania Press. 199–210.

———. 1941. *Disease, Religion and Society in the Fiji Islands.* Monographs of the American Ethnological Society. Seattle: University of Washington Press. Reprinted 1966.

Spiro, Melford E. 1993. "Is the Western Concept of the Self 'Peculiar' Within the Context of the World Cultures?" *Ethos* 21:107–53.

Stern, Daniel N. 1985. *The Interpersonal World of the Infant: A View from Psychoanalysis and Developmental Psychology.* New York: Basic Books.

Strathern, Andrew. 1973. "Kinship, Descent and Locality: Some New Guinea Examples." In *The Character of Kinship,* ed. J. Goody. Cambridge: Cambridge University Press.

Strathern, Marilyn. 1988. *The Gender of the Gift: Problems with Women and Problems with Society in Melanesia.* Berkeley: University of California Press.

Strunkard, Albert. 1990. "A Description of Eating Disorders in 1932." *American Journal of Psychiatry* 147:263–68.

Suleiman, Susan R., ed. 1985. *The Female Body in Western Culture: Contemporary Perspectives.* Cambridge, Mass.: Harvard University Press.

Tahi, Onneyn Morris. n.d. "Melanesia: A Poem." *Pacific Identity, Pacific Perspective* 12(2):61.

Taylor, Charles. 1991. *The Ethics of Authenticity.* Cambridge, Mass.: Harvard University Press.

Thaman, Randolph R. 1993. "Pacific Islands: Education for Nutrition-Oriented Development (NORD) in the Pacific Islands: Problems, Needs, Capabilities and Prospects." In *Guidelines for Curriculum Content in Food and Nutrition Planning and Management: Proceedings from the Second FNP Workshop, 8–13 November 1982, Jakarta, Indonesia,* ed. R. C. Orozco, I. Jus'at, C. V. C. Barba, and M. Jakarta Nube. Akademie Gizi, Los Banos: Regional Training Program on Food and Nutrition Planning, University of Philippines; and Wageningen: Netherlands Universities Foundation for International Cooperation: 23–31.

Thompson, Laura. 1940. *Southern Lau, Fiji: An Ethnography.* Honolulu: Bernice P. Bishop Museum.

Thomson, Basil. 1908. *The Fijians: A Study of Decay of Custom.* London: William Heinemann.

Tiko, Samisoni. 1988a. "Alien System" (Letter to the editor). *Fiji Times* November 12 p: 6.

———. 1988b. "Draft Constitution" (letter to the editor). *Fiji Times* September 28 p: 6.

Toren, Christina, 1990. *Making Sense of Hierarchy: Cognition as Social Process in Fiji.* London School of Economics Monographs on Social Anthropology 61. London and Atlantic Highlands, N.J.: Athlone Press.

Tronto, Joan C. 1993. "Care." In *Moral Boundaries: A Political Argument for an Ethic of Care.* New York: Routledge.

Tsongas, Paul. 1986. *Heading Home.* New York: Vintage Books.

Tuivaga, Jessie. 1988. "Fiji." In *Pacific Women,* ed. Taiamoni Tongamoa. Suva, Fiji: Institute of Pacific Studies of the University of the South Pacific.

Turner, Bryan. 1982. "The Government of the Body: Medical Regimens and the Rationalization of the Diet." *British Journal of Sociology* 33:254–69.

———. 1984. *The Body and Society.* Oxford: Basil Blackwell.

———. 1992. *Regulating Bodies: Essays in Medical Sociology.* London: Routledge.

Turner, James. 1984. " 'True Food' and First Fruits: Rituals of Increase in Fiji." *Ethnology* 23:133–42.

Turner, Victor. 1964. "A Ndembu Doctor in Practice." In *Magic, Faith, and Healing: Studies in Primitive Psychiatry Today,* ed. Ari Kiev. New York: Free Press.

———. 1967. "Muchona the Hornet." In *Forest of Symbols.* Ithaca, N.Y.: Cornell University Press.

Wadden, Thomas A. et al. 1989. "Dissatisfaction with Weight and Figure in Obese Girls: Discontent but Not Depression." *International Journal of Obesity* 13:89–97.

Weiner, Annette. 1976. *Women of Value, Men of Renown.* Austin: University of Texas Press.

White, Geoffrey M. 1985. "Premises and Purposes in a Solomon Islands Ethnopsychology." In *Person, Self, and Experience,* ed. Geoffrey White and John Kirkpatrick. Berkeley: University of California Press.

White, William C. and Marlene Boskind-White. 1981. "An Experiential-Behavioral Approach to the Treatment of Bulimarexia." *Psychotherapy: Theory, Research and Practice* 18:501–7.

Williams, Thomas. 1982. *Fiji and the Fijians.* Vol. 1, ed. George Stringer Rowe. Suva, Fiji: Fiji Museum.

Wiseman, Claire V. et al. 1992. "Cultural Expectations of Thinness in Women: An Update." *International Review of Eating Disorders* 11 (1): 85–89.

Young, Michael. 1979. *Ethnography of Malinowski.* London: Routledge and Kegan Paul.

Zegans, Leonard. 1987. "The Embodied Self: Personal Integration in Health and Illness." *Advances (Institute for the Advancement of Health)* 4(2):29–45.

Index

aesthetic ideals and body shape, 27–29, 37–38, 46, 50–51, 57, 128, 176–77 n.1

agency: and the body, 2, 6, 31, 37, 52, 125, 129–31; and the self, 2, 6, 129–31

Ali, Ahmed, 174 n.11

Alibhai, Naznin, 37–38, 41, 44, 144, 153, Appendix C

alienation, 136; and illness experience, 31–32, 115–16, 123, 125; of self from body, 30–33, 56, 123–25, 130–31, 134, 177 n.4; of self from community, 56, 102, 111, 123–25, 130–31, 133–34

American: attitudes toward illness, 124; attitudes toward weight and body shape, 45; cultural preference for body shape, 28; prevalence of obesity and overweight, 41–43. See also Western

anorexia nervosa, 2, 30, 33–35, 114, 131, 173 n.1 (intro.), 177 n.2, 181 n.26, 188 n.1 (Chapt. 6). See also disordered eating; eating disorders

appearance, 56; and body shape, 36, 56, 156–70; commentary on, 50; dress, 28, 54–55, 87; hair, 28, 53, 55; importance of, 18, 33, 52–55, 128, 179 n.10

appetite, 2, 33; as a marker of illness, 81–82, 181 nn.24–25, 182 n.27; control of, 30, 32, 72, 181 n.26; loss of, 81, 83, 97–99, 131, 181 n.27, 182 nn. 28, 32, 186 n.32; monitoring of, 37, 56, 81–84, 89, 129, 180 n.19, 182 n.32, 188 n.1 (Chapt. 6); *macake*, 81–84, 131, 181 nn. 23, 26, 182 nn.28–30

authority: chiefly, 15, 17, 175 n.20; hierarchical, 19; over body, 37, 127–31; respect for, 17, 19–20

beauty, 28–29; and body shape, 29. *See also* aesthetic ideals and body shape; appearance

Beit-Hallahmi, Benjamin, 177 n.4, 187 n.4

Bell, Rudolph M., 34

Belshaw, Cyril, Figure 1.2, 174 n.11

Bilu, Yorum, 177 n.4, 187 n.4

bodily cultivation, 177 n.5; and care, 58; as a collective enterprise, 5, 58, 84–85, 129, 133; as a personal endeavor, 133–34; in Fiji, 27–28, 37–38, 45–46, 51–52, 56–57, 66, 84, 128–29, 134, 177 nn. 7, 12; 188 n.1 (Chapt. 6); in Western cultures, 29, 34–37, 45, 56, 123, 127–30, 133, 177 n.12

body, 175–76 n.23 and agency, 2, 6, 31, 37, 52, 125, 129–30; and identity, 2, 6, 31, 37, 52, 56, 85, 102–3, 127, 129–31, 133–34; and knowledge, 100–101, 122, 125, 131, 183 n.8, 186 n.35; and self, 2, 5–6, 26–27, 31–32, 35–36, 85, 102–5, 109, 123–25, 127–34, 176 n.30; and society, 2, 85, 114, 126; and the collective, 95, 109, 113, 115, 119, 127, 129–34; and the community, 28, 37, 52, 55–58, 85–86, 92–93, 104–5, 110–11, 116, 122, 126–31, 133, 187 n.3; and the cosmos, 100, 114, 127, 131–33; bodily demeanor and respect, 17, 20–21; boundaries, 2, 104; commodification of, 35–36; objectification of, 30–31, 35–36, 56, 130, 133–34, 188 n.1 (Chapt. 6); social appropriation of, 5–6, 27, 104–5, 110–13, 116, 119, 125, 130–31, 187 n.3. *See also* bodily cultivation; body shape; embodiment; embodied experience